D1204393

THE BRETHREN

The

BRETHREN

*A Story of Faith and Conspiracy
in Revolutionary America*

BRENDAN
McCONVILLE

HARVARD UNIVERSITY PRESS

CAMBRIDGE, MASSACHUSETTS

LONDON, ENGLAND

2021

First printing

Publication of this book has been supported through the
generous provisions of the Maurice and Lula Bradley Smith
Memorial Fund.

Library of Congress Cataloging-in-Publication Data

Names: McConville, Brendan, 1962– author.
Title: The Brethren : a story of faith and conspiracy in
revolutionary America / Brendan McConville.
Description: Cambridge, Massachusetts : Harvard University
Press, 2021. | Includes bibliographical references and index.
Identifiers: LCCN 2021010226 | ISBN 9780674249165 (cloth)
Subjects: LCSH: Counterinsurgency—North Carolina—
History—18th century. | American loyalists—North Carolina. |
North Carolina—History—Revolution, 1775–1783. | North
Carolina—Politics and government—1775–1783.
Classification: LCC E230.5.N8 M33 2021 | DDC 975.6 / 03—dc23
LC record available at https://lccn.loc.gov/2021010226

For Griffin

C ONTENTS

Introduction: The Brethren   1

1   Along the Sound   11

2   Protestants   26

3   Revolution   43

4   July Fifth   66

5   Conventions of the People   82

6   The House of Fear   101

7   Becoming Known, Becoming Loyalists   127

8   The Sword and the Scale   150

9   The Return of the Father   174

10   Aftermaths   190

Conclusion: A Great Change of Seasons   210

NOTES   217

NOTE ON SOURCES   273

ACKNOWLEDGMENTS   279

INDEX   281

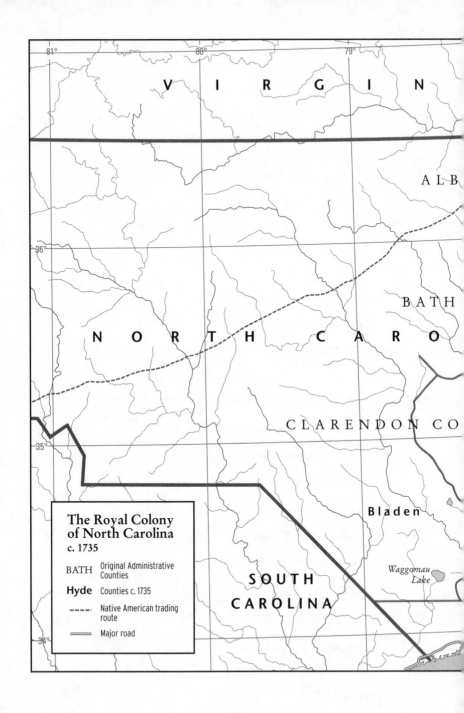

The Royal Colony
of North Carolina
c. 1735

BATH Original Administrative
Counties

Hyde Counties c. 1735

‑‑‑‑‑ Native American trading
route

═══ Major road

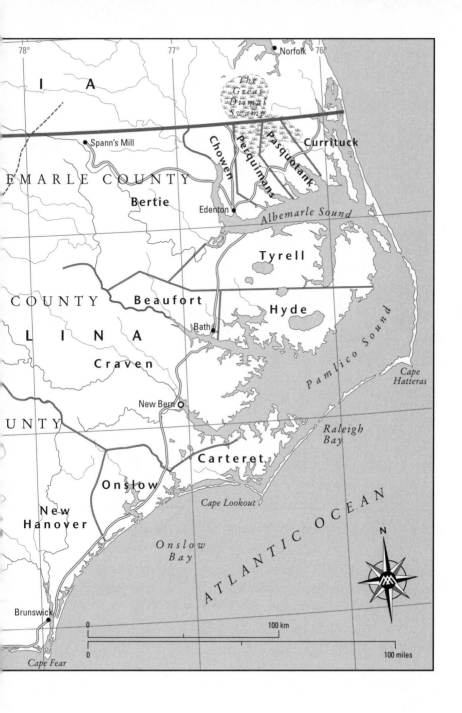

THE BRETHREN

INTRODUCTION

The Brethren

ON JULY 5, 1777, an emergency message reached North Carolina governor Richard Caswell. The state's leaders received an endless stream of such express notes throughout the Revolutionary War, bringing word of military disasters, demands from the Continental Congress for money and troops, explanations of political developments in other states: the expresses never ended. This message, though, brought Caswell especially troubling news. It warned that a "traitorous Conspiracy" of loyalists had formed in the Albemarle Sound region and had perhaps already spread to every county in the state. These plotters intended to "assassinate all the leading men" in North Carolina's revolutionary government—including the governor himself![1]

Caswell immediately moved to crush these rebels against a republican future. Militia units loyal to the state arrested dozens of conspirators, snuffing out the planned coup just before blood was to be shed. This would-be uprising quickly came to be known as the Gourd Patch, or Lewellen, Conspiracy, the former name referencing a rallying place of the plotters, the latter taken from the conspiracy's purported leader, Martin County militia captain and justice of the peace John Lewellen.

For 240 years the Gourd Patch Conspiracy has been understood as one of a string of loyalist plots that rocked revolutionary America. A group of conspirators planned to incite a diversionary slave uprising and seize the state armories in the Albemarle region during the resulting turmoil. The plotters would then slaughter the revolutionary elite and welcome British troops into North Carolina. It fits perfectly with scholarly understanding of what loyalist conspiracies and uprisings were all about. What else could it be?[2]

What else could it be wasn't the question that inspired my research into this conspiracy. Over time, though, I came to believe that the year-long period of unrest that culminated in the planned coup in the summer of 1777 did not *begin* as a loyalist uprising at all. Rather, clashing ideas about the character of liberty and the Revolution's goals caused the unrest that led to the plot to kill North Carolina's revolutionary leadership. In dispute initially was not the issue of loyalty to the British Empire, but the question of what spiritual and political values would shape the new order's constitution and political culture.

The unrest began in the late fall of 1776 when Protestant yeomen and planters in the state's Albemarle region became uneasy about the actions of an increasingly coercive revolutionary government. As the American military situation deteriorated that autumn, the state's revolutionary leaders began to pressure communities to provide men for military formations, this in spite of traditional Anglo-American apprehensions about standing armies and forced drafts. These same leaders publicly advocated for a French alliance despite centuries of Anglo-American hostility to that Catholic absolutist power. Albemarle yeomen viewed these actions as antithetical to the Protestant political values that they understood as not only compatible with the Revolution, but the very reason a revolution could occur and was occurring.

Fears about the state government increased at the end of 1776 when fourteen delegates in the state's constitutional convention tried to inject what they understood as enlightened principles into the state's new republican constitution and political culture. These delegates attempted to exclude Protestant political values from the new state oaths and rites. They came to be known as the Fourteen, men with heretical beliefs antithetical to liberty and a free society as the mass of North Carolina's Protestant yeomen understood those things. The fourteen delegates publicly questioned both the Holy Trinity's existence and the Bible's divine origins. And they continued to assert unorthodox spiritual-political beliefs in public and private even after they failed to purge all Protestant political practices from the state's formal political rites.

Rumors about the fourteen delegates' beliefs intensified fears that the revolutionary government had been compromised by a popish plot involving heretics and the French. In the state congress's aftermath, planters and yeomen in the southern and western Albemarle region began to organize to save Protestantism and Protestant liberty from these threats. The movement they called "the Brethren" and what the state leaders would later call an association or "the Association" was centered in Martin, Tyrrell, and Bertie Counties but had support in a number of other North Carolina counties as well.[3]

The Brethren's leaders initially denounced the fourteen delegates and focused their efforts on defending Protestantism and Protestant political culture in the new state. They developed governing institutions and a recruiting structure, wrote a constitution to define the movement's values, and created a system of oaths and rites. But the movement underwent an ideological change early in the summer of 1777 when revolutionary committeemen and militiamen unwilling to accept any criticism of the fragile republican order threatened to arrest Brethren leaders. These threats led the Brethren's founders to consider a bloody coup in favor of the king that would involve a diversionary slave uprising. This change in direction alienated many of the rank and file, who believed themselves to be defending a revolution in favor of Protestant liberty, not undermining American independence or disrupting the state's racial order. They gave evidence to state officials in late June and early July, and the thoroughgoing crackdown ordered by Governor Caswell followed.[4]

It seems a strange tale from an obscure place. The newspapers mentioned it only briefly, and no writer penned a pamphlet about it. But the voices embedded in a hundred pages of primary documents reveal a story of profound ideological change. I am arguing that the Gourd Patch Conspiracy reflected an abrupt, destabilizing shift in the understanding of liberty during the period of independence. For generations, a militantly Protestant, virulently anti-Catholic worldview had stabilized the British Empire and defined it as free. Paradoxically, that political worldview became, in 1774 and 1775, the primary ideological framework that drove Americans' revolutionary mobilization against the empire.

But in the rapidly changing situation that developed after July 4, 1776, the public assertion of these Protestant political values came to be understood as evidence of treasonous, loyalist designs against the new republican order. This jarring alteration in the political meaning of Protestant liberty evidenced the depth of the military crisis that encouraged the infant republic to seek an alliance with its traditional and much-hated enemy, Catholic France. It also manifested a growing intellectual conflict in that society over the relationship of spiritual faith to republican liberty that began then and remains unresolved even now. The Gourd Patch Conspiracy expressed that conflict at the moment of its birth.[5]

The Brethren is the story of how people in one place experienced this change as a lived reality. While we can understand what was happening then through abstract ideas about paradigms shifting, for those living in the Albemarle the moment of independence was a time of fear and bewilderment during which the familiar became strange and neighbors sometimes turned violently against each other. The beliefs that they imagined they all shared in harmony suddenly became instead publicly contested; the supposedly unbreakable link between liberty and Protestantism that was at the center of their political understanding fell into question. The until-then-uncontroversial question of the role of spiritual faith in American political culture suddenly burst into public life and has remained there ever since.

The study of Protestantism's impact on the revolutionary generation's politics would seem a logical scholarly focus. In 1776 most Americans were Protestant, admittedly of many denominations. They had grown up in a militantly Protestant British Empire and received their political education via Protestant pulpits and a print culture that carried the message of a righteous Protestant polity. Provincial political rites and celebrations educated British Americans in a specifically Protestant understanding of liberty, property, and the nature of a free government. The yeomanry effectively knew nothing about the Enlightenment, and enlightened thinking cannot be said to have played any meaningful role in shaping their revolutionary consciousness.

Instead, scholars have long marginalized and even aggressively ignored the revolutionary generation's Protestantism and its role in the Revolution. A generation of academics interpreted the Revolution as originating in a poorly defined Enlightenment, or English oppositional ideology known to only a few admittedly important writers or political leaders, or growing class tensions. At times scholars have focused disproportionately on certain figures because they were understood as religious skeptics or seemed somehow modern, and have ignored the spiritual-political views held by the vast majority. A distorting tendency developed to describe the

Revolution's ideological character as uniformly "republican" or "liberal," and to privilege what was secular and related to ancient Greece and Rome.[6]

Scholarship that did engage the issue of religion and the Revolution moved in fixed directions. This body of literature focuses overwhelmingly on the separation of church and state, the First Great Awakening's influence on revolutionary action, and secularization. Certainly much has been learned. But these approaches have a teleological quality that encouraged the perception that the Revolution was intended to create the secularized America of the late twentieth and early twenty-first centuries. Which it was not, at least not in a direct sense.[7]

A lack of primary sources enabled the tendency to attribute to the yeomanry beliefs that don't seem on reflection to be historically logical. We simply don't often see the mass of farmers or goodwives interrogated about their beliefs. And this has historically silenced the 90 percent of free white population who lived in the countryside, had limited education, if any, and had only sporadic contact with governing institutions.

The manuscripts created in North Carolina in 1777 allow the yeomanry to speak. That many among them were those I call "X" men—not the Marvel Comic superhumans, but instead the illiterate who could signify their historical existence only by making an X on documents—only magnifies these documents' importance. The political views of such illiterates are almost always beyond our grasp. Their participation in what happened in North Carolina in the year after independence provides a rare, almost unique portal to their thoughts as they lived upheaval and revolution.

These voices admittedly come to us through records created by a hostile state. The revolutionary leadership's manipulation of language in their quest to legitimate their rule has made it difficult to tell stories like that of the Gourd Patch Conspiracy, or to understand the yeomanry's revolutionary consciousness. Loyalist and patriot, whig and tory, conspiracy and plot, republicanism and reaction—these labels deployed by the Revolution's leaders to cement their control became ideological masks that obscured the complexity of beliefs and behaviors that drove change in the period around independence. In the decades and centuries after 1783, politicians and scholars adopted this language to explain the period, obscuring still more what drove people to act in 1776 and 1777.[8]

This complexity also puts into question how scholars have used the idea of "sides" and fixed political identities in the Revolution. Clearly these need to be reexamined. Surely they were real, but they were also permeable and flexible. Men answered some militia mobilizations and then ignored others; resisted drafts; or fought for both sides. The Protestant political values evident in all the political communities that emerged during the Revolution enabled these changes. Movement between camps was easier ideologically than we have imagined because they shared a common ideological rootstock in Protestant political culture.

A new Revolution emerges when we pull away the accepted rhetorical masks of political identity. The depositions, trial records, and correspondence that record the unrest in the Albemarle makes it clear that as the Revolution unfolded, a Protestant worldview informed actions in free white society. Even though that does not fit with much of the scholarship on the Revolution's ideological origins, it makes good sense given that society's history and spiritual faith. What we hear when we listen to them was not designed to make twenty-first-century Americans comfortable with the revolutionary generation. But it should lead us to reconsider received wisdom about the Revolution's ideological structure.

The American Revolution was not a war of religion. But it was a searing upheaval among particularly religious people. Their ideas about sacred and secular, and politics and faith, fundamentally differed from our own and shaped their understanding of what the relationship of God to political man should be in the new order.

They did not abandon these beliefs in 1776, or 1783, or 1787, and such beliefs became a driving force of change thereafter. This view of revolutionary mentality makes good sense if we read American history forward rather than backward. When we do read forward, new opportunities for research and debate about the Revolution emerge in abundance. If we ignore that approach, we risk losing the authentic voice of this vitally important American generation.

Are you willing to defend Protestantism from popery and heresy? Will you stand by others to protect faith and family? Can you help those drafted against their will or who no longer want to serve? These are not seen as the Revolution's great issues. The southern wheat fields where this movement grew are not Carpenter's Hall, or the Old North Church, or Concord's North Bridge. These North Carolina farmers seem to have been meant to live and die and be forgotten as a new revolutionary world consumed the provincial society that had shaped them.

But profound changes at the dawn of American nationhood that we have neither fully understood nor fully appreciated are evident in this story from North Carolina. The words of those involved during the rise and fall of this movement suggest that many did not experience the revolutionary upheaval as a linear march to secular liberation. Nor did many of them hold views consistent with modern ideas about freedom that were, paradoxically, established in opposition to the Protestant liberty the yeomanry sought to uphold.

Would liberty have a soul in the new republic, or would a secularized liberty be the soul of that republic? That was the central question at stake, but there was no immediate answer to it. Indeed, it has never been finally answered in our political culture.

The chapters that follow explain how one region's planters and yeomen came to fear for their faith as well as their rights at independence. I suggest how structural changes in economic and spiritual relations late in the colonial period created the unrest's deep preconditions; examine the imperial breakdown; evaluate how the war destabilized eastern North Carolina; trace the creation of the Brethren's association by yeomen and planters disaffected from those revolutionary state's leaders who publicly professed unorthodox spiritual and political values; reveal the conflicts that led the movement's leadership to consider a tory coup; and consider the role of the ensuing crackdown in creating new republican institutions for a new revolutionary order.

The Brethren is a story of ideological transformation in the Revolution as experienced in North Carolina's wheat fields and half-drowned forests. That vantage frees us from received wisdom and suggests that the entire revolutionary period can be studied anew.

A note to the reader: Use of the invaluable depositions, affidavits, correspondence, and court records that underlay this study did not come without challenges. Perhaps the most daunting was determining the spellings of names. Unsurprisingly, given that many of those deposed were illiterate, and spellings had yet to be standardized among the literate, names were recorded with a variety of spellings that sometimes almost obscured who was speaking or being discussed. For example, the name of John Lewellen, who was understood as the leader of the movement, was also recorded as John Luellen, John Lywellen, John Lewelling, Lewhellen, and John Liwillin. The name of James Rawlings, the movement's spiritual leader, was also spelled as Rollins, Rollin, Rawlins, and Rawlin. Daniel Legate, who played a central role among the Brethren, was also recorded as Leggett, Leget, Legett, Leggatt, and Legit. The family name of Brethren David Taylor was in spots spelled as Tailor. Brethren John Garrett was also recorded as John McGarrett. The name of Brethren William Brimage was also given as Brimmage, and that of Richard Faggan was also given as Fagan, Feggan, Faggans, and Fagin. The name of Salvanas Buttrey was also spelled Salvinas Buttery and Salvinas Buttany. The name of Brethren leader

James Sherrard was also spelled Sherrod, Sherod, Shearrard, and several other ways. The first name of state leader and feared heretic Whitmel Hill was spelled in a wide variety of ways. I have standardized to one form in the text but left the original spellings in quotes drawn directly from primary sources.

A second problem of names grew from the presence of multiple family members with the same name in the Albemarle region in 1777. In those cases, I have tried to provide some guidance as to which person was speaking.

I would finally note that the spellings of the names of counties, towns, rivers, and geographic features also varied. Again, I have standardized those spellings in all cases when it is appropriate to do so.

ALONG THE SOUND

THE PLOT TO KILL North Carolina's leadership grew from the tremendous ideological forces unleashed by the American Revolution. But they occurred against a pattern of long-term structural changes in a society founded some hundred years earlier. Those changes in the political order, social structure, and economy provided the canvas for the 1777 events. Clashing empires, mass migration from the north and across the ocean, changing tastes generated by the intensification of trade, and resulting transformations in the structure of society—these all intersected with the Revolution and shaped the lives of the generation that lived it.

Charles II's restoration to the English throne in 1660 led to North Carolina's founding. Among the things on Charles's mind as he ascended that throne was how to reward those who had remained loyal to the House of Stuart after the execution of his father, Charles I, in January 1649 amid the English civil wars. In March 1663 Charles awarded eight of these loyal men the right to establish a proprietary colony south of Virginia, giving them the power of government as well as ownership of the soil. This grant would eventually become South and North Carolina.[1]

It was the first of a number of gifts of entire colonies given by Charles to royal relatives and loyal courtiers after 1660. New York, New Jersey, and Pennsylvania were all granted to those in the Stuart monarch's good graces. These proprietors also received governing rights and ownership of the soil. And in all these proprietary colonies, chaotic seventeenth-century beginnings eventually gave way to political and economic integration into the British imperial order that emerged at the end of the seventeenth century.

The Carolina proprietors faced the same question that all who received these massive grants confronted. What would they build on the fringe of their world, and how would they make it profitable? They eventually charged one of their number, Anthony Ashley Cooper, with framing a government for their new world empire. Cooper, soon to be the Earl of Shaftsbury, had a most remarkable helper in this task, his secretary and doctor, John Locke, patron philosopher of the world to come. The pen-and-ink utopia they created expressed seventeenth-century dreams of a society based on a kind of mixture of hierarchy, gross exploitation, and benevolence alien to our modern sensibilities. Their charter incorporated some remarkably progressive ideals while allowing for both aristocracy and slavery.[2]

It failed even before it could be implemented. The proprietary government actually established in Carolina was partially modeled on that of Restoration Virginia. In all likelihood, Virginia governor and Carolina proprietor Sir William Berkeley created this alternative framework. He was the first magistrate to actually assert sovereign powers in Carolina, and he appointed the Albemarle settlements' first true governor, William Drummond, in 1664. The frame of government that actually went into effect reflected Berkeley's views about the new colony's governance.[3]

That government never worked well. The proprietors struggled to control so large a territory, and social unrest was common. Divergence in economic interests between the northern and southern portions would eventually lead to South Carolina's establishment as a separate colony in 1712. Continuing turmoil in North Carolina encouraged the royalization of the colony's government in 1729.

From 1731 until the Revolution, the imperial government appointed royal governors and the legislature's upper house for the colony while the assembly was elected by propertied freeholders. The London authorities believed that such a mixed and balanced royal government would help stabilize their often troubled colony.[4]

The problems of governance that plagued early North Carolina in large part grew from a pattern of settlement that began even before Charles II had granted the colony to his loyal courtiers. Migrants from Virginia arrived in the Albemarle Sound region beginning in the 1650s and early 1660s. Over time they displaced by war or other means the numerous Croatan, Tuscarora, and Siouan-speaking peoples indigenous to what came to be known as the Albemarle region. Some of these new migrants from the north sought to escape bondage, some were members of the Society of Friends who fled Virginia for religious reasons, and many went seeking land. Peoples from Germany, Switzerland, northern Ireland, Scotland, and other parts of northern Europe eventually joined them. The forced migration of enslaved West African peoples into the region further diversified a society more ethnically and racially varied than that of Virginia or England.[5]

Although these communities initially had varied economies, over time many Albemarle lives came to center on growing, curing, and exporting tobacco. The area's tobacco production was important enough in 1670 that Maryland and Virginia leaders invited the Albemarle region's tobacco growers into negotiations to limit planting to stabilize prices. In 1672 Albemarle planters began to use tobacco as a currency, and a year later, tobacco growing had become so widespread that the Crown made efforts to enforce duties on tobacco shipped from the Albemarle region.[6]

The Albemarle region's basic spatial structure reflected tobacco's importance. The crop demanded plentiful flat land and access to the sea to export the harvest. This meant that European home-steads would snake around the sound and towns would be few and far between. That pattern of settlement remained evident at the time of Revolution. On July 4, 1776, the counties around the sound remained a rural world of dispersed homesteads with few towns or villages. A traveler crossing the sound going north to south on that first day of independence would have stepped off the ferry at Windsor Landing, one of the southern shore's more cosmopolitan areas. The urban core there consisted of two taverns, a store, and the ferry landing.[7]

The Structure of Society

Rural did not mean bucolic. In the eighteenth century, a planter elite that exploited African slaves to grow tobacco and produce other commodities for export had established themselves atop the Albemarle counties. Below them, a few were above middling, others middling, many others worse off, and a mass of white servants and African slaves found themselves temporarily or permanently trapped at the bottom of the power structure.

The society's hierarchical nature is evident in tax lists and will inventories created right before the Revolution in the southern Albemarle counties that spawned the Brethren. Land and slave ownership data are the most suggestive evidence about social structure. Land records from Tyrrell County reveal that about 13 percent of the county's white male freeholder population each owned more than 500 acres in the 1750s. A much larger group, about 56 percent, held between 100 and 500 acres, and about 30 percent owned less than 100 acres. About 20 percent of the white male population owned no land at all.[8]

A surviving 1774 tax list from the Brethren stronghold of Bertie County, examined alongside the will inventories from the same county, reveals similarly uneven distribution of wealth in the form of human beings. Overall, 44 percent of Bertie households had slaves. These slaveholders constituted the society's top half in terms of wealth. A tiny subset of gentlemen owned dozens of slaves and held thousands of acres. In Bertie, Doctor Robert Lenox stood atop the pyramid. He owned thirty-three people in 1774. This elite group also included Brethren William Brimage. He served as a judge on the colony's admiralty court in 1769, acted as grand secretary of the colony's Freemasons, and had a host of other social connections. Brimage held thirty or more slaves who worked 10,000 acres in Bertie and other counties. Brimage ruled over his kingdom from his mansion house, Westbrook. He lived a comfortable life until the crisis of 1777 altered his existence forever.[9]

A small privileged outer group orbited around this elite nucleus. These lesser gentlemen owned about 5 percent of the county's taxables. Those in this outer elite circle had eleven or more slaves, and substantial landed property in most cases. Bertie County's Armistead family in many ways exemplified these lesser gentry. The family's progenitors in North Carolina, William and Anthony, the younger sons of a well-established Virginia family, moved to North Carolina and purchased lands in Bertie County around midcentury. They then married into the same locally prominent family; William Armistead married Sarah Jordan in 1756, and Anthony Armistead married her cousin Mildred Jordan shortly thereafter. Using slave labor, they produced commodities and established a trade between Bertie County and the Norfolk region of Virginia.

The Jordan-Armistead house, built in the early eighteenth century, gives a good sense of how these minor gentry lived. A dual-chimney, two-story red brick home, it stood alone in a rural landscape dominated by individual homesteads and tiny villages rather than urban centers. It was comfortable but not grand, with sleeping quarters above and social and work space below.[10]

Other factors allowed individuals to claim gentry status under certain circumstances. Birth and kinship, ethnicity, and education also played a role in establishing a person's genteel status. Lawyers, merchants, and even teachers might also be considered gentlemen by virtue of education or kinship connections. At 1750 the gentry families at the social order's apex had been intermarrying for decades, forming a regional elite. Families with ties to Virginia dominated one wing of this elite; the other wing contained immigrant gentlemen from the British Isles and those with ties to the planter elite that emerged in South Carolina in the eighteenth century.[11]

A much larger group of yeomen orbited around these great and petite gentlefolk. No complete yeoman's home in the southern Albemarle survives today, but these houses were likely similar to though more modest versions of the Jordan-Armistead home, with wood rather than brick the primary building material and clapboarding on the exterior. Large families lived in what were usually homes with no more than three, sometimes four, rooms.

A sharp division existed in this yeomen group between those who held slaves and those who did not. Those who did own slaves had one to four people in bondage and were usually wealthier and of modestly higher status than those in the 56 percent of free white households overall that had no slaves. Most Brethren were drawn from the yeomanry, though it is not possible in many cases to determine who among them owned slaves or what was their overall wealth.[12]

The lives of these slaves are largely hidden from us by a lack of records. A 1755 census recorded the Albemarle region's population to be about 23 percent African and African American. It is worth noting that two-thirds of adult slaves at that time had been born in Africa. The sources are largely silent about their views, but they no doubt perceived their new environment through the lenses provided by African cultures. By 1767 about 36 percent of the Albemarle's population were enslaved, and one-third of these were born in Africa. A very considerable number of the enslaved had been in the West Indies before being sold into North Carolina. At independence North Carolina had 60,000 to 70,000 enslaved people out of a population of approximately 300,000. The tobacco-growing eastern counties had the most slaves, with the greatest concentration in the northern Albemarle region. Fears about these slaves shaped events in 1777 at a critical juncture.[13]

Saying that an intermarried elite dominated an early modern agrarian society or that gross exploitation defined many lives is as commonplace as noting that the sky is blue. Every place in the British Empire in the Western Hemisphere dominated by commodity crops had a similar pyramid-shaped hierarchy and enslaved populations. Not only is that well known now, but in that time many people accepted brutal inequality as normal. They may have bitterly resented it, but they knew it as the way the world worked. Only the bonded servants and the enslaved, relentlessly exploited day in and day out, resisted this order of things by flight or violence.[14]

Edenton, on the sound's north shore, was the only urban island in this rural sea. Formally incorporated in 1712, the town lay at the point where the sound received the Chowan River and other rivers of eastern North Carolina and southern Virginia. William Byrd described the Edenton courthouse as "having much the Air of a Common Tobacco-House" in the eighteenth century's first decades. He noted that a Church of England minister who accompanied him preached "in the court-house, for want of a consecrated place." The local gentry homes paled in comparison to the grand residences already appearing in the Virginia Tidewater.[15]

By the time Byrd wrote his dismissive account, though, Edenton had become an administrative and communication center and a major port. It served as the colony's capital between 1722 and 1743. The presence of a customs house allowed planters to send tobacco and other agricultural goods directly from Edenton to London and throughout the empire, and to receive commodities and news from Britain, the British West Indies, and other mainland colonies in exchange. The town also straddled the major north–south road that ran from Virginia to Charleston, South Carolina, and served as the Chowan County seat.

The town's architectural refinement in the eighteenth century expressed its growing importance as a portal for cultural influences flowing from Britain. By 1776 the town's public buildings no longer resembled the tobacco sheds of William Byrd's imagination. The crude courthouse that Byrd so cruelly dismissed decades before had been replaced by a distinctive brick building that survives today as one of the South's finest examples of Georgian architecture. St. Paul's (Anglican) Church in Edenton demonstrated the same refinement. The congregation that had worshipped in the courthouse in 1730 met in a fine brick church, its interior finished in a simplified, and dignified, Georgian style. The refinement of spaces reflected the tastes of an educated elite. Between thirty and forty formally trained lawyers, as well as merchants and educated planters, lived in Edenton and its immediate environs by 1760. Although to us Edenton would seem like a village, with about 125 homes in the 1770s, it served them as an intellectual and cultural as well economic and legal center.[16]

Despite this refinement, cosmopolitan visitor Ebenezer Hazard was underwhelmed with the town in 1777. "Edenton," Hazard recorded in his travel diary, "is a dull disagreeable place." True, perhaps ... but it was the only town they had amid an endless rural expanse.[17]

This sketch of eastern North Carolina's origins and structure suggests a conservative agrarian society. But by 1750, profound changes had begun in the Albemarle region. One of the most important of these involved crops. Grains and cereals began to supplant tobacco as demand for the former grew and demand for tobacco stagnated. This change intersected with what happened in 1777. The movement to save Protestant liberty expressed the beliefs of yeomen who embraced the shift to grain and cereal in the Albemarle.

Reign of the Plow

The Brethren arose in the seven counties—Bertie, Martin, Tyrrell, Pitt, Edgecombe, Halifax, and Hyde—that bounded the Albemarle Sound to the south and west. There were wealthy gentlemen there, and a very considerable number of African slaves, but yeomen and their families dominated demographically. The agricultural cycle ruled them with an iron rod, relentless, unending, unforgiving, the harvest completed only to find the tasks for the next year's planting already under way. This monarchy of the plow would not be overthrown until the coming of machines in the nineteenth century initiated a new order.

The subjects in this vast rural kingdom viewed innovation warily. Yet in the decades before independence, Albemarle planters and yeomen embraced a profound change by increasingly planting wheat and cereal crops for commercial export and moving away from tobacco.

This structural shift in agricultural life and the Brethren's appearance were somehow linked. The sources from the period, admittedly qualitative rather than quantitative, indicate that the Protestant association's supporters were yeomen who overwhelmingly raised wheat, cereals, and corn. Tobacco is not mentioned in any of the depositions or correspondence generated around what happened in 1777.

This is noteworthy because tobacco's hegemony in eastern North Carolina had continued well into the eighteenth century. In 1764 Governor Arthur Dobbs would report to the London authorities that "Tobacco thrives here" and was "of a better kind" than in Virginia. The soil, he stated, yielded more than it did in the fields of their neighboring colony. It was a quality crop grown in abundance for the Atlantic marketplace.[18]

By the time Dobbs wrote, though, changes in the tobacco markets were already impacting growers' bottom line and working against the continuation of tobacco's hegemony in the region. The arrival of agents from British tobacco houses who purchased tobacco directly from the growers was one of these changes. Before 1750, prominent planters with connections to British traders and tobacco houses had acted as middlemen as well as growers, marketing their poorer neighbors' tobacco for a fee. This helped keep large plantations profitable and tied the yeomen to the gentry economically and socially. The major planters began to lose these profitable middleman roles when British tobacco firms began to send agents, called tobacco factors, to the Chesapeake and North Carolina's Albemarle region. These factors began to arrive in the 1750s and 1760s and drove tobacco prices lower by offering payment in gold or providing consumer goods directly to often hard-pressed yeomen tobacco growers. Such tactics lowered overall profits for the yeomen, but provided them with immediate cash in hand and loosened the great planters' social and economic control over them. The factors' arrival helped create downward price pressure in the Atlantic tobacco markets overall as purchasing directly at lower cost encouraged British merchant houses to undercut one another's prices. By the 1770s this price pressure was evident throughout the empire of tobacco.[19]

The perception that too much tobacco was flooding the market also made the crop less attractive. Even as he celebrated the tobacco crop's quality in 1764, Governor Dobbs reported that a perception existed in North Carolina that tobacco had become "overstocked." That meant that overproduction was pushing British tobacco markets toward one of the periodic tobacco busts that plagued colonial growers in the seventeenth and eighteenth centuries.[20]

Such price collapses threatened to bankrupt gentlemen tobacco planters, because growing the crop involved high fixed costs. Large tobacco plantations required heavy investment in slave labor. Tobacco also assaulted the soil, exhausting its mineral nutrients in a matter of years. That meant the constant acquisition of new land in order to open new fields. Shipments to tobacco houses in Britain involved risk of loss as well as the cost of transport. With all these concerns, the crop had begun to seem less viable.

Grain and cereal crops became more attractive to planters and yeomen as tobacco lost its appeal. These crops required fewer hands to grow and did less damage to the soil. Grains and cereals could be sold in any market, local or Atlantic, or transformed into easily preserved and transported alcohol. By the 1750s a trend toward exporting wheat and corn that had begun in the Chesapeake had spread to the Albemarle. In 1753 the assembly was forced to pass "An Act, to prohibit the Exportation of Grain in time of scarcity" designed to control those who "for private gain" exported corn and wheat during dearth.[21]

Contemporaries commented on this crop shift. In 1764 it was reported to the Board of Trade in London that farmers and planters as far south as the Cape Fear District had recently "increased in sowing wheat" to win their living. North Carolina's last royal governor, Josiah Martin, noted that until midcentury, Carolina farmers grew what he called "Indian Corn" as the main cereal or grain crop and used it primarily for local consumption and to sell to local plantation owners who needed to feed their slaves. Martin, by speaking to yeomen he encountered, also learned that "after the example of the Virginians" more and more of them had begun planting wheat at the expense of other crops, meaning primarily tobacco, and had expanded corn production as well.[22]

Export of grains and cereals to other colonies became common. In 1772 Governor Martin temporarily banned the grain trade due to a drought that threatened to create a dearth in the colony. When the rains returned in the summer of 1773, Martin toured the northeastern part of the province and reported to the London government that in the Albemarle counties "Great quantities of wheat will be raised there this year, and I think it inferior to none I have ever seen."[23]

Population growth and a resulting increase in population density probably further encouraged Albemarle yeomen to shift to wheat and cereal growing. The colony's population more than doubled between 1720 and 1740, and then more than doubled again by 1770. While this growth was most explosive in the interior, immigration and a high local birth rate created very substantial population increase in eastern North Carolina as well. The average farm size in the counties directly abutting the sound shrank steadily. Yeomen living on smaller plots of land became more common in the Albemarle region as the population grew. Tyrrell County farms averaged about 280 acres in the 1770s, and those in Perquimans and Pasquotank Counties on the sound's north shore averaged about 230 and 166, respectively, among the lowest averages for freeholders in late eighteenth-century North Carolina.[24]

Wheat and cereals were more economically viable on these smaller farms. These crops demanded less initial investment; fewer middlemen were involved in its sale; fewer laborers, slave or indentured or free, were needed to grow a profitable crop; and more markets existed for it. Grains and cereals became the crops of the future for yeomen. Tobacco remained important—North Carolina exported over a million pounds to Great Britain in 1770. But by then the time of grain and cereals had come.[25]

Tobacco's gradual loss of hegemony seems to have caused less trauma in the Albemarle than did the parallel development on the eastern shore of Maryland and in the Virginia Tidewater region. North Carolina had always had a more diversified agrarian economy, and during earlier tobacco busts people had grown wheat and other cereals to make due. Logging and production of naval stores also played important roles in northeast North Carolina's economy. In 1765 Governor William Tryon reported that the colony produced not only tar and turpentine, but "Barrels, Hoops, Staves, Shingles, Rails, Posts and Pails." Others exported the sound's wealth, dried herring and shad, through Edenton.[26]

This acknowledged, the crop shift impacted social and political relations and somehow influenced the Brethren. The cycle of planting and reaping, life and death and renewal, connected with wheat and corn played a noticeable role in the Protestant associators' lives. The depositions from 1777 repeatedly mention episodes involving yeomen cultivating wheat and corn, and meetings in wheat- and cornfields, as when Thomas Harrison recalled being approached about joining the movement in "his sons Wheat Field." None of the depositions mentions tobacco cultivation or its export, or fishing or logging. Grain crops provided economic independence from planter control, and that may have encouraged the yeomanry to follow out the imperatives created by their spiritual-political values regardless of the views of gentlemen revolutionaries. Some Brethren must have been tobacco planters or engaged in other economic activities. Certainly some held slaves, who tended to be used most extensively in tobacco cultivation and in the production of tar and naval stores. But the depositions about the unrest strongly suggest a movement dominated by wheat- and cereal-growing yeomen.[27]

Our views about the early American period and the Revolution have often been shaped with a focus on those at the top, the Founding Fathers, or, more recently, by examining the enslaved. The white yeoman population that lay between these poles dominated free society demographically and acted as the base of formal institutional politics. But they remain in many respects historically mysterious. Scholarly interest turns to them from time to time, but a lack of documents clearly expressing their views has frustrated efforts to understand their roles in revolutionary change.

Yet there could be no Revolution, no war for independence, nor a popular sovereignty without these yeomen. The actions of one man helped make historically visible how these farmers lived this great upheaval of their times. He is interesting to us not because he was extraordinary, but instead because he embodied so many trends evident in North Carolina's free population in the eighteenth century.

John Lewellen

Around 1760 yet another man migrated from Virginia to the southern Albemarle. He was between forty and forty-five years old, a husband and a father, and owned land and plied the shipwright's trade in Norfolk County, Virginia, near Portsmouth. But the opportunity to be more in the Albemarle pulled him away to the south. In North Carolina he won his living primarily from the land. He became, first, one of the ever-increasing number of yeomen, and then a more substantial property owner. He held hundreds of acres in Martin County north of the Conetoe Swamp, and became a slave owner. A man with a temper. A Church of England congregant.

He eventually received formal recognition of his status by being appointed justice of the peace and militia captain in Tyrrell County in the old order. He retained these positions in Martin County when the provincial assembly split Tyrrell County in 1774 to form that new county.[28]

This was John Lewellen. John Luellen. John Lywellen. John Lewelling. John Liwillin. John Lewellen. All the same man. The person named repeatedly as the leader of the Brethren in 1777. His name in its many variants appears from time to time in the records from the provincial period, and again after independence. He lived the great changes that shaped the eighteenth-century Anglophone world—the north-to-south wave of migration in British America; the royalization of colonial governments; the structural changes in Atlantic tobacco markets and population growth that set in motion a shift from a tobacco culture toward a wheat- and cereal-growing economy in eastern North Carolina; and the imperial crisis itself.

One more change impacted this man intimately: the Christian evangelization of the vast American countryside. Protestantism shaped his self-perception and that of those who followed him. Their morality and their political views, as well as their spiritual perception, flowed from their religious identity. A series of structural changes in the Church of England between 1750 and 1775 linked Protestant yeomen and planters like John Lewellen to imperial Protestant political culture in a new and more intimate manner. The Church provided Lewellen and countless others with knowledge of this world and channeled their hopes and fears concerning the next. The yeomanry's beliefs about God and man shaped their revolutionary consciousness in 1774 and 1775, and led to the Brethren's creation in 1777.[29]

2

PROTESTANTS

"ABOUT THE TIME OF laying the Constitution of Government," remembered Martin County farmer James Rawlings, "a general [militia] muster was held at the Court House of Martin County." This was either the December 1776 militia muster or the March 1777 muster. There Rawlings encountered John Lewellen and John Carter. They began to talk to him about their growing fears that the country "was Like to become subject to popery." Lewellen went on to say they needed "Relief and had though [thought] on means proper, and hop'd for a blessing" on their efforts. In the weeks that followed, the two men contacted Rawlings again and he became a key part of their crusade to save the Protestant commonwealth.[1]

Lewellen had good reason to approach this particular militiaman. He wasn't just a farmer; Rawlings served as a Church of England lay reader in one or more of the simple Church chapels spread across the Albemarle countryside. It is necessary to go deep into the region's religious history to understand why that seemingly minor post gave Rawlings a heightened value to those who would build a mass movement in the North Carolina countryside. The Church of England ministers who began arriving in eastern North Carolina in the mid-eighteenth century were faced with the problem of reaching a population littered across a vast rural landscape. These ministers established preaching circuits to reach a dispersed yeomanry, sometimes covering hundreds of miles in a single year as they moved among an archipelago of churches and rural chapels in eastern North Carolina. It was all part of the realignment of Protestantism to fit the needs of a vast empire whose populations did not live in nucleated towns, villages, or cities.[2]

With ministers absent for months at a time, lay readers became the population's key spiritual and intellectual leaders. This is what made James Rawlings so valuable to those who led the Brethren. Lay readers ran the chapels and churches day to day, and these places became the centers of life for a previously unchurched rural population. The lay readers joined with the ministers to introduce central aspects of the British Empire's Protestant spiritual-political worldview to their dispersed congregants. Anti-Catholicism, anti-popery, Francophobia, fear of an overreaching state and standing armies, hostility toward social and spiritual deviants: in 1763 these beliefs held together an empire that stretched from the Ganges in India to the Great Lakes in America. But in 1774 these same beliefs would guide the growing rebellion against that very empire, and in 1777 the Brethren re-tasked Protestant political idioms yet again to describe the unhappy realities of their independence.

Protestants and Princes

The ideological strut that would motivate the revolutionaries in 1774 and 1775, and shaped the Brethren's worldview, had its roots deep in the British past. The Glorious Revolution of 1688–1689 and its aftermath created the context that encouraged the use of this loose bundle of militantly Protestant libertarian political ideas and idioms that had been current in English politics since the Elizabethan era to stabilize and legitimate the eighteenth-century empire. The formal embrace of these concepts at the end of the seventeenth century led directly to the efforts to spread the Church of England in the colonies, which in turn shaped the yeomanry's worldview when they confronted their own revolutionary crisis seven decades later.

In that Glorious Revolution, James II was driven from his throne by William of Orange, Stadtholder of the Netherlands, and his English wife, Mary, backed by a Dutch army as well as by many in the English establishment. At issue were James's Catholicism, which was decidedly at odds with his subjects' overwhelming Protestantism; his reputed pro-French attitudes; his policies that undermined the Church of England's position as the state church; and the birth of a Catholic male heir to him and his Catholic second wife, Mary of Modena. This infant would, if allowed, be able to carry forward Catholic rule over Protestant Britain deep into the eighteenth century.

The revolution of 1688–1689 may have been glorious, but it was also unnatural in the extreme. James was William's uncle, as well as his father-in-law; Mary was James's daughter from his first marriage to the Protestant Ann Hyde! Nephew/son-in-law and daughter overthrowing the royal father: it weakened divine right, patriarchy, and indivisible primogeniture. The family dynamic involved amplified the shocks caused by this extraordinary event and led writers and speakers who supported James's overthrow to emphasize that William and Mary acted as Protestants to save the realm from popish tyranny. These writers insisted that Rome and France would control any Catholic English monarchy, and that Catholic rulers inevitably sought to establish tyranny over men's souls as well as their bodies.[3]

The Convention Parliament of 1689 and subsequent parliaments that settled the British constitutional order formalized the realm's Protestant character and succession by excluding Catholics from the British throne. This is what ultimately brought the German Hanoverian prince who became George I to the British throne in 1714. His claim to that throne depended foremost on his being

Protestant; a large number of Catholic royals had better genealogical claims but were excluded from inheriting because of their
religion.[4]

So it was that an idiom of protest used to denounce Catholicism, political popery and arbitrary rule with a simplistic theory of
government attached to it came to rest at the ideological core of a
complex, militarized, global empire. Remarkably, this ideological
strut held that empire together for eighty years. The circumstances
helped; anti-Catholicism and anti-popery gained special power and
popular appeal as Britons became locked in a desperate, intermit-
tent world war with France and her mostly (though not solely)
Catholic allies between 1690 and 1815. This specifically Protestant,
Francophobic, anti-Catholic worldview seemed to explain much
about the endless conflicts that raged across the eighteenth century
and legitimated Britain's monarchs as defenders of Protestant liberty from the Gallic foe.[5]

This spiritual-political-historical perception was evident in
North Carolina and the other colonies by 1700. Around that time,
books and pamphlets explaining the historical genealogy of the
struggle against Catholicism and political popery began to circulate in the colony. Works such as *Historical Collections out of several
Grave Protestant Historians concerning the Changes of Religion in the
Reigns of Hen. 8, Ed. 6 Queen Mary and Q. Elizabeth* and *Observations on a Journey to Naples wherein the frauds of Romish Monks and
Priests are Discovered* revealed the popish threat's origins to those
on the imperial fringe. These writings made good sense to people
who lived with French, Native American, and Spanish enemies on
their northern, western, and southern frontiers. Those Carolinians
who could read learned their Protestant history from such publications that reflected the empire's ideological core.[6]

Any sustained spiritual-political education that yeomen in
the Albemarle countryside received, though, would come from the
Church of England's pulpits. Actions by imperial authorities in the

twenty-five years before independence led to that church becoming a central part of life in the rural Albemarle. The ministers who began arriving around 1750 built institutions well suited to serving and educating the rural population from which the Protestant associators arose in 1777. Anti-popery and fear of Catholic powers and Catholics generally, intense disdain for spiritual heresies, and fear of standing armies controlled by absolutist rulers: British Americans' self-perception as a free people depended on these ideals and lessons offered from Protestant pulpits. Balanced government and the rights of an Englishman and/or Britons that we have enshrined as the rootstock of our freedom rested within this Protestant political culture.[7]

The People and the Church

It is hard for us now to imagine North Carolina as a Quaker colony. We think about its past and present so differently than we do that of Pennsylvania and western New Jersey. And yet in the seventeenth century the Society of Friends was the most assertive religious group in North Carolina. This changed in the early eighteenth century when the rising threat of renewed imperial warfare and increased economic integration led to a power struggle between Quakers and Anglicans. The Church of England became legally established early in the eighteenth century, but only at midcentury did the prompting of several activist royal governors lead the Society for the Propagation of the Gospel (SPG) to send more Church ministers to North Carolina. These Churchmen planted the Protestant libertarian worldview that legitimated the empire in the Carolina countryside. Paradoxically, this same worldview would lead North Carolina yeomen to revolution in 1775, and then to gather as the Brethren in 1777.

The Quakers established themselves in the Albemarle in the 1670s during a period of intense proselytization by the Society of Friends. They became a major force in the colony's politics, and one Friend, John Archdale, acted as the colony's proprietary governor in the late seventeenth century.[8]

The tensions with France and her allies that would erupt into Queen Anne's War (1702–1713) led planters and administrators with strong ties to the London government to move to displace the Society of Friends and their allies from the colony's power structure. They saw the Quakers as an impediment to imperial defense and economic integration. The Church of England's establishment via the revised Fundamental Constitution of 1698 and the Vestry Act of 1701 expressed these efforts. The Vestry Act at least nominally established five Anglican parishes and a tithe system to support Church ministers.[9]

These developments came at the same time as the Society for the Propagation of the Gospel in Foreign Parts was founded (1701) to spread the Church of England to the rest of the empire. Granted a charter by William III near the end of his reign, the establishment of the Society created hope among North Carolina's Churchmen that the national church would soon truly root and expand in their colony. The actions of Church of England clergymen like Richard Marsden, who preached ten times, administered communion, and baptized 144 children and nine adults who "had been educated Quakers" when he stopped in the Albemarle in 1706 seemed to realize some of these hopes. Such developments caused consternation among Albemarle Quaker, and a protracted conflict developed between Quakers and Anglicans, along with others. It all culminated in the 1711 unrest known as the Cary Rebellion, in the aftermath of which Friends were forced from the government. In 1715 Governor Charles Eden and the assembly further formalized the Church's establishment.[10]

The Friends, though, need not have worried about the Church of England quickly establishing a real spiritual hegemony. Henderson Walker, writing to the Bishop of London in 1703, noted that even though North Carolina had been settled for fifty years, "most part of 21 years on my owne knowledge without Priest or Altar." Church of England authorities made haphazard attempts to address the situation, but visiting ministers could not build a permanent base for the Church. The difficulties of ministering to a widely dispersed population conspired against any easy solution. As Church minister and Quaker apostate George Keith informed the London authorities in 1704 in regard to North Carolina, ministering to "soe scaterd a people" was nearly impossible.[11]

It was especially difficult given that the SPG could not get ministers to go to the province. Some Church ministers simply refused to go. In 1716, for example, the Reverend Ebenezer Taylor wrote from St. Andrews Parish, South Carolina, to complain to Church authorities in London that his efforts to get one of a number of Church clergymen in his colony to "officiate as the Society's Missionary in North Carolina" had failed. At an assemblage of ministers gathered to consider the question of how to meet the colony's spiritual needs, "not one of them but my self only, gave his Vote for any one of their going to North Carolina." The offended group then promptly voted to send Taylor himself, a commission he vigorously sought to avoid.[12]

The clergymen the colony did attract early in the eighteenth century often left much to be desired. Thomas Bayley [Baylye] exemplified them in many ways. Expelled from Virginia for "vile actions," he arrived at Edenton and promptly began to drink heavily, demanded to preach in the courthouse, and when refused, defied authority and broke in "in a rioutus" manner. He later fled to Pasquotank County on the sound's north shore to continue his ministry. He seems perhaps superior, though, to the Reverend Daniel Brett, clergyman at Pamlico, North Carolina, described simply as

"Bret a Scandelous Fellow," and also to the Reverend John Barnett. When the Bishop of London listed the latter as a licensed clergyman for the colony, he added "bad man" next to the entry.[13]

The shortage of preachers and consecrated space became chronic. "I believe," wrote the Virginian William Byrd in his famous *History of the Dividing Line,* that Edenton "is the only metropolis in the Christian or Mahometan world, where there is neither church, chapel, mosque, synagogue, or any other place of public worship." Byrd noted that when the SPG actually sent missionaries to North Carolina, they were either "too lewd for the people, or . . . they too lewd for the priest." Ministers, Byrd remarked, often left their charges as spiritually adrift as they found them.[14]

In 1740 this spiritual neglect seemed set to continue. Only five Church of England ministers served North Carolina's population of 200,000 free and enslaved persons, and the assembly refused to work with the SPG to support ministers in the colony. Even the long-established Anglican parishes in the counties along the Albemarle Sound usually had no ministers, and their half-built churches proclaimed to all an enfeebled spiritual life. In 1741 George Whitefield wrote the Bishop of Oxford that there were "but two settled Missionaries" in all of North Carolina.[15]

This began to change in fits and starts in the mid-1740s. The massive migration into the colony from the north and from Europe attracted the attention of the SPG leadership. Around 1745 they began sending more Church ministers to North Carolina to serve this growing population.[16]

Two activist royal governors further spurred the Church of England's growth in response to the movement of these masses of unchurched people into their domain. These governors, Arthur Dobbs (1754–1765) and William Tryon (1765–1771), repeatedly lobbied Church leaders to send North Carolina more and better ministers. In the 1750s Dobbs complained to the London government about the "want of a sufficient number of pious Clergymen." He asked for increased support as tens of thousands of people arrived in the colony, most unaccompanied by spiritual shepherds. He got the clergy's pay increased and got a vestry bill through the assembly in 1764 that funded the building of parsonages and the purchasing of glebe lands (lands designated for the support of ministers within parishes) for Church ministers. This 1764 Vestry Act further called for a ten-shilling poll tax to maintain the Church. Dobbs had worked persistently to make the colony attractive to Church clergymen.[17]

William Tryon further expanded the Church's footprint when he became governor in 1765. Tryon believed the growing numbers of dissenters in the colony "would come over to the established religion [the Church of England]" if sufficient Church clergy could be put in place. He reinforced the Church's status by getting the Orthodox Clergy Act through the assembly. It provided for more incomes and glebe lands for Church ministers and placed them under the Bishop of London's ultimate control in an effort to gain the Bishop's patronage.[18]

In 1768 Tryon successfully lobbied the assembly to renew the 1764 Vestry Act. He personally provided financial help to complete St. Paul's Church at Edenton, and went on to encourage the completion other Church buildings in the colony. In 1769, viewing the flood of people coming into North Carolina from other colonies, Tryon wrote to the Bishop of London asking for permission to induce Church clergymen from those same colonies to come as well as a way to increase the overall number of Church clergymen in North Carolina. When Tryon departed in 1771, at least eighteen Church ministers were active in the colony. These new ministers settled in the eastern counties, largely those along or near the Albemarle Sound.[19]

The Church of England that developed in the Carolina countryside after 1740 did not look like the colonial Anglican Church that exists in scholarly imagination. That fantasy Anglican Church was formal, largely urban, with elaborate churches and church rites conducted by ministers ordained in London. Church ministers are portrayed as rabid opponents of evangelical-style preaching, itinerancy, and the plain style of Baptists, Presbyterians, and later Methodists who began flooding into the southern interior at midcentury. But in fact the late provincial Church of England had much in common with these supposed enemies.[20]

Mobile Christianity

The institutions created by Church of England ministers in the eighteenth century challenge our understanding of colonial Anglicanism. The mobile Christianity we associate with evangelical Baptists and Methodists in the early republic had its roots, seemingly paradoxically, in what we have imagined was a staid and urban colonial Church of England. The Church was a leader in the use of itinerancy, circuit riding, and lay readers to serve the spiritual needs of British America's growing agrarian population. Simply put, the provincial Church of England that tended souls and spread the Protestant-imperial worldview that shaped the Brethren's thinking looked radically different from the staid Church of historical imagination and a lot like the Methodist Church that developed after the American Revolution. Circuit-riding ministers moved along rural traces that served as the eighteenth-century's fiber optics, linking rural chapels and churches. Lay readers—the James Rawlingses of that world—played vital roles as they led prayers and held congregants together during the ministers' long absences.

This provincial Church emerged in equal part by design and by local innovation. London Church authorities realized that only a mobile ministry could reach so dispersed a population. The Anglican ministers who began arriving at midcentury were often sent as semi-itinerants, given a zone by the SPG to preach in—north of the Albemarle Sound, south of the sound, western counties—rather than the traditional parish structure that had supported the Church in the home islands since the English Reformation. This was a logical approach to the situation in the colonies, and these ministers traveling from place to place encouraged the appearance of simple chapels across the countryside. With so few ministers and so dispersed a population, there seemed to be no other way to reach needy souls.

The paucity of records makes it difficult to determine exactly when individual chapels appeared, and it is unclear if knowledge of all of them has survived historically. But we do know these chapels appeared in one county after another beginning in the 1740s. In Bertie County, a Brethren stronghold, the vestrymen in the Northwest Parish supported preaching at six private homes, the Bertie County courthouse, and a structure called Maney's Chapel in the 1740s. Halifax County, some of whose population became caught up in the 1777 unrest, had at least six chapels or simple churches by 1760. In 1764 the Reverend James Moir reported that Northampton County had "a Church & 3 Chapels, at which I officiate alternatively." By 1774 the St. Paul's Parish centered in Edenton had five outlying chapels.[21]

The country chapels' ritual spaces diverged radically in appearance from the Church of England's churches in London, Williamsburg, or even Edenton. These tiny spiritual outposts were usually log huts or spaces in private homes set aside for worship. The Reverend Alexander Stewart described one as "a most miserable old house ... [where] ev'ry shower of Rain or blast of wind blows quite through it." Stewart regularly visited thirteen such chapels in Pitt, Beaufort, and Hyde Counties, to the sound's immediate south and west. The meeting spaces had, Stewart bitterly noted, an unintended egalitarian character.[22]

These simple chapels became the filling stations of the spiritual highways that began to snake through the half-drowned landscape of eastern Carolina as more Church ministers arrived and began to preach in different locales. These ministers created spiritual webs in the countryside as they rode circuits between these chapels at loosely fixed times each year. Their journeys connected one chapel to another and to the empire that ruled them all. In September 1749 Edenton's Reverend Clement Hall went to Granville County, which lay west of the Albemarle, preached a number of sermons and "Churched 50 well disposed women & Baptized 184 children." Hall eventually returned home, but soon again departed to ride his preaching circuit in the eastern Albemarle. By November 1749 Hall had ridden about 200 miles, preached fourteen sermons, and "Bapt 265 white & Black children & 4 Black adults." In 1751 he complained that illness had kept him from a trip of 400 miles through his "South Mission," the area south of the sound that would be the Brethren's stronghold, where he ministered to eighteen congregations at least once a year.[23]

The circuits and chapels became the dominant spiritual institutions in eastern North Carolina. The Reverend James Moir preached in Bertie County, "in Hartford County," and was active in Edgecombe County as well as at his home base in Northampton County. The dispersed agrarian majority could be reached no other way. Such tactics proved so effective that in April 1767 Governor Tryon reported to the SPG that "religion is making very regular progress in this province," by that meaning the Church of England was growing.[24]

The frequent absence of trained ministers and the crude nature of the chapels impacted Church rites, though again the precise character of these revisions is often beyond our historical grasp. James Moir reported in October 1764 that although he at one time had tried to restrict communion to "the Church" in Northampton "on the Festivals," he had in the previous decade begun to administer it "also at the Chapels & sometimes in private houses" in the countryside. But that created problems; twice when he preached in the countryside in the summer of 1764 "there was no communion, there being no Churchwardens to provide the elements which too often happens when I cannot carry them along with me." Sometimes people would, he further complained, attend services at several chapels and receive the Lord's Supper more than once.[25]

Circuit riding encouraged spiritual authority in the chapels to devolve down to lay readers like James Rawlings. The ministers' infrequent visits meant that these lay readers led weekly prayers and headed committees of trustees that handled the congregation's business. They became important sources of knowledge of the world as well as day-to-day spiritual leaders. In 1756 lay readers provided over three-fourths of the population with their primary spiritual guidance. Nine years later, lay readers served the rural chapels "where no clergy can be procured, they have two, three or four" such places of worship in each county.[26]

Who were these lay readers and how did they come to their place? Francis Veale described the Church of England's average lay readers as "a Tayler or Some old Pirate or Some Idle Fellow" chosen by those "religiously Inclin'd" who would "Read the Service of the Church of England & then He Hacks out a Sermon." We should assume much license in this account as the supply of literate former pirates was by the mid-eighteenth century quite limited.[27]

There is no contemporary account of a reader being selected in the Albemarle. Literacy would have been one key prerequisite, devotion to the Church another. The yeomanry's role in these appointments, or whether church wardens existed at all chapels, is unclear. But it is clear that the preachers who moved between churches and chapels, and the lay readers who ministered to congregations in the ministers' absence, tied agrarians more firmly to the Protestant empire. Such forgotten people were the spiders whose webs made that empire real.

The services in the Church of England chapels were based on the Book of Common Prayer. The SPG pointedly sent copies of the Book to rural chapels to guide prayers and rites there. A volume shipped to Governor Tryon in the 1760s reveals these prayer books as a source not only of liturgy but of a rudimentary education in the norms of Protestant political culture for those attending the country chapels in the southern Albemarle. This particular Common Prayer volume was intended as a "Gift . . . for the use of the Chapels in North Carolina." The governor awarded it to the chapels in the "Society Parish in Bertie County," a Brethren stronghold in 1777. The book delineated the prayers "for the 5th of November, being the Day kept in memory of the Papists conspiracy" of the Catholic Guy Fawkes in 1605 as well as the prayers to be used to remember Charles I's execution in 1649, to mark Charles II's restoration in 1660, and to celebrate George III's coronation. This volume also provided "Prayers and Thanksgivings upon several occasions" as well as instructions on Church rites and liturgy.[28]

Another volume used in the Albemarle also outlined the services to be used on November 5, as well as how to conduct services on important national and Protestant anniversaries. Such services provided the listeners with a Protestant national historical identity by warning against the dangers of popery and Catholics. We also know that Church ministers and lay readers led weekly prayers for their Protestant princes in the southern Albemarle in the 1770s. Their refusal to stop doing so became a major political issue late in the imperial crisis. A dispersed population with a high degree of illiteracy received their primary Protestant political education from the chapel pulpits.[29]

For certain, published sermons and volumes on theology and politics sent by the SPG reinforced the Protestant political culture's norms in North Carolina. Among those sent or recommended were *Preservations against Popery 2 Volume fo.; Trap against Popery,* as well as attacks against the heretical and Quakers, such as *Waterlands Importance of the Trinity,* and several anti-Quaker works. These volumes defined the British Empire's spiritual-political orthodoxy in the mid-eighteenth century.[30]

By the mid-eighteenth century newspapers were also spreading these values among the literate in North Carolina. Writers in the *North Carolina Gazette* persistently used anti-Catholic political idioms to explain the world to readers, as when a writer reminded his readers during the Seven Years War of William and Mary, who "delivered us from Popery and arbitrary power." In the same issue Governor Dobbs published a proclamation calling for a fast day to pray for divine assistance in defeating the French and Native Americans. The governor assured his readers that these dreaded enemies intended to deprive British Americans "of their Holy Protestant reformed Religion, their Liberties and Possessions, and fixing Gallican and popish Slavery, Superstition and Persecution, over all this Continent." He warned that the war grew from the actions of "a Combination of Popish Powers" who intended to use the conflict to destroy the "Protestant Religion and Liberties of Europe."[31]

Colonial authorities also promoted public celebration of formal imperial holidays. These celebrations—the monarch's coronation, birthday, the queen's birthday, Pope's Day (Guy Fawkes, November 5)—were designed to reaffirm loyalty to the Hanoverian dynasty and a free Protestant political culture. In what towns and villages existed in North Carolina, the special prayers and preaching that marked these days was followed by cannonades, flag raisings, processions, parades, military demonstrations, bonfires, preaching and ox roasts. These so-called red-letter days educated the population, literate and illiterate, in the empire's political culture.[32]

The role that print, rites, and processions played in political education in the Albemarle countryside remains unclear because of gaps in the sources. Because literacy was nowhere near universal, and publication runs were limited, the role of print in spiritual-political education had to be limited. How many yeomen from the countryside saw and participated in political rites and holidays? Many? or none? There may have been celebratory bonfires in rural North Carolina on imperial political anniversary holidays, but the lack of diaries and newspaper accounts keeps knowledge of such things largely beyond our grasp. In the 1760s, Anglican cleric Charles Woodmason, traveling deep in the North and South Carolina interiors, did record seeing drunken backcountry men celebrating the Protestant king's birthday.[33]

The most logical assumption is that the Protestant political language used during the crisis in 1777 flowed from the chapels. John Lewellen attended a country chapel at Hamilton, Martin County, and chapel lay reader James Rawlings provided spiritual guidance to the movement and acted as one its leaders. We also know that some associators like Pelog Belote believed that the Protestant association was "an Engagement to support the Religion they had been used to," meaning by that circuit-riding Anglican ministers and chapel services led by lay readers, although most Brethren saw the movement as a general defense of Protestantism and Protestant political culture.[34]

Country chapels, lay readers, and some semi-itinerant ministers—it all sounds pretty mundane. They become a lot more important, though, if we think of these preachers and lay readers as the agents who inserted a coherent spiritual-political worldview into the countryside and built the institutions and community ties that maintained it. Most Americans lived in the countryside in 1776. That worldview proved adaptable to a social order and physical landscape quite different from that in England and even in American towns. And it proved to be a potent political mobilizer in a variety of contexts.[35]

Around 1750, structural changes began in North Carolina that came to overlap with the crisis that led to independence. A shift to a grain-cereal-corn economy was apparent in the Albemarle region, and Edenton waterborne trade with the rest of the empire increased in the same period. Church of England chapels were being created as more Church ministers arrived, and preaching circuits were established to provide spiritual instruction and a spiritual-political worldview to the rural mass settled to the south and west of the Albemarle Sound.

In 1774 and 1775 these changes intersected with the political crisis that would transform the world. Ironically, the Protestant worldview that had made the far-flung empire real to its millions of subjects also made the Revolution possible. What began as a revolt against a Parliament believed to be tainted by Catholic intrigue became a profound revolution against imperial authority that destroyed provincial North Carolina and called into question central aspects of its social order. Those involved explained the dramatic changes around them through the spiritual-political idioms that drove the Brethren to organize and that ultimately came to be seen as antithetical to the American cause.

3

REVOLUTION

"THE SEDITIOUS COMBINATIONS," an exasperated Governor Josiah Martin told his royal councilors in June 1775, "that have been form'd, and are still forming," in the aftermath of the fighting in New England were destroying royal North Carolina. Martin, a former British army officer and scion of a well-connected Anglo-Irish family, was horrified by "the violent measures they persue in compelling his Majesty's Subjects by various kinds of intimidation" to join what had become a swelling uprising. Using the "usurped Authority of committees," these rebels were forcing fellow subjects into ad hoc armed groups and revolutionary militias. Martin believed that the actions tended toward "the dissolution of the Constitution of this Province," a prophecy that would be fulfilled in a matter of months.[1]

We in the twenty-first century often have a hard time accepting the American Revolution as a close relative to the convulsive bloodbaths that followed in France, Russia, China, and elsewhere. In popular eyes at least, our Revolution still wears an intellectual or even whimsical character, with gentlemen in ruffled shirts debating in a manner suggesting they were about to break out into song. It seems fundamentally different from other revolutions and a testament to America's exceptional character.

Josiah Martin, though, and every other person who lived through it knew the American Revolution as a time of violent change that began with a profound spiritual-political crisis. The turn toward open rebellion began in the spring of 1774 when Americans became convinced that a popish plot had infected the London government. The beliefs that preachers and lay readers had spread through the countryside in the 1750s and 1760s, the very perceptions that made them all British and Protestants, were used by colonial writers in 1774 to mobilize the population to resist popish enslavement by the imperial government. London's control broke down month by month in 1774 and 1775 as Americans refused to obey royal officials whom they understood to be controlled by covert Catholics in the imperial administration's highest reaches. The growing fear that the king himself had been compromised by this popish plot destabilized the critical relationship between faith and imperial sovereignty essential to the British constitution's proper functioning in America.

Conventions and committees of safety basing their power on a loosely defined popular sovereignty had already seized authority in most of North Carolina by the time Governor Martin made his angry declaration in June 1775. Committee-led mobs attacked those they labeled as enemies of the people, beginning the process that created the rhetorical political identities of loyalist, tory, and disaffected. By 1776 colonials' successful appropriation of imperial Protestant political idioms had destroyed the intellectual-emotional logic that made British America real. As strange as it seems, ideologically, the empire died of itself.[2]

The Motives of Rebellion

The Revolution came suddenly to British America in 1774 when a severe ideological dislocation undermined imperial control. The empire's core political values of anti-popery and anti-Catholicism abruptly turned cancerous that year as Protestant British Americans came to believe that a Catholic-led plot had compromised the British ministry at its highest levels and eventually engulfed the king himself. The empire spasmed violently as provincials turned its core organizing principles against the very imperial actors and institutions that were supposed to embody these principles. The perceptions that had held the imperial British world together for a century were used to indict the London ministry's actions in a manner that fractured the empire in less than eighteen months. Accepting this as the primary ideological origin of the imperial collapse is essential to understanding how a decade-old, diffuse protest movement about constitutional rights suddenly became a true revolutionary upheaval.[3]

What occurred in the decade before 1774 had inspired deep doubts about the intentions of some government ministers and the British Parliament. North Carolina experienced unrest during the Stamp Act crisis (1764–1766), just as every other colony had. A Wilmington mob burned a stamp collector in effigy and conducted a mock burial of "Liberty." Then a mob forced the actual stamp collector, William Houston, to resign. Several other North Carolina towns also hung effigies and held mock funerals for "Liberty."[4]

But at the beginning of 1774 the empire still held. Most colonials remained willing British subjects with an agrarian-imperial-Protestant understanding of what lay beyond their fields, to the degree that they thought about the wider world at all. They remained loyal to George III, "his Most Sacred Majesty King George the Third," as a proclamation of Edenton's respectable freeholders put it as late as August 1774.[5]

This helps explain North Carolinians' initial reaction as the crisis that followed the Boston Tea Party unfolded. The Moravian leader Traugott Bagge noted in 1774 that many in North Carolina considered "the acts of the other colonies" in support of the Tea Partiers "as madness." Most Carolinians continued to believe that the empire existed in large part to protect the liberty and property of Protestants from political popery and foreign Catholics.[6]

British history, though, provided ample warnings that these beliefs might be turned against the London ministry. In 1774 the anti-Catholic and anti-popish idioms so central to creating British identity and legitimating George III and the Hanoverian dynasty retained a powerful, though long-obscured, subversive potential. Unlike divine right, anti-popery, anti-Catholicism, Francophobia, and related concepts did not provide blanket support for monarchy as a system. Indeed, they had repeatedly been used against established authority in the past. Writers deployed them during the English civil wars to delegitimate King Charles I's authority. The commonwealth governments that appeared after that monarch's execution in 1649 used these idioms to normalize their authority. Anti-popish and Francophobic languages had enabled the Glorious Revolution and formally legitimated the Protestant monarchs who took the throne after that upheaval.[7]

But the London authorities did not remember their own past until it was too late. Just how dangerous Protestant political culture's core beliefs were became apparent in mid-1774, the time of rebellion. What began as another year in the empire became in short order a time of profound upheaval. Provincials interpreted legislation passed by Parliament as evidence that popish plotters had compromised the imperial administration in order to destroy the empire and Protestantism itself. This interpretation made coherent the diffuse disorder that had plagued the empire since 1763. The resituating of anti-popery and anti-Catholicism from an ideology of institutional legitimation to a platform from which to criticize the imperial order destroyed the empire's institutional logic in a matter of months.[8]

The Intolerable Acts and the Quebec Act drove this alteration in Protestant political ideology's location in British American society. This legislation dealt with two distinct problems. The

Intolerable Acts punished Boston for the Tea Party. The destruction of the British East India Company's property in December 1773 pushed imperial authorities to crack down hard. Parliament passed a virtual economic death sentence on Boston by sealing its port to all waterborne trade. London revoked the Massachusetts Charter, effectively placed provincial courts under London's direct control, and appointed Thomas Gage military governor. It limited town meetings in all Massachusetts communities and upended other aspects of local control. In colonial eyes this established a military despotism and threatened the rest of British America with the same.[9]

The Quebec Act that soon followed convinced provincials that the legislation coming from London grew from a concerted Catholic-led ministerial conspiracy designed to enslave British Americans body and soul. Viewed from London, the issues at stake were complex. Imperial authorities had agonized about what to do about French-speaking, Catholic Quebec since the armies led by generals Amherst and Wolfe had captured New France during the Seven Years War. How much of their French culture and beliefs would be allowed to survive in the British Empire?[10]

The London government wanted to create a template for integrating peoples who were different from Protestant Britons into the imperial order. In 1774 they finally settled Quebec's place in that order in a manner that from a modern perspective looks decidedly open-minded. The Quebec Act protected the Catholic religion in Quebec and allowed Catholics there to take loyalty oaths without mentioning Protestantism. The legislation put French civil law largely back in place, thus doing away with trial by jury in some cases, and made no allowance for an elected assembly. The act also joined the vast trans-Appalachian interior won from France in the Seven Years War to Quebec administratively. By accepting many French practices in their new colony, the imperial ministry wanted to demonstrate their cosmopolitanism and strike a balance between integration and acceptance of local norms.[11]

It all seemed rational in London. Punish those who had destroyed the British East India Company's property in Boston, and show toleration to French-speaking Catholics in Quebec. For British Americans, though, the legislation, taken together, signaled that popery had infiltrated the empire's very heart.

With the acts, North Carolina awoke politically. Even quite sober colonists began to fear that a time of tyranny had come. The wealthy Edenton lawyer Samuel Johnston Jr., who would eventually be elected governor of republican North Carolina, became intensely apprehensive about events. He had largely kept his thoughts about the imperial crisis out of his correspondence until 1774. But when a British friend informed him that Parliament had brought in a bill for "shutting up the port of Boston" in response to the Tea Party, everything began to change. Within months his correspondence became political, and ultimately seditious, in character. Writing in reference to the Intolerable Acts, Johnston told a British friend that "no people who had ever tasted the sweets of freedom would ever submit to them.... They [meaning the British ministry] have now brought things to a crisis."[12]

The Carolina jurist James Iredell went through a similar transformation. Iredell was British-born, the poor relation of Henry McCulloh, one of colonial North Carolina's greatest landholders. His kin ties to McCulloh had led to Iredell's appointment as comptroller of customs at Edenton in 1768, at the tender age of seventeen. His life at Edenton centered around his official port duties, building his budding legal career, and wooing Hannah Johnston, sister of Samuel Johnston Jr., a campaign crowned with success when she agreed to marry him in 1773. Revolution was the last thing on his mind. In fact, Iredell became crown attorney for Hertford, Tyrrell, and Perquimans Counties during the imperial crisis and accepted the post of collector of customs at Edenton in 1774.[13]

But news of the Intolerable Acts and the Quebec Act abruptly reoriented his attitudes toward imperial politics. While he denounced mobbing, he expressed his belief that the crime done by the Tea Partiers hardly merited a punishment that could "scarcely be told without horror." An entire town received a death penalty for the actions of "30 or 40." The Intolerable Acts expressed the British ministry's arbitrary character and Parliament's "condescending meanness."[14]

The Quebec Act intensified Iredell's radicalization. The legislation completed "the tower of Despotism," indulging the French-speaking settlers in "all their prejudices.... in favor of *arbitrary power.*" Worse yet, the legislation made Catholicism, "persecuting in its principle, and horrid in its influence on the morals of Mankind," a legally recognized faith in the province, and did nothing to protect Protestant settlers' religious liberties.

Iredell found it all unacceptable. A French government had been created in British America's very bosom. Such a province was not English in "spirit, in principle, in dignity." Further, the London ministry's administrative union of the western interior to Quebec left the British colonies surrounded and allowed for "the propagation of the Romish Faith, and of despotic principles" in the North American interior. In the months that followed, James Iredell would pen two important pamphlets, *To the Inhabitants of Great Britain* and *The Principles of an American Whig,* that helped establish the intellectual basis for independence. Little could Iredell suspect that the path to his eventual appointment as associate United States Supreme Court justice would intersect with the Brethren in Edenton's courthouse. In September 1777 he would find himself acting as the state's prosecutor of a strange group of loyalists who had plotted to kill Governor Richard Caswell. When he read their depositions, he may have recognized that their spiritual and political views were like his ... in 1775.[15]

One Carolinian after another asserted that the Intolerable Acts and the Quebec Act expressed a perverse thirst for unlimited temporal power fueled by spiritual corruption. They used the Protestant political languages that had bound the British Empire tightly together for over eighty years to indict the imperial leadership. "Lord North [prime minister of Britain]," explained one North Carolinian in 1775, had secretly become "a Roman Catholick." George III's crown, the same man continued, "tottered upon his shoulders," for he had "established the Roman Catholick Religion in ... Quebeck." Others insisted that Quebec's re-enslavement was a key step in the British ministry's diabolical design "to establish Popery" throughout North America.[16]

In western North Carolina, Rowan County's alarmed residents feared that London's satanic forces would murder them all. They believed that Lord North and Britain's North American military leader General Gage intended to set the Native Americans on them in order to rip "Infants from the wombs of their expiring mothers" and roast Protestants to death. County whigs called on the yeomanry to "rouse like one Man in Defense of our Religion from Popery, our Liberty from slavery, and our lives from tormented Death." Indeed![17]

Suspicion began to extend toward George III himself. A tavern keeper in eastern North Carolina stated with assurance "that the King and Parliament had Established the Roman Catholick Religion ... in Quebec ... and did intend to bring in popish principles into America." This same rural philosopher declared that by advancing this popish plot "the King had forfeited his Coronation Oath" that called on him to defend Protestantism.[18]

People in every colony used this framework to subvert imperial control. The Georgia legislature declared that the Quebec Act had granted "little short of a full establishment, to a religion which is equally injurious to the rights of sovereign and of mankind." According to one Georgia minister, Parliament intended to establish "a hierarchy over them similar to that of the church of Rome in Canada." New Yorker Samuel Avery described the Quebec legislation as the plan "to Subjugate the Colonys." He believed it had been introduced "by Lord Bute who is . . . a Relation to the Pretender [Bonnie Prince Charlie of the Stuarts, the ruling family whose Catholic branch was deposed in the Glorious Revolution], and is said to be of the Romish Religion." London lost control in every colony as the belief took root that the imperial leadership had been corrupted by a popish plot. The very beliefs that had been used to formally legitimate the Glorious Revolution and held the empire together now split it apart.[19]

The speed of that collapse is startling. As early as August 1774 freeholders in Pitt County in the southern Albemarle declared that imperial tyranny had led sovereign power to revert "to the people as the foundation from whence all power and legislation flow." Governor Martin reported to London that those provincials who had "traitorously propagating the most base, scandalous and monstrous falsehoods of the Kings religious and political principles" drove this transformation in order to seize power for themselves. These rebels used the language of anti-popery to defame "the sacred character of the best of princes." The perception that the Protestant prince had embraced popish principles caused the empire's inner logic to disappear in America.[20]

Stressing these anti-Catholic and anti-popish idioms' importance does not mean that no one invoked natural rights or referenced the classical world as they denounced the London authorities. They did, in North Carolina and elsewhere. Nor is it to suggest that structural change and social conflict were not in play in the revolutionary crisis. They were. But the appropriation of the Protestant libertarian discourses that had stabilized the empire until 1774 played a central role in explaining the unfolding crisis to an agrarian Protestant population with limited literacy, and ultimately undermined imperial control.

Seen within this context, Americans' rapid change from loyal Protestant subjects in love with their monarch to antimonarchical revolutionaries becomes easily understandable. A bold stand against traditional authority could be aligned with the vast majorities' traditional beliefs and historical understandings in the empire. And it explains why the empire so suddenly collapsed into civil war and revolution after a decade of low-level conflict that, while troubling, did not seem to foretell a dramatic, world-altering upheaval.

The yeomen who would shape much about the Revolution's course did not understand these developments, or themselves, from the high vantage point of an unknown future national identity. Nor did they find motivations in the writings of the authors at the center of often-cited twentieth-century academic treatments of eighteenth-century ideology. The Intolerable Acts and the Quebec Act led North Carolinians and Protestant British Americans everywhere to believe that America would soon fall under popish absolutism, and with that understanding the society edged ever closer to revolution.

Order broke down in this strange political twilight as popular conventions and ad hoc committees of safety seized power. The committeemen soon launched a disjointed and violent offensive against the people's enemies. Examining their reign makes the American Revolution look . . . a lot more revolutionary. By 1775, Edenton, New Bern, and the other parts of North Carolina came to be in some ways like Paris in 1793 or St. Petersburg in 1917, in miniature, with increased humidity. The time of the committees of safety had come.

Come the Committees, Come the Terror

With the royal government corrupted by a popish plot, the belief "that right [of government] again reverts to the people" spread rapidly. It remained unclear just who, or what, constituted "the people," given the circumstances. It began an agonizing conversation. Again and again throughout the revolutionary and early national period, bitter debates would erupt about who constituted the people and which institutions could speak for them. The ad hoc popular conventions and committees of safety that appeared suddenly in 1774 were Americans' first answers to this dilemma. Provincials claimed these bodies were the institutional manifestation of the people's primordial authority as understood in the British constitutional tradition.

British Americans knew about popular conventions and ad hoc committees long before the imperial crisis. Committees of safety had formed in the British Isles during the English civil wars (1642–1651), and on both sides of the Atlantic during the Glorious Revolution (1688–1690). Conventions and committees had also appeared in parts of the British American countryside during the prolonged disputes over property rights that began there after 1740. Colonials understood them as extraordinary institutions that emerged when rulers violated the people's rights or when normal institutions failed for any reason. They would be used to correct the British constitution, and then be disbanded when normal constitutional practices resumed.[21]

What began in British America in 1774 was on a whole other level. With the Intolerable Acts and the Quebec Act, the great mass of people awoke politically and moved to reclaim their sovereign power from a popishly tainted imperial administration that threatened them body and soul. Extralegal conventions which began to be called in mid-1774 in one county after another to meet the growing threat from London assumed local power as imperial institutions withered away. These county conventions were mass meetings of freeholders, some held at county courthouses, others under local liberty trees, and still others in local taverns. Commentators proclaimed these county conventions to be the people in their most primordial institutional-constitutional manifestations, reemerged to assert their sovereign power in the face of a tyrannical ministry.

Even as these conventions sprang to life, their hard-minded siblings, the committees of safety, began to emerge across North

Carolina and the rest of the colonies. In some cases conventions appointed committeemen, in others town meetings or county free-holders authorized their creation, and some committees formed on the initiative of those involved. The committees enforced consumer boycotts of British goods, organized resistance to popish ministerial authority, and maintained order in the locales as imperial control waned.[22]

A colony-wide congress that met at New Bern in August 1774 legitimated the authority of the committees of safety that had already appeared and ordered a great increase in both the numbers of committees and their powers. The conventioneers called for the formation of county committees of five. These five committeemen would be elected by freeholders who swore loyalty to the whig cause at their county courthouses the third Thursday in October.[23]

Many locales used these recommended procedures to form committees. Freeholders meeting at the Wilmington courthouse, in the region to the south of the Albemarle, elected committees in this manner. Those who attended "united themselves under every tie of religion and honor" to stand together to defend North Carolina until a reconciliation "upon constitutional principles" between London and the colonies could be worked out. The convening freeholders further swore to obey the committees in all matters related to the ongoing struggle.[24]

The New Bern convention's instructions were, though, just recommendations. Committees continued to appear under a variety of circumstances, and with varied structures. Samuel Williams saw a "number of People assembled at the Court House" in Anson County "chose a Committee of 19 men." He heard one man say the king had violated his coronation oath, thus freeing Carolinians from their imperial allegiance. In Surry County, the committee of safety, proclaiming "Liberty or Death" as well as "God Save the King," instructed militia captains to "call their Companies together . . . in Order to chuse three in each respective Company as Committee

Men." Pitt County freeholders created a county committee of an astonishing ninety-eight men in June 1775. Committee formation accelerated throughout 1774 and 1775, with some following the New Bern guidelines and others ignoring them.[25]

The Hillsborough Provincial Congress that convened in August 1775 sought to bring order to this chaos of county conventions and local committees. The Hillsborough delegates created a hierarchy of committees designed to control North Carolina as the royal government disappeared. They divided the state into six defense districts and called on freeholders to elect a committee of safety composed of twelve men in each district. Local committees were to form subcommittees of "secrecy, Intelligence and Observation," to communicate with other towns and districts about public enemies who might be moving between communities. The convention delegates instructed committeemen to "Examin all suspected Persons," punish those who would not support the cause of liberty, and act as "a superintending power over the Town and County Committees."[26]

The delegates further determined that in each county a committee of not less than twenty-one freeholders should be formed. The major towns would have committees of fifteen people, and in every other town that had a right of representation in the assembly a committee of seven would be formed. By then, at least twenty-six counties out of thirty-two had committees of safety of some kind, often with different structures and agendas. Certainly, the southern Albemarle counties of Bertie and Pitt had county committees, although gaps in records make it unclear when they formed in Martin and Tyrrell Counties.[27]

The delegates also asserted the committees' control over the militia, whose importance increased day by day amid the growing turmoil. The congress brought the standing militia units under the committees' authority and dissolved the ad hoc independent militias that had formed in 1774. They saw these independent units as interfering with "the regulars and Minute [man] service." Individuals could still form companies on their own initiative, though, subject to "regulations of such Committees" as existed in their local areas. The conventioneers further ordered local committees to speed military preparations in case the fighting raging in New England spread south.[28]

From these county and provincial conventions the petite American terror of the committees of safety sprang. Tasked with maintaining the boycotts against Britain, controlling prices as demands for commodities dramatically increased, ensuring acceptance of the new polity's paper currency, and dealing with the people's enemies, the committees seized control. Situation by situation, the committeemen tightened their grip on the society by redefining what constituted political crimes, until the boundaries between public and private, social and political, words and actions, completely collapsed.[29]

The American Revolution in North Carolina began in earnest with this change. A new political world of interrogations and mob attacks developed as provincial norms against violence fell away. Committeemen started to hunt down liberty's enemies, using intimidation, mobbing, and torture to establish their authority. A wrong word, the sale of forbidden articles, sympathy for beleaguered royal officials, thinking wrong thoughts, being born in Scotland: these could make you an enemy of the people.[30]

Rebellion had swallowed protest, and now revolution consumed the rebellion. The use of intimidation and violence to sustain committee authority became systematic in 1775. When Rowan County merchant Maxwell Chambers raised prices in May 1775, he became an "Enemy to the common cause of Liberty" for defying the Continental Congress's edicts about trade. The committee published his name in the South Carolina papers as a person hostile to the cause. Thomas McKnight, who refused to swear loyalty to the rebellion, complained in July 1775 that a Joseph Jones threatened to get committeemen to "tar, feather and burn me, together with my property" as an enemy of the people. Merchant Hugh Montgomery, on the other hand, "generously acknowledged" his error in raising prices and accepted committee authority. He received far friendlier treatment as his reward.[31]

Even those who supported the cause found the use of sustained torture against the people's enemies troubling. A committee-led mob "tarr'd & feathered," Edenton's Robert Smith remarked, "two poor devils last week and sent them over to Tyrell," the county on the Albemarle's southern shore, for additional punishment for some unspecified political crime. They did this, Smith reported, to demonstrate their power. "This week," he continued "they threaten to serve all my countrymen [he was Scottish] the same way, Mr. Johnston [Samuel Johnston, also born in Scotland]. . . . and my self it seems are to be excepted" because of their known patriotism. Scots were seen as likely allies to a popish imperial ministry because of the Highlanders' traditional support of the deposed Catholic Stuart king James II and his eighteenth-century heirs.[32]

Yet Smith continued to back imperial defiance. In his own way he had become as radical as those who had turned to terror to enforce their revolutionary will. "No treatment I may receive," he declared, "from the over heat of their zeal shall make me to desert a cause, which I . . . had more at heart than life."[33]

Other Albemarle gentlemen, though, were more alarmed as traditional means of controlling mobs began to fail. Edenton whig Samuel Johnston warned correspondents that the established elite were losing control. Johnston told North Carolina congressional delegate Joseph Hewes that only the most aggressive intervention "of some of the old members of our committee" had kept the situation in the town from really getting out of hand. Eventually even members of local committees of safety believed to have conservative views found themselves questioned by other members, the former suspected by the latter of a lack of ardor for the looming struggle. It went on and on. An Edenton mob paraded "a certain Gentleman . . . of great fortune" deemed hostile to the cause of liberty because he insulted revolutionary militiamen. The mob tarred and feathered the unlucky target at the town whipping post and then burned his coach.[34]

Violence carried out by committeemen against those they deemed opponents: this transformed imperial defiance into revolution. And it transformed those targeted from "farmer" or "neighbor" into "enemy of the people," "tory," or "loyalist." As the Revolution blossomed, the society fell into distrust and disorder.

The committees' aggressiveness in dealing with the budding Revolution's enemies led to the restructuring of the ad hoc power arrangements that had been agreed to at the Hillsborough convention. The Provincial Council became the Council of Safety. The convention abolished the committees of the six districts, which had never really become effective. The key power relationship now became that which existed between the North Carolina Council of Safety and the town and county committees.[35]

Royal officials could do little but watch as sustained violence brought down the imperial edifice. In May 1775 Governor Martin requested a royal standard and called loyal subjects to rally to fight for the king. But it was not enough. A month later Martin glumly reported that the committees had taken power. When the "incendiaries" failed to win someone to their cause, they seized the property of the loyal, tarred and feathered the recalcitrant, and otherwise threatened the king's faithful subjects "even with death." The governor fled to a British warship when rebel forces burned Fort Johnston in July 1775. He denounced the Second Continental Congress as the wellspring "of these foul streams of sedition" that via "the committees have overflown this once happy land." Martin told London that revolutionary committees dominated everything "to the distance of an hundred miles [from the coast]." He thought it impossible to govern without British regulars to assist him.[36]

By late 1775 the committees had become the local government and judiciary in every North Carolina county. As early as June 1775 the Moravian leader John Michael Graff noted that in Mecklenburg County, the rebels "have unseated all Magistrates and put Select Men in their places," meaning committeemen. In March 1776 Martin informed London that "little Tyrannies . . . under the denomination of Committees" now controlled North Carolina. Martin returned to the state later in the war, when Cornwallis invaded North Carolina, but his efforts to restore royal government failed. Martin ended his days as he began them, in Ireland, dependent on his prominent Anglo-Irish family, watching America from afar.[37]

The committees' power became irresistible as the Revolution unfolded across the political landscape. Even holy men found themselves questioned, slighted, attacked, and expelled if they defied the revolutionary authorities. The people's reign had indeed begun.[38]

The Committees against the Clergy

In 1775 a worried Reverend Daniel Earle, minister of St. Paul's Church in Edenton, wrote to Church of England's leaders in London to explain the clergy's dire situation in North Carolina. Earle, like Governor Martin, was a Protestant Anglo-Irishman, born at Bandon, Ireland. He had arrived in Edenton in 1757, become minister of St. Paul's in 1760, and established an extensive preaching circuit in the western Albemarle. Now, in 1775, he saw the empire's central spiritual strut in North Carolina under siege. Church ministers could not, he wrote, fulfill their duties without giving "umbrage to the Inhabitants." By continuing to pray for the king and royal family, and in some cases urging imperial fidelity, ministers found themselves removed from their pulpits, deprived of their pay, and finally "proscribed by the Committees." The

Reverend Earle believed that the "case of the clergy [in North Carolina] is very critical."[39]

That the Church of England liturgy required such prayers was immaterial. In the revolutionary crisis that developed in 1775, committeemen repeatedly accused the Church of England clergy who prayed for the royal family of hostility to the American cause. The Reverend Earle believed that "if the most ... eloquent Divine in England" tried to convince them otherwise, he would only inflame the situation further. The wily Earle escaped violent persecution; he had publicly denounced imperial taxation in 1774, but he knew the key to his preservation came from never publicly praying for anything other than "peace, good order and a speedy reconciliation with Great Britain." Nonetheless, Earle's congregants tried to starve him out by refusing to pay his salary or otherwise provide for him. He awaited better times as a herring fisherman, the waters of the sound his solace in a world turned upside down.[40]

Nowhere is the committees' revolutionary character more evident than in their interactions with Protestant ministers who would not conform to the emergent political reality. The right to disagree disappeared in that season of revolution. The pulpits' centrality as communication hubs convinced committeemen in many locales not to leave in place clergymen who might in some way threaten the cause of liberty. Committeemen used threats and withheld pay to force ministers who seemed sympathetic to the empire from their pulpits. With these expulsions, the spiritual communities built by preachers and lay readers in the Albemarle in the three decades before independence came under intense stress. The Brethren arose in this vacuum created in 1775–1776.[41]

The imperial crisis had already ruptured many norms when committeemen began threatening clergy in 1775. Until then, British American society found violence against licensed Christian ministers unacceptable. There had been formal actions, sometimes violent, against wandering Quaker preachers in the seventeenth and eighteenth centuries, and against unlicensed Baptist evangelicals in Virginia in the eighteenth century. Some of these incidents were quite unpleasant. But for someone to threaten or attack an orthodox minister, or deface or damage a Protestant church in an iconoclastic attack, went well beyond the pale.[42]

Church ministers' continuation of prayers for the royal family after 1774 caused this norm to rupture. These prayers played a central part in the Church's liturgy, but they became more problematic week by week as the king came to be directly indicted in the popish plot and the committees became more confident in asserting their power. By 1775, North Carolina revolutionaries had decided they could no longer stand the affront to liberty posed by these prayers. Honest Protestant subjects should not be praying for a popish monarch; truly Protestant clergy should not be urging them to do so.

When the committees ordered the prayers stopped, Anglican ministers became trapped between local politics and British patronage, and between oath-sworn duty and deference to provincial concerns. Initially they refused to comply. The ministers understood local political concerns, and they wanted to avoid political conflicts whenever possible. And yet they also acknowledged the monarch as the Church's head and the empire's father, and they depended on the Bishop of London and the Archbishop of Canterbury for their appointments.

The Church ministers were forced into silence as committee-led violence and intimidation against them intensified. The Reverend James Reed, for example, Anglican minister at New Bern, came under scrutiny when he refused to preach on a general fast day ordered by the Continental Congress in July 1775. He declared that as a missionary for the Society for the Propagation of the Gospel, he could not join in the fast and would lose his livelihood if he did. The committee of safety ordered his vestry to suspend him. Then some of his own congregants rebuked him as he prayed for the king;

they famously shouted, "Off with his head!," leaving it unclear which head they meant. Reed soon fled his pulpit.[43]

Ministers in the other Albemarle counties had similar experiences. The Reverend Nathaniel Blount of Martinborough in Pitt County was one of several ministers who not only tended his own flock but rode the circuit of rural chapels in the southern Albemarle area that spawned the Brethren. Blount's refusal to stop praying for the royal family attracted the Pitt County committee of safety's attention in July 1775. They ordered the church wardens to advise Blount "That the People Desires he may withdraw from his agreement as the only method to Unite People of the County." And with that, his twenty-year contract to preach and serve the community came to an end. Bertie County Church of England minister Reverend Francis Johnston, who served several chapels in that county, at some point came under committee scrutiny. By 1777 he had been sent into exile, eventually ministering to a parish in Jamaica. Other Church of England ministers soon fled their pulpits out of loyalty to the Crown or from fear of the committeemen.[44]

The committeemen also scrutinized dissenters who preached pacifism or nonresistance or both. More than one Baptist preacher found himself called before committees for advocating pacifism or passive obedience to authority. In August 1775 the Rowan County committee reported that "Mr. Cook, the Baptist preacher" appeared before them. Cook "in the most … humiliating Terms" apologized for signing a protest against the cause of liberty that circulated in the Yadkin River region. He acknowledged his error in opposing the "Rights and Liberties of the Nation in general and American Liberties in particular," and begged the committeemen to educate him politically. No one could speak against the cause without inviting retaliation on some level.[45]

The Halifax Congress that met in May 1776 moved to permanently end the threat posed by the Church of England. The delegates declared that while church vestrymen would still be elected as tradition demanded, on Easter Sunday, they would not be seated until "subscribing the [loyalty] Test recommended by the last Provincial Congress." Only then would they be "declared legal vestries." The committees held the ministers to the letter of this decree. When Bertie County Anglican preacher Francis Johnston refused to take the new state's oath of allegiance, feeling it contradicted his loyalty to the king as his church's spiritual head, the local committee forced him to stop preaching.[46]

At independence, the revolutionaries disestablished the Church of England, but simultaneously brought local church governing structures further under the revolutionary government's control. The state authorities proclaimed liberty of conscious. But ministers would feel the full weight of sedition laws if they used their pulpits to encourage defiance of the new order. Despite our historical perception that the Revolution broke church–state unions or created freedom of religion, at its birth the revolutionary state sought control of the pulpit. They had to; the pulpit was too central to be left outside their control. The threats and attacks initiated a process that reoriented crucial spiritual-political relationships in the Anglo-American world, but in a manner not in line with our historical understanding of the supposed separation of church and state. The committees sought, not liberty of conscious, but to control theology as well as behavior. Linear interpretations of the spiritual and the political early in the revolutionary period tend to obscure more than they clarify. [47]

The Church had become deeply engaged in community life in eastern North Carolina in the years before 1775–1776. Church ministers, church wardens, and lay readers came to regulate social relationships and provided the very basic support that enabled society to function. The records of St. Paul's Church at Edenton give a strong sense of this engagement. When congregant Joseph Mansfield fell ill, church wardens paid Elizabeth Chappell fifty shillings to care for him. Peter Barns needed a "shirt & Trowsers," which the Church provided; Rachel Walton received five shillings, eight, to help him purchase them. Thomas Price received three pounds and one shilling to care for an unnamed woman of color for three months. The list of people helped or cared for by St. Paul's went on and on.[48]

At least some chapel congregants provided similar assistance. When people in Currituck County in the north Albemarle petitioned Governor Martin for permission to establish a chapel, they asked for permission to raise funds "for maintenance of the poor" and other "charitable intentions." The chapel lay readers and the circuit-riding preachers created community networks in the countryside that enabled and regulated life there. People met, married, and often buried their dead in or within feet of their churches and chapels, the cycle of everyday life tied to the spiritual.[49]

The suppression of the Church created a lasting spiritual and social vacuum in the countryside. In the spring of 1777 the Reverend Earle reported to London that the new state constitution placed all denominations on an equal footing, rendering the Church's situation in North Carolina "very precarious." Reverend Willis told the SPG that he had been "driven from his mission for 2 years' past" by the revolutionary turmoil. Although some preaching occurred at Edenton and elsewhere in the Albemarle after independence, the Church of England effectively disappeared from North Carolina in 1776 and would not come back for nearly twenty years. When it did return, it manifested itself as unhappy fraternal twins: the Methodist Church and the Protestant Episcopal Church.[50]

The committees' actions disestablishing the Church might be understood as a triumph for religious toleration, but people in the Albemarle experienced it as a major, and enduring, loss. With the yeomanry's normal sources of comfort and routine in times of crisis unable to provide them with succor as the Revolution intensified, their anxieties, as well as their hopes, became free to flow in other channels. And that would encourage the Brethren to emerge.

In colonial minds, the famed balance that had defined British constitutionalism before 1765 had disappeared entirely by 1776. This disruption was not just about the balance of power between metropole and colonies or king and Parliament. Balance in the British Constitution was never just about the institutional relationships between the branches of government. Only in a Protestant spiritual-political order could balance be maintained, and in 1774–1775 the colonists came to believe that Protestant political culture had been undone at the imperial core by popish leaders.

On January 1, 1776, provincial North Carolina no longer existed. Force wielded by the committees of safety held society together to the degree it was held together at all. Political views ran from extreme pacifism to militant whiggery to imperial loyalty. To understand what changed in those crucial months between that day and the Brethren's appearance early in 1777, we need to come to a better understanding of what happened immediately after independence. Surely there is no more mysterious date in American history than July 5, 1776.[51]

4

Julr Fifth

Early in July the congressional delegates in Philadelphia issued the Declaration of Independence and ordered it proclaimed
in America's towns and villages. At Halifax, North Carolina state
leader Cornelius Harnett read the Declaration to a boisterous crowd
that then carried him around the little town on their shoulders. In
every state raucous celebrations broke out as American independence was announced to the world.[1]

But by late summer the party was over. At the end of August
imperial forces defeated Washington's army at Brooklyn Heights
in New York and soon drove the Continental Army from Manhattan. The disintegrating American forces fled across New Jersey
in the fall of 1776. The resulting strains were felt from Maine to
Georgia. In North Carolina, trade collapsed, committees of safety
enforced order where it existed at all, and British cruisers lurked
along the coast. Confidence in the state's paper money eroded day
by day, and by the fall that currency was already being counterfeited.
Price inflation took hold, and salt and other essentials came into
short supply. Little wonder that when asked to describe the times
in those months, Albemarle yeomen gave one answer: "very bad."[2]

Amid this chaos state leaders began to adopt positions that
seemed to the state's yeomen to repudiate all historical logic and
the very rationale for the Revolution. The revolutionary government

made increasingly arbitrary demands for troops and began to advocate for a military alliance with Catholic France—the sworn ancient enemy of all free Protestants. Worse yet, rumors began to circulate that some leaders had strange spiritual and social beliefs that seemed to threaten the Revolution itself.

The yeomen did not understand these unhappy changes through a national mythology that had yet to be created. American republican identity could offer no guidance as it had yet to be formed in any meaningful way. All these farmers had to guide them was the past. Within months after independence, Albemarle yeomanry were viewing at least part of their revolutionary leadership as contaminated by the same popish forces that had infected the imperial administration. In the broadest sense it expressed the general suspicion in revolutionary America toward anyone in power, even the people's representatives serving in a republican government.[3]

These suspicions led the yeomanry to again mentally resituate the idioms and beliefs embedded in Protestant political culture. What had been perceived as shared political values and the general motivation for revolutionary mobilization became in their hands a tool to criticize elements in the new republican state who were publicly abandoning the values of free Protestant society at the very moment of independence. In applying the logic contained within Protestant political culture to elements in the revolutionary elite, the Albemarle yeomanry effectively again reverted those Protestant political idioms to their historical usage as tools to criticize and delegitimate a popish-heretical government.

Abandonment and reapplication: this process expressed a profound ideological divergence in the revolutionary political community in North Carolina and indeed everywhere in America in the months after independence. And that divergence helps explain the startling transformation in which the values and political language that had mobilized the population in 1775 become increasingly identified with loyalism and reaction by 1778. Ancient ideas about

Protestant liberty became institutionally unmoored in the maelstrom of war and revolution and diplomacy, their original starring role in the empire's demise ultimately forgotten by a society in need of a different origin story.

"Defend & Protect All Drafted, Distres'd or Opprest Persons"

In the fall of 1776 it became obvious to those who won their living from the soil that they were trapped between two mighty forces—revolution and war, on the one hand, and the relentless agricultural cycle that dominated their lives, on the other. With the fighting raging in the Mid-Atlantic, the state's demands for troops and militia mobilizations intensified even when all hands were needed at home to take in the harvest and prepare for spring planting.

No matter what we believe about the revolutionary generation's civic virtue, the need to eat had a primacy that could not be challenged. Despite the impression left by our prevalent national mythology, the minutemen's time—the period where volunteers rushed to defend the country—passed as quickly as it developed. Even in the heady days of 1775, militia units failed to muster, men tried to avoid service, and chronic problems plagued recruitment efforts. But the military effort had to be sustained if independence was to be won and the Revolution succeed.

The North Carolina Provincial Congress that met in August 1775 had initiated the military mobilization that would soon become permanent, coercive, and troubling to many. The mobilization created difficulties even as the provincial congressmen tried to plan it. "Our principal debates," the congress's president Samuel Johnston correctly predicted, would be "about raising troops." After heated words, apparently over the appropriateness of creating a standing army in a free commonwealth, the delegates agreed to assemble 1,000 soldiers for what became the state militia line, and to rearm and reinforce local militias wherever possible. They also laid plans to raise several Continental regiments and six minuteman units of 500 each.[4]

By the fall of 1776 the state leaders knew they would need many more troops for a longer period of time than they had imagined the year previously. There was no escaping it as the British repeatedly pummeled Washington's ragged army and the Mid-Atlantic militias collapsed in the face of the imperial onslaught. To get that manpower, the American leadership began to behave in manners that seemed at odds with the Revolution. The Continental Congress pressured the states, the states pressured the counties, and the counties pressed the parishes and town. It devolved toward raw coercion amid a revolution in defense of liberty. They had become what they had all feared in 1775: a coercive government demanding money and troops.

The leaders turned to bounties, to quotas, and finally to impressment to get troops into the field. The Albemarle region bore the brunt of the initial efforts to man North Carolina's military formations when the calls for troops intensified during the disaster-filled fall of 1776. The state government did not intentionally overburden the region. The Fifth State Congress, the same body that would write the state constitution, authorized the creation of three regiments for Continental service. These regiments' leading officers were all from the southern Albemarle, and beginning in December 1776 they began recruiting heavily in Bertie, Martin, and the nearby counties where the Protestant association took shape and spread.

These officers tried to get men to enlist voluntarily by promising bounties. Such noncoercive efforts had been used without problems in the imperial wars. But they immediately caused resentment in 1776. Voluntary enlistments depleted the local manpower supply at a time when the economy was in shambles and men were needed at home more than ever to reap and sow, and to guard against slave insurrection. The efforts failed anyway; no matter how much bounty money they promised, officials again and again failed to reach recruitment goals via such means.[5]

The Continental Congress's demand for troops intensified early in 1777. Congressional delegate Thomas Burke told Governor Caswell in March that Congress was "using every endeavor to recruit a strong army" to mount a campaign in the spring. Their efforts, he continued, "will be ineffectual if not earnestly seconded by the States." He urged Caswell to focus on recruitment and told him Congress would work with the states or without them to raise the forces necessary. A few weeks later Burke told Caswell, "Our recruits come in very slowly, & I fear there is very great abuse in the recruiting department."[6]

Desperate state leaders turned to coercion to fill out formations. They employed forced drafts and impressments, practices that had a long and unsavory history throughout the British Empire. The state government placed troop quotas on towns and counties and authorized forced drafts to try to meet the quotas. It seemed the only way to sustain the war, even though it violated principles of limited government and self-determination that underlay the Revolution. People resisted actively or passively. The harder the state leaders pushed in order to prosecute what quickly became a desperate war, the less the population linked liberty with independence or equated military service with support of or acquiesce to the Revolution. The fact that the rebellion in part began in opposition to the threat posed by a standing army only exasperated the problem.[7]

The yeomen who associated to defend Protestantism in 1777 frequently expressed hostility to the sustained efforts to force them into military service as a primary reason they supported the movement. Yeomen and planters needed to be at home at crucial moments in the agricultural cycle no matter what the military situation. Southern Albemarle yeoman Joseph Taylor expressed the countryside's sensibilities about the agricultural cycle's domination of their lives even in wartime. Men needed to be in their fields; he strongly objected to men being drafted against their will "in Crop time." William Tyler also believed there should be no drafts or mobilizations "in Croop time." Men taken from their families, kept from the all-important planting and harvesting, their children left to starve—it was unacceptable. Both men joined the movement to save the Protestant commonwealth in 1777. Joseph Taylor, William Tyler, and every other yeoman in the Albemarle needed to reap and sow. There was no other way.[8]

William Hyman would later swear that he joined the Brethren to "Defend & protect all drafted, Distres'd or opprest persons," people taken against their will. If the state could coerce them, how could they be said to be a free people? Lemuel Hyman simply thought it wrong for men to coerce men to fight. He found it hard to tolerate men being "prest or carried away from their Wives and children" against their will. Benjamin Harrison felt the exact same way. He believed it right to defend anyone being "pressed to go to War against there will." Tyrrell County's Stephen Garrett associated with the Brethren so men would not "be pressed to go to the war against their will." Most of these men expressed no hostility to the American cause, or even aversion to service to that cause in an emergency. Resistance to popish tyranny should be stout, but it could not be coerced in a free commonwealth.[9]

The need for men in the fields reflected a central social reality of the yeomen in the southern Albemarle. Over half the yeomen had no slaves. Those who did own slaves had only one or two and often labored with their families beside those they owned. And those who had more slaves feared their servants as much as they needed them. Anxiety about a potentially rebellious slave population influenced resistance to drafts and mobilizations in eastern North Carolina. When the struggle for independence and the yearly struggle to survive conflicted, the latter always took precedent. If these yeomen linked their draft resistance to any broader political worldview, it was to the pillars of Protestant political culture—Francophobia, anti-popery, and anti-Catholicism. Only tyrannical governments like that in Bourbon France tried to create standing armies and coerce their populations in such a manner.[10]

The state quickly defined draft resistance or avoidance as treasonous, but the drafts and impressments failed anyway. The authorities could not meet troop quotas for the state line or the Continental Army, and they never did. Even in the midst of the crisis in the summer of 1777, when it seemed that the revolutionary government was under the most dire threat, recruitment and drafts disappointed all expectations.

The demands caused by the war created an ideological dislocation everywhere that came to the fore in North Carolina in the months before yeomen associated together to defend the Protestant state. The imperial unrest had begun in part in reaction to problems caused by the empire's maintenance of a standing army in peacetime. Such formations were seen as the tools of tyrannical, popish rulers. But with independence, traditional fears met the realities of having to fight rampaging imperial forces determined to crush the rebellion. American authorities who had denounced standing armies and expressed confidence in the civic virtue of yeomen militia were soon forced to create the Continental Army and to pressure local militias and state lines for help as one crisis followed another during the eight years of fighting.

The dramatic developments of 1776 drove a stark transformation in the political location of the beliefs embedded in Protestant political culture, and the forced drafts were only part of it. For in their quest to save the Revolution from imperial armies, the revolutionary leaders began to repudiate liberty's entire political-historical logic. They began talking about allying themselves with Catholic France. They wanted a deal with the devil.

Francophobia

The fear of France inculcated into British Americans from childhood continued to reign in their hearts on July 5, 1776. Anglo-Americans saw Bourbon France as the wellspring of all geopolitical evil. The British monarchy's legitimacy in the eighteenth century rested on its role as defender of British Americans and all Protestants from the French and Romish threats. This understanding that had come into being with the Glorious Revolution fully bloomed within the long imperial war between Britain and France that began in 1690 and didn't really end until Wellington bested Napoleon at Waterloo. The epic Seven Years War (1754–1763), fought largely against Catholic France and its Native American allies, had intensified Francophobia in Anglophone America still further. For provincials, no greater earthly enemy existed.[11]

But the diplomatic and military context that emerged at independence led North Carolina's leadership to join the leaders in other states to advocate for the unthinkable: an alliance with Bourbon France. The yeomanry prepared for the worst when rumors began to circulate in the fall of 1776 that this alliance would soon be signed, and actual French people began appearing in North Carolina. History and theory taught that Catholic France would use any opportunity to subvert free Protestant polities. The Revolution of 1775, against popery and tyranny, was in danger of being lost.

It is surprising that the reaction to the quest for a Franco-American alliance has not been understood as more central to ideological change between independence and the Yorktown victory in 1781. The revolutionary leadership denied their history and their God by courting France, in the process creating political-ideological fractures in the American cause. The Brethren grew in this conceptual fracture. Responses in other states took different forms, but collectively they are critical to understanding the Revolution's ideological and political character.

In North Carolina, private discussion of a Franco-American alliance by revolutionary leaders began shortly before independence. The Edenton attorney Samuel Johnston told several correspondents that America could prevail if "France and Spain would join us cordially and risque [risk] a war with Great Britain in Exchange for our Trade." Worldly souls like Johnston believed an alliance with Europe's Catholic powers was the only way the independent states could survive their fratricidal duel with the world's greatest military power.[12]

Talk about an alliance became public immediately after independence, and along with it came suppression of the anti-Catholic and Francophobic public discourse that had mobilized the population to revolutionary action in 1774. North Carolina's delegates to the Continental Congress began writing to as many people as possible about an impending French alliance. The Congress, they reported, was "endeavoring at a foreign Alliance, and have some hopes of success." In 1776 and 1777 newspapers repeatedly published reports that "a French war" against Great Britain "was inevitable," as a writer in the *North Carolina Gazette* put it. Continental Congress delegate Thomas Burke, believed to be a closeted Catholic, publicly promoted this league with France.[13]

Amid all this, a wave of actual French people began arriving in Edenton and other parts of North Carolina late in 1776 and early in 1777. French merchants and tobacco concerns sent agents and factors eager to enter the trade formally dominated by British tobacco houses. Jean Blair, living in Edenton, reported that "there is a whole Cargo of French folks come in." Two French women arrived with this group, "two very fine Ladies with a great many fine things and New Fashions." They walked about the town talking "of Balls and entertainments," and within a short period several French merchants threw a ball. The Protestant Albemarle's capital made home to aristocratic French women and licentious French merchants throwing galas during a war—suspicious indeed![14]

The French presence in the state seemed to grow as each month passed. Early in 1777, as tensions over forced drafts raged, a French officer, Major De La Port, openly aided by Governor Caswell, began roaming the countryside trying to enlist people, ostensibly to assist the American army. The French major discussed his plans to recruit Frenchmen then in Charleston, South Carolina, and march them into or through North Carolina. Given the society's history, what could possibly go wrong with such a plan?[15]

It got worse and worse. At the exact moment the unrest reached its brief zenith in early June 1777, Richard Caswell gave extensive help to another group of French officers. These "four French Gentlemen" had arrived in the state on their way to join the Continental forces in the north; Caswell provided them with comfortable carriages to help them on their way. To cap things off, state leaders then warmly greeted the Marquis de Lafayette as he passed through the state on his way north to join Washington's army. Little wonder anxiety should be high about French involvement in a popish plot against the state. Actual Catholic Frenchmen were wandering all over North Carolina raising soldiers, aided by the state elite.[16]

On July 5, 1776, the Albemarle yeomanry still saw the French as a deadly threat. Nathan Hallaway testified that when he was recruited into the movement to defend Protestantism in North Carolina, John Carter told him, among other things, "that the French was coming in that the gentry was joining them to bring in the popish Religion." This created great fear in Hallaway and other Albemarle yeomen.[17]

Lay preacher James Rawlings shared with David Taylor and others his fears about the new government and the French. Rawlings believed that "the Congress had given up the Country to the French to be governed by them, and then Popery would come into the Country." In such a turn of events, they might have been sure that 99 percent of American yeomen, whatever their proclaimed political allegiances, would have joined them in resisting this intrusion. The historical conditioning that painted the French as the enemy of all liberty-loving Protestants went too deep for it to easily disappear when the empire imploded.[18]

Leaders had generated this talk of an alliance in large part to restore hopes for victory among an already war-weary population that knew American forces had been badly defeated in New York and New Jersey. State leaders ignored the fact that this union with the ancient enemy seemed unnatural in the extreme to many. For most of those living in the dislocated revolutionary reality that existed in the months after July 4, advocacy of a French alliance and the efforts to force men into standing military formations quickly came to be seen as part of the same disastrous whole.

How could they fight for liberty while bound to its most intractable enemy? By publicly discussing a French alliance, state leaders inadvertently contributed to a rumor-fueled climate that made themselves vulnerable to charges of popery and covert Catholicism. The same leaders who had denounced the Catholic toleration inscribed in the popish character of the Quebec Act and the Intolerable Acts now seemed to be determined to make a deal with the true enemies of all free Protestants, when they should have been trying to create a free Protestant polity.

Francophobia was hardly confined to North Carolina. In some areas there was a swelling belief that the alliance represented a dark conspiracy to put America under the French king's control. This fear played a role in debates over state constitutions in Massachusetts and New Hampshire at the end of the 1770s. In the former state, it led to a, from the modern prospective, bizarre outburst by Protestant townsmen across the state against use of the word "Christian" in the Massachusetts constitution of 1780. "Christian" seemed to invite in "his Most Christian Majesty" the king of France. Bay State yeomen struggled to get this wording struck from the document, to be replaced by something far more reassuring: "Protestant."[19]

Talk about an alliance that defied all historical logic awakened ancient fears. Protestantism and a revolution in favor of free Protestant government seemed to be under attack from within the republican political community. From imperial pillar, to instrument of rebellion, to idioms used to voice fears about the new republic's foreign policy: a series of rapid transformations occurred in the public and private use of a specifically Protestant, Anglophone political language. This discourse had become unfixed, unconnected to any specific institutional structure, but still potent among the general population.

These shifts evidence a disturbing fact: at independence some elements in the revolutionary leadership tried to disconnect the Revolution from its own ideological origins and historical foundation. It was in that strange conceptual wilderness that the North Carolina yeomanry met and recoiled from the American Enlightenment.

Enlightenment Unwound

The unorthodox beliefs that unsettled the political order right before and after independence were rooted in the general Anglicization and refinement evident in many walks of provincial life late in the imperial period. The same ships that carried away tobacco and grain brought in European goods and British tastes. This growing cosmopolitanism expressed identification with London and the gentry's sense of being separate from the rest of provincial society. Albemarle gentlemen Anglicized their person and their leisure time in the decades before the Revolution in imitation of the British aristocracy. They donned periwigs created in Britain so they might look like British gentlemen, wiped their brows with silk handkerchiefs, wore British wools and linens, and otherwise imperialized their appearance. Thus attired, they gambled, danced, raced horses, and bet on cockfights just as British gentlemen did. As early as 1737, Edenton gentlemen John Bricknell noted that North Carolinians loved cockfighting. Not considering the local avian talent up to the home island's standards in regard to bird-to-bird combat, Edenton residents beseeched merchant traders to supply them with "Birds . . . From England and Ireland."[20]

If it had just been silk handkerchiefs and aggressive British roosters, Anglicization would have remained largely uncontroversial, at least in the short term. But it wasn't. Texts flowing from Europe into Edenton, and educations received outside North Carolina, led some Albemarle gentlemen to adopt irregular spiritual convictions that became bitterly divisive once fully released into public life by the Revolution. The theological tenets contained within enlightened literature were simply too radical for most eighteenth-century people and spoke against the Protestant spiritual and political beliefs that held their world together.[21]

British America had seen occasional public spats between gentlemen who embraced unorthodox spiritual beliefs, on the one hand, and Protestant clerics and lay believers, on the other. They occurred in the Albemarle, in other parts of North Carolina, and in every other colony. In the early 1770s James Iredell, a devout Church of England congregant, described the writings of "professed Deists" then circulating in Edenton as "Libertine." Such men, he continued, led "Immoral Lives," the character of which made them "dread an Account hereafter," thus encouraging them to deny that the hereafter even existed.[22]

Though Iredell used the term "Deists" to describe them, these heretical Carolinians held unorthodox beliefs along a wide spectrum. Some denied Christ's divinity, the Holy Trinity's existence, and the Bible's divine origins. Others seem to have had Arian beliefs, seeing Christ as a separate being from God the father; or to have been Socinians, rejecting the Trinity and denying Christ's immortality or His universal atonement. Or they simply held other unorthodox views.

These beliefs did not unravel the empire. The primary ideological axis, that which mobilized the mass to action in 1774 and 1775, grew from the imperial-Protestant political culture that had shaped their worldview in the eighteenth century. The enlightened in North Carolina were small in number, perhaps no more than several dozen, and in 1774–1775 the popish London ministry and the imperial armies seemed to be much bigger problems than a small number of people's private spiritual convictions. That the enlightened tended to be well-educated gentlemen, many of whom still attended Sunday preaching in Protestant churches, made them less threatening than they otherwise might have been. The concepts central to enlightened political discourse—liberty, property, virtue, fear of corruption—seemed no different from those at the center of Protestant political culture. The awareness that these terms might have different meaning to different people had yet to come.[23]

By mid-1776, though, some had started to become frightened by the efforts of enlightened men to introduce unwanted spiritual novelty into the new political order. While we have long understood the Revolution as a product of enlightened beliefs that brought the hope of liberation to an oppressive age, for America's yeomen political salvation could come only in a Protestant political order. By advocating for principles that seemed anti-Christian, elements in North Carolina's state government seemed to be acting against the Revolution itself as it had been understood in 1775. The beliefs expressed at the convention by a group of delegates who came to be known as the Fourteen seemed to promise North Carolinians enslavement of their souls as well as their bodies. The revolutionary republican state needed not to embrace enlightened liberation but to be saved from it.[24]

July 5, 1776

On July 5, 1776, American identity and ideas about freedom as we think of them did not exist. And yet the rebels against London's authority were no longer fully British. They had become trapped in a conceptual dilemma that engulfed newly independent America and drove change early in the revolutionary era. The Albemarle yeomanry's efforts to navigate in that unknown expanse led them first to associate to defend Protestantism and community, and then to become entangled in a murderous conspiracy against the republican state. It all expressed their fears about the Protestant commonwealth's fate and a Protestant American Revolution now forgotten but central to them.

On July 5, 1776, most American yeomen held views about Protestants and Catholics, God and man, right and wrong, threats and liberty, that were broadly similar to those held by the Albemarle yeomanry who associated in 1777. These views were expressed by people of all imaginable allegiances. Anti-Catholicism and anti-popery and Francophobia had played the central ideological role in holding the empire together and were seen as the pillars of true Protestant liberty. Paradoxically, these idioms also starred in the great drama between 1774 and 1776 as colonials used them to indict the very imperial institutions that were dependent on these discourses.

These ideological strands inherited from British America, stripped of imperial references, continued to shape behavior on and after July 5 as the realities of independence acted to change their political meaning and location. Growing rumors about a French alliance, combined with resentment about forced military service, leveraged this change. Although it was rural, the southern Albemarle abutted two major communication passageways, the north–south road between Virginia and Charleston, South Carolina, and the sound itself. This let information, often in the form of rumors, flow quickly into and around the area, which intensified the sense that something had gone drastically wrong.

The Albemarle yeomen are interesting, and historically troubling, precisely because their beliefs on July 5, 1776, were broadly representative of America's free white majority but do not fit into what we accept as the revolutionary generation's primary ideological and political categories. The writing of America's revolutionary political history has depended on the reality of a secularized republicanism based in classical virtue or a kind of nascent liberal individualism as the revolutionaries' primary motivation for action. And our contemporary inability to acknowledge the centrality of a Protestant worldview to the vast majority in that society because of our own political concerns has crippled our ability to understand the period any other way.

The values embedded in Protestant political culture were incompatible with both enlightened education and the diplomatic situation that developed at independence. But there was more to it. The idioms of Protestant political culture threatened elements in the emerging order precisely because they could be used to challenge the power of a state based on popular sovereignty, or indeed any state. Popery, heresy, or lust for arbitrary power—these were the common burdens of all mankind and all orders, and had to be confronted by a free Protestant people.

A new political contract could secure them from these threats. But when the congress called to write a republican constitution for North Carolina assembled late in 1776, it became apparent that the popish-heretical infection evident in the empire had already spread into the revolutionary leadership. Debate within the convention exposed fundamental disagreements within the American cause over the Revolution's character and the new order's spiritual-political constitution that could not easily be resolve. Would the upheaval produce a Protestant commonwealth? or an enlightened, secularized, neoclassical polity? or a hybrid, or something else? In North Carolina, this conflict led to the plot to kill the revolutionary elite.

5

CONVENTIONS
OF THE PEOPLE

ANGLO-AMERICAN POLITICAL theory provided a means to end
the revolutionary turmoil that had engulfed the nascent states.
New political contracts created in special constitutional conventions would allow Americans to end the rule of ad hoc institutions
that began in 1774 and exit the state of nature. At independence,
though, Americans knew these special conventions only through
their reading of political theory. Between late 1775 and 1778 that
abstract knowledge gave way to a gritty political reality. Americans in eleven of the thirteen onetime British provinces, plus
those in the rogue proto-state Vermont, formed conventions, congresses, or special legislative sessions to create new republican
governments.

These conventions became the solution that created new crises.
Bitter disagreements broke out everywhere over what type of constitutional structures would best secure the Revolution, how the institutions they created would relate to the British political past,
and what values should shape the republican states' political rites.
These disputes expressed a general confusion about the Revolution's
origins, character, and goals that would last for decades. What kind
of Revolution was it, and what would the new society be?[1]

The North Carolina's convention in the late fall of 1776 conformed to this troubled pattern. The delegates quickly fell into bitter conflict over the new state's constitutional structure and its spiritual-political character. At stake was the legislature's nature, the governor's office, and the role of Protestant faith in the government's formal rites. Their debates exposed a dangerous truth: they weren't all fighting for the same revolution. Not all delegates believed that the Revolution was a defense of Protestant liberty or that Protestant political values were central to its outcome. Not everyone thought that the Revolution should lead to a Protestant commonwealth; fourteen delegates made it explicit that they believed it should not. They denied Christ's divinity and the Bible's literal truth in the quest for a more secularized republic. Stories about their words and actions spread through the Albemarle region in the convention's wake. The growing realization that some revolutionary leaders had expressed anti-Christian views in public led directly to the Brethren and the crisis in 1777.

Constitutional Conflict

Ad hoc rule had already started to play on many nerves when the Fourth North Carolina Provincial Congress met in April 1776. That revolutionary body endorsed a separation from Britain, and appointed a Committee of Nineteen to create a temporary state government to meet the growing emergency. These nineteen men soon erupted into bitter conflicts over what shape the new constitutional frame should take. The conflicts reflected a deep conceptual divergence between those who advocated constitutional novelty and those who wanted to retain as much of mainstream eighteenth-century British constitutional logic as politically possible. Novelty or history? Progress or tradition?

The conflict over institutional frameworks reflected a profound struggle over how or whether precedent and history would be embodied in the revolutionary state. Should independence mark a unique historical origin point for a new society expressed in new institutional structures that in their form embodying the idea of popular sovereignty—namely, a governing structure with a unicameral, single-house legislature at its core? Or would Americans retain the logic of the balanced British constitution embodied in a bicameral legislature with a strong executive, albeit in a purified, republicanized form?

Unicameralism had significant support in the congress. Albemarle gentlemen Wylie Jones and Thomas Pierson, perhaps initially supported by soon-to-be governor Richard Caswell, wanted a unicameral government. The state would be governed by a legislature without a senate, elected by the free white male population over age twenty-one. The executive office would be effectively controlled by the legislature. The central ideas embedded in the concept of popular sovereignty seemed to create an undeniable logic in favor of such a government. The looming imperial separation would lead to the creation of a new republican people stripped of their social pretensions and ranks. This perception seemed to demand one legislative house, an institutional expression of their equality as they exited the state of nature. As a contemporary put it, the assembly needed to be "so near the people as to be an image of their thoughts and wishes, so numerous as to appear to every voter his direct counterpart, so frequently renewed as to insure swift responsibility." This new legislative body's institutional architecture would express the revolutionary leveling of social status in free white society embodied in the term "the people." Political time would begin anew in the revolutionary republic as single-house government would announce separation not only from the monarchical empire but from mainstream British political thought as well.[2]

Other delegates, though, were hostile in the extreme to unicameral government. These delegates rejected a complete conceptual rupture with the British past and demanded a mixed bicameral government with a strong executive that resembled that of the provincial period, freed from the corruption that had destroyed the imperial constitution. Edenton lawyer Samuel Johnston, Allen Jones, along with North Carolina Continental Congress delegate William Lettice Hooper, who was added to the Committee of Nineteen in mid-April 1776, led the efforts to establish this sort of bicameral system.[3]

The conflict between unicameralists and bicameralists became protracted. "We have," Samuel Johnston lamented, "a meeting on it [a new constitutional frame] every evening but can conclude on nothing." The problem was how or even whether to "establish a Check on the Representatives of the people" in a republican order, given that all authority came from the people. Why would the balances so celebrated in the now-corrupted British constitution be necessary in a regime constituted under the auspices of popular sovereignty and in a society emerging from the state of nature with its inherited social distinctions thrown down? These unhappy debates foreshadowed decades of controversy to come over the institutional nature of American's revolutionary freedom. At independence there seemed no easy way forward in North Carolina.[4]

The factions on the Committee of Nineteen tried to compromise. At some point during their meetings, those who wanted a single-house government accepted the idea of an upper house (senate) to act as a check that would inhibit a single-house assembly from becoming despotic. They also consented to property qualifications for assemblymen. But these more democratically minded revolutionaries continued to insist on yearly elections for all offices, an elected judiciary under legislative control, and most controversially, a plural executive. They could not yet bring themselves to give one man executive power.[5]

Demands for a plural executive challenged the central assumption of provincial politics and society: patriarchy, the belief that the rule of fathers was divinely inspired and benevolent in character.

The long-held belief that fathers or father figures should rule shaped early modern European society and the British American colonies more than any individual monarch ever did. It seemed nature's order, fathers ruling families, ministers acting as fathers to their congregants, royal governors serving as political fathers to their colonies, and Britain's Protestant kings symbolically acting as the empire's parent answerable to the Almighty parent of all. Protestantism, they believed, tempered fathers' rule, in sharp contrast with the harsh and authoritarian reign in family and polity in Catholic realms. Protestant patriarchy provided a logic that linked the biological and the social to the political and spiritual in a common framework.[6]

What happened in 1775 and 1776 had called Protestant political patriarchy violently into question. How could it not, with angry crowds putting imperial governors to flight and destroying effigies and symbols of a Protestant father-king become popish tyrant? A wave of iconoclastic violence against royal images and symbols in every state in late 1775 and 1776 proclaimed the imperial father's political death on the Atlantic's western shores.[7]

The revolutionaries advocating for a governing council as the state's executive rather than a singular governor had to confront troubling historical precedents in regard to plural executives. This type of executive council had been put in place in England after Charles I's execution in 1649, and several of the commonwealth governments that followed in the chaotic period between 1649 and 1659 had either single houses or plural executives or both. Many in the revolutionary generation read the history of that violent period one hundred plus years before as a warning from the past about the dangers of single-house republican governments and plural executives. But despite this, in 1776 several states considered using a plural executive, and those who wrote the Pennsylvania unicameral constitution actually created a council to act as that state's chief executive. It continued until Pennsylvania's 1776 constitution was replaced fourteen years later.[8]

In the spring of 1776, North Carolina's Committee of Nineteen reached a momentary consensus for a plural executive. The office was designed as an "Executive Council to consist of a President and six Councellors" to be elected annually. The consensus failed to hold, though, and violent arguments ensued. "A variety of plans," James Iredell reported, "is offered, and night and day wise and unwise heads are ruminating upon them." Convention president Samuel Johnston and other advocates for a single strong governor with a bicameral legislature became apprehensive and refused to warrant the plural executive. Despite attempts at compromise, no permanent agreement could be reached. The delegates empowered a Council of Safety to temporarily govern the state and then adjourned on May 14, 1776.[9]

In August 1776 the Council of Safety set off six months of political turmoil by recommending that freeholders select delegates for a new congress to write a republican constitution. October 15 was designated the day to elect the delegates to what became known as the Fifth Congress, a body tasked with establishing fundamental law for newly republican North Carolina. Intense partisan rancor marred the voting for delegates; violence broke out in some areas at the polling stations. Several mobs burned effigies of Edenton's Samuel Johnston. His advocacy of a British-style bicameral constitution with a strong executive and an independent judiciary made him a special target of those wanting more egalitarian constitutional structures. This opposition kept Johnston from becoming a delegate and enraged his brother-in-law James Iredell.[10]

Machinations about political architecture continued behind the scenes as the convening of the Fifth Congress approached. Second Continental Congress delegate William Hooper, in a private letter to Johnston in the fall of 1776, described Pennsylvania's newly formed unicameral government as "an execrable democracy—a Beast Without a head." Single-house governments, Hooper believed, were a threat to good order. In Pennsylvania the mob had been made "a second branch of Legislation—Laws subjected to their revision in order to refine them, a Washing in ordure by way of purification," Hooper's words referencing the submitting of all laws in Pennsylvania to popular ratification under the state's new constitution.[11]

Such innovations left people like Hooper and Samuel Johnston and James Iredell aghast. They envisioned the new order as a republican version of the old bicameral imperial governments, based on the true principles of Britain's mixed and balanced government. In their understanding, such governments offered an ordered liberty.

Discord over the constitutional form erupted immediately when the Fifth Convention convened in the second week of November 1776. Several delegates invoked John Adams's political writings that militantly favored strong executive bicameral government to support their pro-bicameral position. A copy of Adams's *Thoughts on Government* had been forwarded to the state, to either Richard Caswell or Samuel Johnston, sometime in the fall of 1776. It carried a detailed attack on unicameralism.[12]

A public letter from William Hooper to the delegates at the convention's opening intensified these attacks on unicameralism and brought disputes over constitutional structure again to the forefront. Hooper asserted that "the British Constitution in its purity (for what is at present stiled the British Constitution is an apostate)" was as close to perfection "as any could within the compass of human abilities." Hooper, like Johnston and Iredell, advocated for a republicanized version of the constitution they were in rebellion against. He believed the state constitution should express the British Constitution's "original principles." Hooper lashed out at unicameral government as "a many headed Monster . . . without any check." Such governments, he argued, soon descended into tyranny, as members of the single house "possessed of power uncontrolled, would soon exercise it." Sound governments had to have "another branch of legislation . . . selected for their Wisdom, remarkable integrity, or that weight which arises from property," the factors that provided "Impartiality to the human mind."[13]

Tensions intensified when someone circulated copies of the Pennsylvania and South Carolina constitutions and colonial Connecticut's charter to be consider as potential templates. Real knowledge of Pennsylvania's single-house government with a plural executive reanimated those who favored single-house government. Other models that circulated in the Congress, including the republican constitutions of Delaware, Virginia, New Jersey, and colonial Connecticut's charter were bicameral governments, with some significant differences between them, but with a loose similarity to North Carolina's colonial government.[14]

The conventioneers argued and argued. By early December, though, they found a compromise between tradition and revolutionary novelty. The specifics showed just how far the Revolution in North Carolina would go in its initial stage. Those advocating for a single-house government again accepted an upper house as a check on the assembly. They feared assemblymen in a single house might usurp all authority without such a check. Each county would have one senator and two assemblymen. Both houses would be directly elected. Voting for the senate would be restricted to those holding at least fifty acres and those voting for the lower house limited to those with enough property to pay taxes. The legal system fell under the assembly's domination; the legislature would appoint the superior judges. The document contained a Declaration of Rights derived directly and indirectly from that penned months before by George Mason for Virginia. Slavery would continue, and women would remain completely excluded from formal political life.

The new constitution, though, also encoded the assault on institutionalized patriarchy. In a concession to conservatives, there would be a single executive. He would be elected annually by joint legislative sessions, as would his council, again asserting legislative supremacy. Governors would have to have at least 1,000 pounds worth of property, be over thirty years old, and have been in the state for at least five years. These governors would have very little institutional authority. As in many states, the new legislature assumed patronage and policing powers that in the provincial period had been controlled by royal governors. Joint assembly sessions would appoint the attorney general and militia officers. The governors would continue as captain-general of militia, but only "for the Time being." Any financial powers granted to the executive were for "the Time being" only. The institutional patriarch would be left almost impotent.[15]

Even as the conventioneers struggled to iron out these issues, a clash between the Protestant faithful and the enlightened that would in different forms define much of American political culture thereafter began to manifest itself in the convention. Would the new state government's political rites and processes reflect the European Enlightenment and its values, or preserve elements of the Protestant political culture, liberated from its imperial entanglements, that had shaped Americans' understanding of their liberties and properties for a century? The resulting struggle led to the Brethren's creation when frightened yeomen heard rumors of some state leaders denying Jesus Christ's divinity and the literal truth of the Bible during convention debates.

Revolution and the Problem
of Enlightened Heresy

As the bitter debates over constitutional structure continued in November and early December, another divisive issue suddenly erupted into the congress. What would the spiritual-political character of oaths and public rights in the new polity be? Some delegates held views of a sort that the devoutly Protestant majority understood as spiritually as well as politically heretical. These delegates—those who came to be known as the Fourteen—denied Christ's divinity and tried to get mention of Christ and the Bible removed from formal political rites and oaths in the new common-wealth. Most or all also denied the Old Testament's literal truth and divine origins. Such views were incompatible with the beliefs of mainstream Protestants and their understanding of a functioning of a free—and thus Protestant—political society.

How had these Fourteen come to such radical spiritual-political views? In many ways it was their journeys in the decades before independence that led them to the views they expressed in the provincial congress in the late fall of 1776. Those involved in the unrest in 1776 and 1777, "in particular mentioned Wylie Jones & Whitmell Hill," as the heretical state leaders among the Fourteen convention delegates they feared the most. In these two lives we can understand how the Fourteen came to their views and why they were perceived as a threat to Protestant society and a Protestant American Revolution.[16]

Wylie (Willie) Jones was born to the Albemarle elite. Like many other gentlemen from the region, he descended from a family with its origins in the Virginia Tidewater. His father, Robert Jones, was a prominent landowner and lawyer who served as North Carolina's attorney general under Governor Arthur Dobbs in the 1750s. Robert Jones eventually assumed the position of proprietary quit rent collector as well.[17]

Robert Jones used his prominence to aid his children. He sent Wylie and his other son to boarding school at Eton in England early in the 1750s so that they might become proper British gentlemen, to be separated by their learning and manners from America's boisterous yeoman mass. At Eton, Jones acquired a taste for classical scholarship and an affinity for unorthodox religion. Such questioning of the tenets of mainstream Protestant theology by members of Britain's educated elite became increasingly common in the eighteenth century. Some of these skeptics were deists, others Socinians, still others Arians, and many simply had doubts about one aspect of Christian theology or another. Unlike most others labeled deists in eighteenth-century America, Jones may actually have been one, or close to one. He denied the Trinity and made it clear he did not believe the Bible to be divinely inspired or true. During the Revolution, he cynically referred to evangelicals from western North Carolina counties as "the Saints of the Back Country."[18]

Jones developed other eccentricities as well that played against North Carolina's predominant Protestant culture. On his return from England, he alarmingly pledged himself to a celibate life. Here was a sure sign of Catholic tendencies in the eyes of a Protestant population conditioned historically to equate celibacy with covert papist priests. The origins of his pledge is unclear, and he eventually engaged in a rebellion against it, apparently, by marrying Mary Montfort in 1776 and fathering thirteen children with her, more than half of whom did not survive to adulthood. When one of his young daughters died, he reaffirmed his religious views by composing a poem for her gravestone about the ancient Roman gods, failing to mention Christ, Christianity, or heaven. His will instructed his executors to allow "no priest or other person ... to insult my corpse by uttering any impious observations over my body." A heretic indeed.[19]

Like many other Carolinian gentlemen, Jones joined the Revolution late. He may simply have believed that the crisis would blow over. Or his known attachment to Eton and England may have made him hesitant to act. He had generally been on good terms with royal officials and had served as an aide to Governor Tryon in 1771 during the campaign against the Regulators, agrarian dissidents in the interior who rebelled in the 1760s and 1770s. Jones certainly had something to lose if the Revolution failed. He owned a large estate with dozens of slaves; his enlightened learning had done nothing to temper his tendency to purchase people. He would eventually own 140 people and have a number of white servants as well.[20]

In late 1774 Jones assumed several key leadership roles in the revolutionary movement. He was elected to head the Halifax Committee of Safety in December 1774. That committee then promptly called in a merchant whom they believed had violated the commercial boycott against Britain instituted in the wake of the Boston Port Bill, and interrogated him about his political views. Chosen to represent Halifax in the Provincial Council that met in Johnston County in October 1775, Jones eventually headed the state's Council of Safety and later served in the Continental Congress. Elected as a delegate to the Fifth Congress in the fall of 1776, Jones joined with the thirteen other dissidents in publicly attempting to purge the new constitution and the related rites in the new republican political culture of practices associated with Protestant political culture.[21]

Martin County resident Whitmel Hill's unorthodox spiritual views were equally troubling to those who eventually associated with the Brethren in 1777. A North Carolina native, Hill also received his education "abroad," in his case in Philadelphia at what became the University of Pennsylvania. There he too developed irregular religious beliefs. As with many others holding such beliefs in eighteenth-century America, he acknowledged a supreme God and Jesus Christ's importance, but would not warrant Jesus Christ's divinity or the Holy Spirit's reality. In a letter to a friend, he described himself as an "infidel[s]." His theological opinions tended toward Socinianism, which North Carolina's Protestants would find unacceptable.[22]

Hill was well connected by birth to the provincial gentry and married into the prominent Blount family. His wife, Winifred Blount Hill, also had blood ties to the Williams, a gentry family with extensive landholdings in southern Albemarle counties. Hill had a mansion house, Palmyra, in Martin County and owned substantial property in Martin, Bertie, and Halifax Counties. He too owned slaves, and he never freed them, willing them instead to his

North Carolina
1777

o State Capital

78° 77° 76°

Norfolk

I A

Camden
Currituck
Northampton
Hertford
Chowen
Perquimans
Pasquotank
Halifax

Bute

Bertie
Edenton

Albemarle Sound

Nash
Windsor
Edgecomb
Plymouth
Martin
Tyrell

I N A
Pitt
Washington
Hyde

on
Beaufort

Dobbs
Pamlico Sound

Craven
New Bern

Duplin
Raleigh
Bay

Onslow
Carteret

New
Hanover

Onslow
Bay
ATLANTIC OCEAN
N

Green
Swamp
Wilmington

nswick

ong
ay
0   100 km

0   100 miles

wife and children in his last testament. The London government acknowledged his high social standing and learning by appointing him a justice of the peace in the imperial legal system.[23]

Despite all this, or perhaps because of it, Hill joined the rebellion in 1775 and he quickly gained authority in the emerging order. Elected as a delegate to the crucial Hillsborough congress in 1775, Hill became a member of the Martin County committee of safety and eventually became a colonel in the county's revolutionary militia. In October 1775 he represented Edenton at the Provincial Council that met in Johnston County, and like Wylie Jones he eventually joined the state's Council of Safety. Selected as a delegate to the Fifth Congress, he would stand among the Fourteen who denied Christ's divinity and did not want to use the Bible to swear fidelity to the new order.[24]

Who else were among the Fourteen and how had they come to their views? It is unclear who all of them were, though several are known. The Fifth Congress's president, Richard Caswell, was believed to hold irregular spiritual beliefs; the vice president, Cornelius Harnett, from Wilmington in the southern part of the state, definitely did. Harnett repeatedly expressed views hostile to organized religion even though he was a member of Wilmington's St. James Church. He was a merchant and may have come by his views via books purchased while engaged in trading. He vigorously resisted calls to embrace revealed religion even on his deathbed, and proclaimed his view about religion from beyond the grave. His gravestone bore the phrase "Slave to no sect, he took no private road—But looked through nature up to nature's God," a declaration of rational religious beliefs derived from Alexander Pope's "An Essay on Man." Harnett also did not believe officeholders should have to swear to Jesus Christ's divinity or the Bible's divine origins.[25]

There were stories that another among the Fourteen, Doctor Thomas Burke, was an Irish Catholic. Though born to a Catholic family, Burke apparently never practiced. He had a strong anticlerical streak and wrote repeatedly about the Christian clergy's stupidity. But he was widely believed to be Catholic anyway. As with most of the others, he did not have tightly defined views about what he did believe, though he would later declare himself a "citizen of the world." Burke's presence among the Fourteen may help explain why some Brethren would conflate popery and heresy in 1777, given that he was seen as a heretic-papist.[26]

The views of some of the Fourteen had been known from the time of the Fifth Congress's opening and it quickly became an issue. Delegates from the western counties, supported by others from across the state, openly indicted these spiritual deviants. The Mecklenburg County convention instructed their delegates to deny office to anyone who declared themselves "to be an Atheist or deny the Being of God or shall deny or blaspheme . . . the Holy Trinity." They sought to exclude any believers in the religious-intellectual heresies fashionable among elements in the Anglo-American elite. Other counties sent similar instructions to the convention and later to the new legislature that first sat in 1777. They wanted to introduce "a test by which every person before he should be admitted to a share in the legislature" had to profess that he believed in the Holy Trinity "and that the Old Testament was written by divine inspiration." For most Protestants in the revolutionary generation the acceptance of such acknowledgments were a line in the sand spiritually and politically.[27]

As the debate over the test continued, the Fourteen enlightened delegates asserted in an organized manner their vision of human liberation. They wanted mention of Christ removed from political and legal oaths and the Bible removed from formal rites. The fourteen men had excellent reason to resist the practices common in Protestant political culture; these rites and procedures would have either precluded them and those who believed as they did from the revolutionary government, or forced them to swear to something they did not believe.

The disputes over this issue nearly caused the Fifth Congress to come apart. While Article 31, which barred clergymen from holding public offices, and Article 34, which did away with the Church of England establishment in the state, were both accepted with broad support, the test oaths in Article 32, according to Samuel Johnston, blew up "such a flame that everything is in danger of being thrown into confusion." Wylie Jones led the resistance to the oaths put forward by the western evangelical delegates. A former celibate who refused to publicly acknowledge Christ's divinity and wanted to purge Protestant political rites from the new order: here was a sure enemy to a free Protestant people. The enlightened would no longer tolerate what they now deemed superstition, and Protestant Christians would not warrant heretics shaping the new order.[28]

By the time the Fifth Congress prepared to adjourn in the fourth week of December 1776, even those who might have privately been sympathetic to the enlightened spiritual deviants realized they had to concede. To deny central tenets of Christian theology in a state whose population was almost entirely adamantly Protestant, admittedly of many different churches and sects, endangered the Revolution itself. The political mechanics of their surrender is unclear, but it seemed to involve the heretically minded avoiding a direct oath while reaffirming the new constitution's Article 32 that effectively limited office to professing Protestants. Significantly, Article 32 did not stop Jones, Hill, or Burke from later gaining office. With the nominal acceptance of Article 32, the convention adjourned on December 23.[29]

The failure to de-Christianize political rites and defeat Article 32 should lead us to pause and think about how we understand the separation of church and state in the Revolution. The period of the state constitutional conventions is usually considered the beginning of the full and legal separation of church and state. This is of course true in regard to specific church-state structures. The preservation, though, of Christian tests, language, and rites in the political culture suggests that separation as we have considered it is inadequate for understanding the spiritual-political culture's trajectory of change.

It was not separation as we like to discuss it. Rather, it was institutional disestablishment and a reorganization of spiritual-political language and rites toward a more generic but still potent Protestant Christian character. Formal establishments began to disappear—very slowly in New England—but rhetorical establishments that linked the new political order to Protestant Christianity generally came into being and were soon deeply entrenched.

Stories that some delegates had injected unorthodox spiritual-political beliefs into the debates at the Fifth Congress led Albemarle yeomen to begin to organize against what they saw as a popish, tyrannical threat coming from the new state government. The rumors about the Fourteen and their unorthodox beliefs began to circulate even before the Congress broke up right before Christmas 1776. A revolution against popish tyranny could not be led by those that denied the truth of Jesus Christ and the Bible. Nor could the new state have formal political rites stripped of their Protestant character. Far from being a sideshow, the new government's spiritual character, and its connection to Protestant political culture, became a central issue in 1776 and 1777. When Protestant planters and yeomen in North Carolina's Albemarle region heard rumors of these heresies, they saw the faces of people like Hill and Jones and Burke. And they saw a threat to their core beliefs, posed by people who were supposed to be leaders of the Revolution to defend Protestant liberty but who publicly disdained Protestantism and the norms of Protestant political society that ensured that liberty.

Despite the conclusions of a generation of scholars, enlightened ideas played a limited or no causal role in rupturing the empire. But these beliefs became a major issue in the struggle to determine the character of the America to come after July 4, 1776, and disputes between the faithful and the enlightened have defined American culture ever since. The new constitution announced to all that the provincial world had died. Republican North Carolina's troubling birth had profoundly unsettled the Albemarle yeomanry, and in the Fifth Congress's immediate aftermath, and even perhaps before, they began to organize to resist heresy, popery, and the forced drafts of a government that seemed to be drifting toward tyranny.

6

THE HOUSE OF FEAR

DANIEL LEGATE left his farm in Bertie County sometime in the late winter or early spring of 1777 on a spiritual quest. Yet another scion of a family that had entered the Albemarle from Virginia, he traveled overnight to James Sherrard's home in neighboring Martin County, "to a meeting where one Rawlings was to preach"—James Rawlings, lay reader in a Martin County chapel, the man John Lewellen publicly approached at a militia gathering to discuss the popish, heretical threat facing North Carolina. Preaching had been thin on the ground since the committees of safety turned their attention to the Church of England ministers and the prayers for the royal family in 1775. Before the preaching began, Rawlings took Legate aside and asked "if he did not think they were in danger of losing their Religion, that it was reported that Thirteen or Fourteen persons in the Provincial Congress had objected to the Trinity." Rawlings asked Legate if he agreed that it "would be a good thing if the People were to join in a Society to support their religion," and Legate answered he thought it would be.

Legate agreed to join this movement to support their religion and swore an oath on a book to keep it a secret. Rawlings provided Legate with a stick with three notches and a series of secret signs that culminated in spelling out "B-E-T-R-U-E." Rawlings then sent him to "Senior warden" James Sherrard to hear the movement's "Constitution" read. It was the beginning of Legate's short but extremely active career as a key leader in the movement to save Protestantism and Protestant political culture in North Carolina. Daniel Legate, southern Albemarle yeoman, had entered history as both a subject of and an agent of change.[1]

In the six months between January and July 1777, John Lewellen, James Rawlings, James Sherrard, as well as Daniel Legate and several dozen other men moved through the southern and western Albemarle's fields. In those fields and along wooded paths they held hundreds of conversations with yeomen and planters. Their words turned the fear of popish infiltration, concerns about heresy in the government's upper reaches, unhappiness about forced drafts, persistent Francophobia, and anxiety about the general turmoil into an institutionalized movement.

It was born in Martin County. Called "the Brethren" by some of its adherents and "an association" or "the Association" by state officials, the leadership's powerful message about the threats to Protestantism and Protestant political culture, their willingness to delegate authority, and their deft appropriation and re-tasking of older institutional rites and practices allowed the movement to grow quickly. In the six months between January 1777 and July 1777, the movement gained adherents in Martin, Tyrrell, and Bertie Counties and to a lesser degree won support across the southern and western Albemarle watershed.[2]

This Protestant association grew rapidly as long as defending the faith remained its primary goal. The records that trace its institutional rise tell a story about the migration of political language, beliefs, and practices inherited from the provincial period amid a revolutionary maelstrom. Ideas and institutions traditionally assumed to be bulwarks of Protestant liberty and thus free societies came to be redeployed against an element in the new state government that seemed determined to abandon those cherished principles. The leaders of the Brethren initially intended not to subvert liberty or independence but to protect their very foundation in Protestantism. By 1777, though, anyone forming institutions outside the revolutionary leadership's control risked being defined as hostile to the republican cause, regardless of the institution's ideological origins or the goals of those who formed it.

Fear

Rumors about the strange, heretical spiritual-political beliefs voiced in the Fifth Congress began to spread through the Albemarle in the last weeks of 1776. The Albemarle yeomanry had no idea what the enlightened Fourteen intended by their unwillingness to swear to Christ's divinity or the Bible's divine origins. They did not understand enlightened words in terms of modern ideas of freedom and separation of church and state but instead saw these words as an attack on their Protestant liberty. Who could be more destructive than those who did not embrace the Trinity or understand the Bible's divine origins? Surely they were more dangerous than any imperial army.

Carolina yeomen had no intention of tolerating heresy or Catholicism or Catholic Frenchmen. Why would they? After all, they were in rebellion against suspected crypto-Catholics and popish plotters in the London government's highest reaches.

The vague stories about the heretics that passed after the Fifth Congress adjourned transformed the general uneasy feelings about forced drafts and a potential French alliance that had emerged after July 4 into concrete fears about the Revolution's spiritual-political course. The growing turmoil evident on January 1, 1777, combined with the news from the Fifth Congress seemed sure evidence that the popish and/or heretical plot that had destabilized the empire had now reached North Carolina.

Several among the heretical delegates exhibited behaviors pop-
ularly identified with covert Catholics, and this, along with the
public quest for an alliance with France, explains at least in part why
some conflated enlightened belief and popery. Wylie Jones's pro-
nouncement about living a celibate life was suspicious, as celibacy
was associated with Catholicism. Daniel Legate warned Thomas
Harrison and others that "that fourteen members of the Assembly
had agreed to introduce Poppery & in particular mentioned Wylie
Jones & Whitmel Hill being forward" in these efforts. The fear that
the Fourteen were popish in their intent became entrenched.
William May of Pitt County believed that these spiritually rogue
"gentlemen [were] ... trying to bring in popish Religion," and that
Protestant North Carolinians needed to "keep out popish religion if
we could." John Garrett told Armel Holles (Hollis) the same thing,
"that 14 members of the Assembly wanted to introduce the Romish
religion" into North Carolina and that they had to be resisted.[3]

Other yeomen feared that the Fourteen sought to create a new,
anti-Christian faith centered on idol worship as a way to mask their
crypto-Catholicism. Albemarle farmers Absalom Legate and Peleg
Belote worried that the Fourteen wanted to "impose a new Religion
on the People," and that a faction within the new state government
might be aiding them. In this new faith, they would be compelled to
worship images, something that they "both expressed a very strong
disapprobation of."[4]

It all made perfect sense given the yeomanry's worldview. Who
would benefit most from turmoil first in a Protestant empire and
then in the newly independent Protestant state? Surely it was the
Beast, whose feared Catholic agents would exploit the revolutionary
turmoil to establish a popish-heretical order in North Carolina,
perhaps under French control. A powerful tendency remained in
the eighteenth-century Anglophone political community to inter-
pret any conflict on a vast scale, including the imperial crisis itself,

as resulting from popish plots or foreign Catholic intrigue or heretical efforts to undermine the Protestant religion. The public attack on basic tenets of Protestantism intensified the sense that the revolutionary turmoil ultimately grew from a general spiritual-political crisis that was engulfing the entire Anglo-American world.

It was in this environment that those who formed the Brethren acted. Their call to action worked because they tapped into the society's primary beliefs at a time when it seemed that dark forces sought to undermine those same beliefs. As America reeled from one crisis to the next in the months after independence, yeomen's sense that they might need to fight to defend their faith intensified. A strong conviction took hold that the population needed to act to support "the old & New Testament," as several men who organized the movement put it. They asked people "to stand up for the Protestant Religion" as all indicators suggested a plot existed to destroy that religion's spiritual and civil structures.[5]

While it might be argued that this idea of a defense of Protestantism was imposed on the associators by the movement's leadership, in later conversations and depositions the rank and file used the idioms of anti-heresy and anti-popery and community defense to explain themselves. Even those who examined the Protestant associators for the state courts described the movement as "a certain Religious Society" in the depositions. The Fourteen's efforts to resist the oaths that affirmed their Christianity, and their objection to the state constitution's Article 32 that limited office to professing Protestant Christians, made evident a heretical design on the state's government, and the yeomanry's souls.[6]

The ancient enemies of all free Protestant people stalked them again in late 1776 and 1777, now wearing a disguise of pseudo-cosmopolitanism. Sometime early in 1777 a group centered in Martin County began to organize to meet the threat and preserve their Protestant liberty.

Family and Friends

On an early summer day in 1777 Thomas Harrison walked into his cornfield in Tyrrell County to continue his labors in the endless cycle of planting, weeding, watering, and harvesting that dominated his agrarian world. As Harrison worked away, someone he knew, Daniel Legate, came to see him unexpectedly. Harrison's visitor "asked him if he would join a Constitution to support their religion." Harrison immediately agreed. It was all necessary, Legate told him, because "fourteen members of the Assembly had agreed to introduce Popery" into North Carolina, something they both sought to prevent. Legate was looking for support to fight this new threat, and he knew something important about Thomas Harrison: he was one of a large number of Harrisons wringing a living from the soggy flatlands of Martin and Tyrrell counties. Get one Harrison to associate, get others. At least twelve Protestant associators in Tyrrell County had the surname Harrison by the time the state suppressed the movement.[7]

It is hardly surprising that kinship ties became central to the movement to save the Protestant revolution. Blood ties held early modern societies together on a primal level. In the Anglo-American world, towns and even whole counties were often little more than extended family, or a few extended families, which made institutions and families one and the same in many locales. Family members tended to stand together in times of crisis. Locally prominent men acted as the patriarchal fathers of these kin networks.[8]

Kinship became more important amid the revolutionary turmoil. Only family remained in many locales to support the individual in the time of trouble between the imperial collapse and the appearance of working republican institutions. Certainly this was true in the Albemarle, where the courts had been shuttered and Church of England's ministers put to flight in 1775. Local tradition and blood ties were holding the society together as the Revolution expanded, precisely because British America's institutional superstructure had disappeared amid terror and warfare.

Unsurprisingly, then, the Brethren began with families and friends. Late in 1776 or early in 1777, Martin County freeholders John Lewellen, John Carter, James Sherrard, James Hayes (Haise), and James Rawlings, who were joined early on by Bertie County yeoman Daniel Legate, began to tell family and friends the unsettling stories about heretics, the efforts to bring the French into the war, the forced drafts, and recounted the events that suggested a popish plot. They asked them to join together to defend Protestantism and the Protestant state.[9]

Even a superficial survey reveals the role of kinship in the movement. John Lewellen recruited his own son William and perhaps other kin as well. The Taylor family contributed three members, the Hyman family in Bertie County had two would-be associators, and the Legates in the same county had at least two family members, Daniel Legate and his father, whom he recruited early on. The twelve Harrisons in Tyrrell County who associated were joined by two Durrances, four Garretts, two Everetts, and two Faggans (with a third Faggan in bordering Martin County) who became involved as well. Family bonds and kin networks underlay the Protestant association.[10]

Those who initiated the Brethren also turned to neighbors for support. It is not surprising they should do so. The eighteenth-century yeoman was never autonomous. Neighbors supported one another—during harvest and planting, in militia formations, at prayer, at the birth of children, and at death. These invisible but very real threads held society together in fat times and in lean. People counted on their neighbors in times of crisis, and that encouraged many to join this movement to save North Carolina from popery and heresy. The neighborhood and its intimate contacts had become ever more important as the society suffered repeated shocks in the transition from empire to independence.

Neighbors stood with neighbors. Witnesses described early associator Richard Taylor Sr. as "a near neighbor to Capt. Lewelling." Richard Faggan told John Buttrey he wanted to "geet Every Body" in their neighborhood "of one mind" about the spiritual-political crisis in order to lead them to associate. There must have been many such conversations in the late winter and spring of 1777. When John Hodge considered joining "James Rollins [Rawlings]" in resistance to popery, he took "the advise of his neighbours," before agreeing to hear Rawlings out.[11]

Land records and wills evidenced these neighborly bonds. In 1774, for example, lay preacher James Rawlings acted as a witness for a land transaction in Martin County between the Barbree and Counsel families. Members of these families associated in 1777. In 1775 John Carter and James Sherrard stood together to witness another land transaction and later both would associate. In the same year, Sherrard acted as executor for the will of John Lewellen's mother, Frances. Deeds from Martin County suggest that many involved in the movement lived in proximity to one another in what became District 1 and District 5 in that county.[12]

Blood and friendship acted as the true foundation of a movement built from rural communities rather than imposed upon them. Nervous Albemarle planters and yeomen who saw in the revolutionary turmoil the specter of their ancient spiritual-political enemies created the Brethren.

These neighborly relations were never entirely egalitarian. Deference to local leaders among the original group who built the movement encouraged the Brethren's expansion. In the eighteenth century, people with wealth and power assisted those beneath them in the social structure. In return they expected their views on public matters to hold sway. The Revolution temporarily weakened or even ruptured these norms, but did not destroy them. More than one conspirator noted that John Lewellen had "Great influence . . . over that Neighborhood" where he lived. James Rawlings felt that, as a poor man, he had to defer to Lewellen, and even after his arrest Rawlings continued to fear that Lewellen would use his influence to hurt him. John Stewart of Martin County was told that leading men in his county, including "members of [the provincial] Congress" and some Martin County justices, had associated; this encouraged his own participation. Deference and patronage enabled the movement by empowering leaders to influence clients.[13]

The initiators also understood how planting and harvesting drew rural people together. This provided opportunities to further expand their movement. The eastern North Carolina yeomen who did not have slaves counted on family and friends to plant the earth and reap the bounty. With much of what had been public life in the countryside gone due to the upheaval, informal gatherings linked to the yearly agricultural cycle became central to shaping opinions and to organizing those who would associate. Daniel Legate approached Tyrrell County's William Durrance at the "Reaping at Jonathan Davis's in said County," and the "brethren" approached the remarkably named Bird Land during the same reaping.[14]

Other Brethren approached Armel Holles at that reaping. John Garret asked Holles to help mend a bridle in order to get him alone to discuss the troubled times. Daniel Legate approached yeoman Thomas Harrison Jr. "in his cornfield," and William Brimage spoke to Thomas Harrison Sr. in "his son's Wheat Field." William Howard joined the movement in Jonathan Davis's apple orchard. The leadership was able to build the movement rapidly because they knew the countryside.[15]

These leaders also used militia training days to organize men. James Rawlings's encounter with John Lewellen and John Carter at a militia meeting was only one of several instances where associators discussed the situation in the state at militia musters. With church meetings and court days gone, and public life thus diminished, those who organized to defend the Protestant commonwealth worked in whatever gatherings were available to gain support.[16]

The movement grew because its leaders understood the anxieties created by Revolution in their agrarian world. In a matter of weeks early in 1777, hundreds rallied to support Protestantism and the Protestant commonwealth. As numbers increased, the leaders began to form institutions to control what quickly became a geographically extended movement.

Brethren

Around July 1, 1777, John Stewart returned to his home in Martin County from the Tar River region of North Carolina to find that in his absence a man named Daniel Legate had left a message for him. Legate "wanted to see this Depondent [Stewart] on Business" and that he would be waiting at the home of their mutual acquaintance Thomas Harrison, Senior. Two or three days later, Stewart found himself at Harrison's home, where Legate "began his Discourse by saying that we was like to have a great fall in our Religion" as "sundry Members of Congress had damned the Being of God."

Heresy in the government during war and revolution: it was a desperate situation. Farmers in the Albemarle countryside needed to "form themselves into a society for the support of Religion," by this meaning a body to protect the true Protestant faith. Legate then read him a statement "related principally to religion" and went on to mention that they intended to have "Ministers in the Society," presumably meaning by this restoring the services run by the lay readers who dominated spiritual life in the southern Albemarle before the war. Stewart expressed enthusiasm for a return of their spiritual life disrupted by war.

But when Legate asked him to swear oaths binding him to this new society, Stewart demurred, claiming he intended to move from the area soon. That might have ended it, but Legate then asked Stewart whether he thought another acquaintance, Samuel Black, might not make a good member. Within a week Black and another man, the prominent admiralty judge William Brimage, arrived at Stewart's home to inquire about this new society to support the Protestant religion. Stewart told Black and Brimage that "he knew neither head nor tail of it" but that Daniel Legate did.

The next day Stewart escorted the two men to meet with Legate at Thomas Harrison's house. As Stewart waited, Legate, Harrison, and Brimage disappeared into the woods near the home where Legate administered the movement's secrecy oaths. With that, Stewart headed for home, but Legate had unfinished business. He soon reentered the woods to swear Samuel Black into the movement and administer oaths to him. Legate then turned to William Brimage and offered to make him an official for the movement in Bertie County, an offer that the former judge accepted. Brimage went on to request a copy of the statement of the movement's values that he could read to recruits. Then they all departed.[17]

As the movement extended beyond Martin County across a significant portion of eastern North Carolina, the initiators adapted elements of the institutional practices they had known in the Church of England and the provincial legal system to create a structure to connect their dispersed followers. These became the bones and ligaments that bound the Brethren together in the time of fear. John Lewellen took the lead in creating the movement's structure and rites. Almost all documents name Lewellen as the Brethren's initiator, and it's clear that most Protestant associators deferred to him. He shaped the document that came to be known as the movement's constitution. The conspiracy bore his name for those reasons.

Acknowledging this, yeoman Daniel Legate played a critical role among the Brethren as it began to expand across the southern Albemarle. Legate and his male family members were yeomen of modest means. He lived in Bertie County before and during the war, and owned just a hundred acres in Tyrrell County after the war. He and his immediate family seem to have farmed without slave labor. Those deposed mentioned Legate and his family members most frequently as the people who approached them about associating with the Brethren. The Legates' names appear most often in the depositions that discuss building the movement on the ground. Their participation only highlights what is apparent in all the sources: the movement came from the Albemarle yeomanry and planters, their actions and worldview shaped by what they had known before independence.[18]

Sometime in March Lewellen and the group assembled around him began to articulate a chain of command and an organizational structure for the movement that would become the conspiracy. They recruited local leaders and gave them three specific titles to denote their status in the movement—senior warden, warden, solicitor. These men were empowered to act for the movement in specific geographic areas.

About twelve men served as senior wardens in the Albemarle counties of Martin, Tyrrell, and Bertie. The title of senior warden probably derived from churchwardens, those who served as lay officials in Anglican congregations. The ever-active Daniel Legate told Thomas Harrison in midsummer 1777 that "James Sherrard, Lewellen, and & James Hayes were the Principals concerned in Martin County," and he told Benjamin Harrison that "Stewart, Sherrard, Lewellen, & Hayes" were the leaders in Martin and "Wm. Brimage, Peleg Belote and one Brogden in Bertie." Legate should have included himself on this list. He told Jerosiah Everett that he was "the Senior Warden for the Society." William Tyler of Bertie County and Captain John Garrett of Tyrrell probably also held the title of senior warden. They recruited and knew about the movement's inner plans. Several other senior wardens operated in Tyrrell County, although who they were is unclear.[19]

The senior wardens came from across the social order. William Brimage had extensive land holdings and dozens of slaves. He stood atop Bertie County society. Other senior wardens, though, like Daniel Legate himself, were yeomen. Dedication to the cause, as much as previous social standing, determined who would be included in this circle of leadership that emerged across the southern Albemarle counties. The senior wardens' central role was to bring people into the movement. When the associators appointed Brimage senior warden for Bertie County early in July 1777, the leadership tasked him and other senior wardens with "the gaining & swearing in members to this Association." These men also provided overall leadership to the Protestant associators in their counties and educated members in the movement's goals.[20]

Wardens and solicitors, subordinate to the senior wardens, also recruited for the Brethren. Those so designated held the movement together and drove its growth in a considerable number of places. Wardens felt out community members' views about the times, about Protestantism, about the French alliance, the drafts, and about the heretics in the new order. These men broached joining the movement with likely candidates and referred them to the senior wardens for further instructions. The sources do not reveal how many wardens served, though there seem to have been several in each county.[21]

Others received the title of solicitor. These men were empowered to recruit in specific locales. This title had been used in the imperial period to refer to legal officials and in some cases to attorneys. William Jordan (Jordain) claimed that two leading associators, William Collins and Richard Faggan, "wanted to make an officer of Him, a Solliseter to take in others," for the movement, something he ultimately refused to do. Whether a difference existed between wardens and solicitors is unclear, as is the number of solicitors.[22]

This structure was adapted to the realities of organizing a dispersed rural population. It looked like the networks of chapels and circuits that Anglican ministers had created in the vast southern interior in the twenty-five years before independence or the circuits that provincial judges rode to bring the king's justice to different counties. The Brethren's leaders appointed and empowered the wardens to preach their cause and take in new members in their communities or districts. Circuit-riding senior wardens and wardens united these cells and disseminated instructions, goals, and news. The movement's structure reflected the institutional experiences lived in the late empire.

Devolving the authority to recruit is what enabled the Protestant association's rapid growth in the late winter and spring of 1777. Even the wardens devolved authority, empowering those they recruited to try to bring in their immediate friends and families. Richard Faggan, for example, recruited by Daniel Legate, in short order recruited John Burkey, and soon after recruited Salvanas Buttrey. The devolving of power was so thorough that it is unclear if everyone even knew the original leaders' names when the revolutionary state suppressed the movement. Not all wardens seem to have actually met John Lewellen or his inner circle. The chain of contacts that led several men to solicit is unclear, and not everyone who recruited mentions Lewellen as their primary contact. This decentralization also suggests that individual wardens and solicitors may have explained the movement's goals differently, emphasizing what they thought important, or what they believed would win recruits in their local areas.[23]

When Robert Smith wrote to Governor Richard Caswell after the conspiracy's discovery, he noted that "our neighbor in Martin, upper end of Tyrell and Bertie, are not like long to be quiet." He was right; that was the home ground of the Brethren. There is only one surviving list of those who associated, that of Daniel Legate, and it focused on those counties. Legate recorded speaking to at least fifty-two people. The surviving list kept by Legate, depositions taken when the movement was suppressed, and court records reveal the names of forty-five Tyrrell County men involved to widely varying degrees. For certain, twenty-four Martin County men were involved and twenty-eight from Bertie.[24]

But most of these numbers are derived essentially from the records of only one senior warden, so we can surmise that the membership numbered much higher. Who the other Brethren leaders took in is not known. It is known that at least some carried papers with them, which may have included additional membership lists. They either destroyed their records when the state suppressed the movement, or did not keep written records, or those records did not survive into the modern era. If we had records from the other senior wardens and wardens, the movement's geographic structure would no doubt look somewhat different and the extent of its membership would be made evident.

It is clear that the Brethren had support in counties beyond Martin, Bertie, and Tyrrell. We know the name of only one member in Pitt County, for example, but anecdotal evidence suggests there were many more. Edenton's Robert Smith believed the movement had very substantial support in Pitt County. Thomas Harrison's deposition suggests the same thing—that the movement had substantial support in Pitt, with the specific numbers unknown.[25]

The same was true of other southern and western Albemarle counties. Absalom Legate told one recruit, and probably others, that the movement had support from "a considerable number of persons in Bute, Edgecombe and Martin" counties, although the names of the membership in the former two counties is unknown. William Lewellen also noted members in Edgecombe County, but again who is unknown. Lieutenant Colonel Henry Irwin, writing from Tarborough in Edgecombe County in July 1777, believed that "too many evil persons in this and the neighboring Counties" had joined in this "wicked Conspiracy," although again the exact number and names of those engaged in the wickedness was never stated. Wardens recruited in the town of Halifax and the region surrounding it as well.[26]

At some point John Lewellen and the other leaders tried to extend the movement geographically away from the Albemarle region by sending riders to distant areas. The leaders claimed to have "several persons constantly and Daily riding to increase there numbers." He claimed that the Brethren had contacts deep in the North Carolina interior at Haw River. By late April certain wardens had traveled extensively to try to recruit members in distant counties within the state.[27]

Senior warden James Hays was repeatedly named as being the most active in this regard. Why him? It's unclear, but he traveled hundreds of miles to build the movement. The fact that he was apparently an X man—illiterate—did not inhibit his fellow Protestant associators from directing him to assume this task. It does, though, make it more difficult to determine who he talked to and where he went, as he left no written records to guide us.[28]

The leadership may also have made efforts to recruit beyond North Carolina. The sea and the north–south coastal road that bisected the southern Albemarle provided associators with avenues to dissimilate their ideas to the neighboring colonies. Daniel Legate told another associator that they had extended the movement into "New Georgia." His father, Absalom, claimed that the Brethren had contacts in South Carolina as well as throughout North Carolina. Shortly before the state government suppressed the movement, John Lewellen told James Rawlings that he had sent word about the movement "into Virginia," and that the Brethren had support in the Norfolk-Portsmouth area, the area Lewellen had originally migrated from. That area had strong trade ties with the Edenton region and had a reputation for dissent against Virginia's republican government. This acknowledged, it is difficult to determine whether the Brethren ever had contacts outside the state. Certainly, no one from neighboring states came to their aid when the authorities suppressed the movement.[29]

The Brethren's primary realm was the Albemarle Sound's southern and western shores, with the population in the sound's watershed to the south and west also offering some support. The population in counties on the sound's northeast shore remained largely aloof, at least formally. The Edenton area, as one writer noted, remained loyal to the new state government—"at least none are impeached," as he so diplomatically put—although the movement was believed to have sympathizers there.[30]

Constitutions and Oaths

By mid-April 1777 the Brethren's initiators had appointed leaders in a number of counties and developed institutions to support the movement's further growth. And these leaders also began to establish an institutional process to formally incorporate people. It involved a recruiting script that warned of the popish threat and forced drafts, followed by a system of oaths, initially three in number, with a fourth eventually added, that bound those who would swear allegiance to them. The nature of these conversations and the layers of oaths created different types of associators, with different types of commitment to the movement being expressed by how many oaths people took. It is clear, though, that with each oath the initiate became more enmeshed in the Association and its goals

The recruitment process's formalization and the introduction of an oath system became evident by April 1777. Wardens and solicitors began conversations with potential initiates with a preconceived declaration about the times and how the situation threatened souls. Once having engaged a potential associator, the wardens and senior wardens would reveal that they were forming a movement to fight the fourteen heretical infiltrators in the state government, defend Protestantism, guard against a French conspiracy,

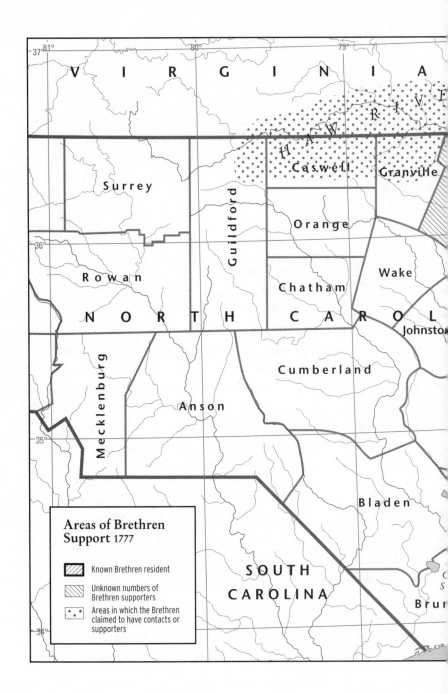

Areas of Brethren
Support 1777

Known Brethren resident

Unknown numbers of
Brethren supporters

Areas in which the Brethren
claimed to have contacts or
supporters

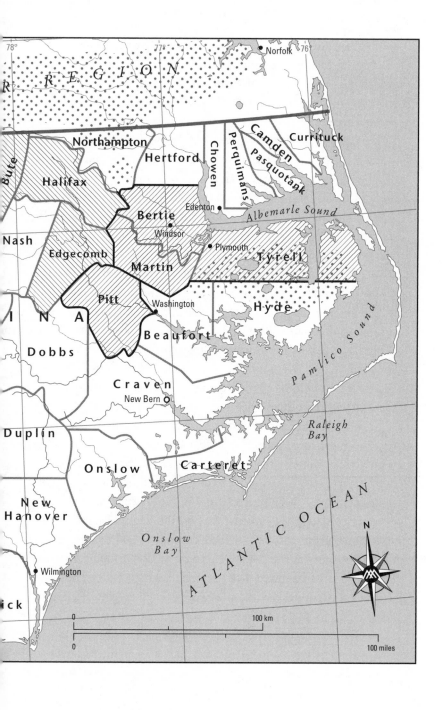

and resist forced drafts. They would then offer the initiate membership in the movement. Hundreds of Carolinians were approached in this fashion. In late March or April 1777 the senior wardens created a series of interlocked oaths to bind the willing to the movement.

The need to explain the movement's values became pronounced as the Protestant association spread across counties and its structure became more complex. This led the leaders to write a statement of beliefs and goals that they called a constitution. As early as mid-March, John Lewellen insisted that "there must be an Instrument of Writing Down to which people Might agree" when they joined. He and his son William appeared shortly thereafter at lay preacher James Rawlings's home and requested that he formally write down what they believed to be the movement's central values. William Lewellen then made copies, "for Martin, Edgecombe, Halifax and think he sd. For Bartee [Bertie] and Teril [Tyrrell]" counties. This document may have grown from the practice of writing a covenant or other articles when founding a new Protestant church, or expressed the rage for constitution writing then current in politics. Or both.[31]

This document has not survived. But the Brethren referred to the document as a spiritual-political statement that bound them to live by the values embedded in the Old and New Testament, to defend Protestantism, and perhaps, to help those drafted against their will. And it became a key tool in the movement's recruiting efforts. Equipped with copies of the constitution, the senior wardens and wardens and solicitors fanned out and in short order created their movement in the Albemarle countryside. Reading this document to recruits was more than a rote statement of values. The movement's leadership used oaths and rites intertwined with reading the constitution to bind the Protestant associators together.[32]

In eighteenth-century America, people took oaths far more seriously than they seem to today. Swearing oaths reaffirmed religious beliefs, announced political allegiance, and asserted allegiance to a common idea of legality. To declare one's allegiance in public or in front of others was to indeed own it, and those who acted contrary to their sworn oaths profoundly threatened their status and reputation. The imperial collapse and the petite terror launched by the committees of safety altered the oaths' usage but not their importance. Oaths became the conduits through which people established new political identities and announced new and old loyalties in a time of violent flux.

Political allegiance in the Revolution came to orbit around oath taking. In North Carolina the end of British America began in earnest with an oath created by the ad hoc government in March 1776 that bound its takers to not aid British forces. They swore not to "by example, opinion, advice or persuasion, endeavour to prejudice the people . . . in favour of Parliamentary Measures or against those recommended by the General and provincial Congresses." In June 1777 the revolutionary government created a new oath that called on citizens to be loyal to North Carolina, to support independence, and to resist "George the Third, King of Great Britain, and his successors" as well as any other "Person, Prince, Power, State or Potenate." They made citizens swear to reveal all conspiracies or attempts against the state government. Words to live by—literally.[33]

We do know generally the oaths the Brethren used. People who expressed willingness to join swore to keep the movement secret, to defend the Protestant faith and community, and to defend those unwillingly drafted into the state militia or the Continental line, or both. At some point the leadership added another secrecy oath, this one designed "to keep the Senior Wardens name secret." Even those who did not join after being approached were sworn to this.[34]

The oaths became a central part of a recruitment rite that emerged in April 1777. John Hodges agreed to associate after warden and lay preacher James Rawlings "offer'd him a Secret." Rawlings handed him "a book and he Qualified him"—in other words, swore him into the movement on the Bible. Peleg Belote recalled that he "kissed the book" twice. The constitution would then be read, or arrangements made for the initiate to meet a senior warden to hear the constitution read. The wardens would then administer the oaths to the initiate. They were offered in succession and the initiate could swear or not at each stage, creating several conditional categories of association. Apparently only those who took at least three of the oaths became full associators, true Brethren. "All that were concerned," recalled one associator, referencing those who were considered full members, "took the third oath."[35]

Yet those who took one or two oaths became somehow involved, and it is evident that many in this ambiguous outer circle tried to negotiate the nature of their future participation with the Brethren. Daniel Legate's surviving list of those among the fifty-two he approached in Martin, Bertie, and Tyrrell Counties who swore one, two, three, four, or no oaths reveals that considerable numbers associated conditionally—in other words, by swearing some rather than all of the oaths. For example, when James Sherrard read the movement's constitution to William Hyman, the latter man objected to "some articles in said constitution" though he swore to others.[36]

Widespread illiteracy among the yeomanry amplified the ambiguity of membership in some cases. A very substantial number who associated could only sign their name with an "X"—the X men—and were known to be illiterate. This impacted the way they understood the movement and their membership in it. When Daniel Legate approached one of the several men named Benjamin Harrison he spoke to, this particular Benjamin Harrison refused to join on the grounds that even though the constitution had been read to him, "he could not read it himself." He did not want to swear allegiance to something he did not fully understand. Harrison did, however, agree to keep the first oath, to keep the organization's existence a secret, and in so doing revealed the intricacies of the use of oaths, and the ambiguities of membership they created. By allowing some people to swear only one or two oaths, Legate and the other senior wardens, warden, and solicitors created a group in the Albemarle who were neither fully associators nor non-associators. They shared values with the movement, but only committed themselves to act in certain circumstances. [37]

Institutions consist of people and the rules governing how they interact. Armed with the constitution, the Bible and/or the Book of Common Prayer, and the oaths, the senior wardens, wardens, and solicitors swore people into the movement in the late winter and spring of 1777. As the movement grew, though, and extended through a number of counties, another question came to the fore. How would members know one another? Fear that the heretics in the state government and the committeemen that did their bidding would discover them led the associators to create a secret set of verbal and visual cues that expressed membership and understanding of the movement's goals. Though crude, it proved an effective as long as the movement lasted.

"By Word and Sign"

As the movement grew and spread, the associators established a system of secret signs, symbols, and code words to allow members to reveal themselves to one another while remaining hidden from the committees of safety. "After," as James Rawlings so aptly put it, "many had come into this society as it was term'd they became known to each other by word and sign." "By word and by sign": These words have a strangely modern feel to them, suggesting an anthropological understanding of how symbolic systems function. This system expressed their values as a Protestant Christian movement even as it allowed them to avoid the prying eyes of the committees of safety.[38]

The system of signs they created reflected the movement's origins among yeomen with limited education. When deposed, one

associator after another mentioned that simple sticks with three
notches carved into them played a central role in the movement's
communication system. The three notches' exact meaning is unclear
other than to designate membership in a movement that had me-
tastasized across county boundaries. The most likely explanation is
that it stood for the Christian Trinity. It is also possible it meant
that the bearer had taken three oaths, but that was never made
clear and it seems that people who had not taken three oaths were
given sticks.

It was simple, but it worked, as the numerous depositions taken
in 1777 attest to. The sticks became totems of membership as the
Brethren spread across counties. Peleg Belote received a stick with
three notches when he joined the movement. He was to show
warden James Sherrard the stick to alert him that Belote had associated. When John Carter recruited Nathan Hallaway [Hattaway],
he administered him the oaths and gave his new co-conspirator
"a stick with three notches which stick" to carry with him when he
visited John Lewellen. That stick, he continued "let Lewellen know
that he was Entered into their Society." Then, after Lewellen had
confirmed that Hallaway or anyone else carrying such sticks understood their meaning, he would unveil the movement's inner values.
Hallaway swore on "a Book" to "join with him if the people was
Drafted" against their will.[39]

Displaying the stick in some cases led to a preset verbal exchange
involving secret passwords and rehearsed dialogue designed to acknowledge membership. "A person possessed," testified John
Clifton, of the secrets, "was to have a stick with three notches" to
display to others he might encounter. When asked "what that was
for, he was to answer 'a sign.'" Upon it being inquired "what sign,"
the conspirator was to reply "'the sign of a secret.' The Inquiry,
being . . . examined in these words 'Have now that Secret?' . . . was
to answer 'I have' that the words 'BE TRUE' were then to be let."
These exchanges rapidly became stylized. The parties would pro-

nounce the letters in quick succession, to "letter" as one of them put it, "begin first says B, 2d E, first T, 2d R, first U, 2d E," thus spelling out "Be TRUE." One wonders how the numerous illiterate members used these, given that they could not even sign their own names.[40]

Other cues referenced the movement's origins as a defense of Protestant Christianity. Protestant associator Charles Rhodes testified that Daniel Legate taught him "to shut three fingers of the left hand and draw the fore finger over the Face" to signal to others that he knew the secret. Again, this most likely stood for the Christian Trinity or the three oaths. After giving this sign, the signifier was told to let out the letters "INRJ," abbreviation for Jesus Nazarenus, Rex Judorum—Jesus of Nazareth, King of the Jews.[41]

It was not always possible to reveal one's stick or call out letters without raising questions. For such situations the leaders developed less overt hand and body signals that allowed members to identify themselves to other associators. Conspirators were to rub their left forefinger "over the right arm, nose or chin or any part of their body [!] the other person being of their party, will ask him what he points at, (answers) a secret, have you that secret." No doubt more than one North Carolinian in those disquieted days left a riding companion mystified by their rubbing, and perhaps fearing one of the period's all-to-numerous skin infections.[42]

It seems surreal, a Monty Python sketch in a world askew. Men were moving around eastern North Carolina carrying sticks with three notches and asking one another if they knew the secret sign, and telling each other, if they did, to "BE TRUE." Others frantically rubbed their noses and legs with their left forefinger and asked whether you knew the secret or shouted "R" at you to see if you would respond. It seems funny now, and yet for them it was deadly serious. People had been tortured for a lot less between 1774 and 1776. While their efforts at secrecy might be seen as evidence of the Brethren's subversive intent, it is important to remember that from the beginning they feared that the popish, heretical conspiracy had been at least partially successful in penetrating the committees of safety and the new government. They wanted to avoid discovery by the heretical papists; they wanted to BE TRUE to INRJ.

"Conspiracy." The Revolutionary War's victors used this word to discredit all those who opposed them. And historians in the twentieth century used it to criticize aspects of American culture they did not like, especially in the wake of the McCarthy hearings in the 1950s. What happened in the Albemarle in 1777 suggests that this labeling has obscured central forces of change in the early revolutionary period. The Brethren grew from a Protestant value structure traditionally associated with the defense of liberty. Those who joined feared state leaders who had been polluted by popery and heresy. The Fourteen were heretics whose political-spiritual beliefs seemed much like the beliefs of those in the London ministry who had sought to deny Americans their liberty in 1774. The Albemarle planters joined together to save the state from this threat. In so doing, they created the preconditions for a clash over the meaning of the Revolution itself in the summer of 1777.

7

BECOMING KNOWN,
BECOMING LOYALISTS

IN LATE 1776 and early 1777, eastern North Carolina's yeomen rallied to defend Protestantism and to resist forced military service. The evils they had been taught to fear their entire lives—popish plots and tyrannical Frenchmen, heretics and an overbearing government tearing men from their harvest to serve in standing armies—had arrived amid the revolutionary chaos. The changes that came with independence seemed to undermine the Protestant liberty that had for generations shaped their self-understanding as a free people. The Revolution of 1775 had developed in support of those beliefs. The Brethren grew rapidly in number as long as their movement appeared to be defending the values embedded in this libertarian Anglo-American spiritual-political worldview.

Confrontations along some forgotten trails in the southern Albemarle revealed that by 1777 some in the revolutionary government saw this Protestant political worldview as dangerous and subversive. That revelation came when committeemen and militiamen threatened John Lewellen and some other leading Brethren with arrest as tories. The revolutionary leadership and their supporters in the counties would accept no criticism of the immature republican state's actions or its members' enlightened beliefs. The use of a Protestant political language to warn against the French, against heresy, and to speak in opposition to forced drafts smacked of sedition against the nascent republican order. By that summer the language of Protestant liberty that had been the traditional ideological pillar of a free people had again radically shifted its political position. It had become a weapon in a struggle over the course and nature of the Revolution, used as a discourse of criticism to assert a specific vision of liberty in a manner that some viewed as threatening the republican state.

As American freedom took shape, elements within the revolutionary leadership redefined central tenets of Protestant British liberty as hostile to an independent republican state. That enlightened political ideas had virtually no popular constituency in that early period of upheaval did nothing to temper this tendency. When this new freedom established its historical hegemony, it made what preceded it, and had made it possible, invisible. This occurred even though Protestantism was almost universally seen in the English-speaking world as essential to a free society. When the Albemarle's revolutionary leadership threatened John Lewellen, they exposed how fraught this central ideological transformation was.

This is not to say that loyalism was created solely by committee persecution in revolutionary America. Loyalism was a complex, varied, and at times contradictory identity within the fractured Anglo-American political reality that existed in the revolutionary period. However, it is to say that some of those who created a republican state during a bloody war caused a jarring ideological dislocation when they disowned the predominant ideas of liberty in the English-speaking world. That dislocation helps explains a central, unrecognized ideological paradox that emerged early in the Revolution and impacted all the political communities in the English-speaking world: by 1778 the beliefs that drove the Revolution in 1775 were being identified as counterrevolutionary.

Angry Words

Late in 1776 or early in 1777, John Lewellen began to tell others that the heretics in the North Carolina government intended to make the state "subject to popery." He wanted to seek relief from their plotting "and hop'd for a Blessing on the Indeavour." Lewellen talked openly about these threats. He did not advocate violence against the state or its leaders. He served the revolutionary state as a militia officer as well as a justice of the peace. Lewellen sought redress and to halt the drift toward popish government.[1]

The Brethren did not begin as a tory uprising at all. Ironically, members believed themselves to be responding to a popish, heretical, tyrannical conspiracy *against* Protestant liberty and the new state. It was a plot possibly inspired by the hated French, the traditional enemy of all free Protestant people, who were already rumored to be preparing to enter the war. This again suggests they did not think it a rebellion against the Revolution per se but a defense of Protestantism.[2]

Nor did the movement's constitution or other writings advocate a tory coup. When deposed during the movement's repression, James Rawlings denied that the constitution discussed a violent uprising. "It is," he testified, "certain none of these vile proceedings [meaning the later talk about a violent coup against the state] were inserted in their writings but very repugnant to them." The writings bound them to live by moral laws and the "old and new testament." The state government had copies of the constitution, and nowhere in the copious documentation created during the movement's suppression did they challenge this description. In 1777, swearing to oppose popery and idols did not make anyone loyalists. It made them normal at the very moment events violently redefined normality.[3]

It was a series of angry confrontations that altered the movement's political character. In early or mid-May, John Lewellen encountered committeeman James Mayo on some unnamed rural path. Mayo was part of a locally prominent Albemarle family that had migrated like so many others from Virginia to North Carolina in the 1740s. They owned considerable land in Martin County as well as in several other southern and western Albemarle counties. By 1776 James and his brother Nathan had become active revolutionaries and were heavily involved in the southern Albemarle's revolutionary militias and committees. James was a member of the committee of safety in one of the counties, probably Martin. His brother Nathan was appointed justice of the peace for Martin County in 1776 and became a militia captain in the same county, at approximately the same time that John Lewellen was appointed to the same positions and ranks in the same county, both serving in the same unit with the heretical Whitmel Hill. Nathan also owned land in Pitt County and served on committees there. When the Church of England collapsed in the southern Albemarle in 1776, Nathan joined the Baptist Church's chapel at Flat Swamp in Pitt County.[4]

When James Mayo encountered John Lewellen, he accused him of being an enemy of the people. More clashes soon followed for Lewellen as he had words with "Whitmel Hill," spiritual deviant Wylie Jones, and others who threatened "to take him [John Lewellen] up for a Tory," with Mayo being the first to make that threat. What specifically sparked these clashes remained unstated specifically. But Lewellen's views about the state leaders' embrace of popery and heresy, and specifically his views about Whitmel Hill and Wylie Jones's spiritual beliefs played a central part in it.[5]

James Mayo may have heard of Lewellen's views directly from the source. The two families knew each other. Lewellen's family held lands in Martin County near those of Nathan Mayo, who had been involved in a land conveyance to John Lewellen on extremely favorable terms in 1772, suggestive of a long-term relationship between the families. Lewellen may have tried to recruit James Mayo on that rural path. Or another Protestant associator may have tried to recruit James Mayo or Nathan Mayo. Certainly the Protestant associators did try to recruit James's brother William Mayo. He was invited into the movement but refused and reported the offer to the authorities before the Brethren became generally known. William quite possibly spoke to his brother James about what had happened, and this may well have been the source of James Mayo's knowledge of the Brethren.[6]

Albemarle committeemen and militiamen saw the Protestant associators' words as a challenge to the revolutionary state. Criticism of Hill and Jones was criticism of the Revolution; both played key roles in the committees of safety and / or the revolutionary militias as well as being members of the new state leadership. By 1777 Wylie Jones was an assembly leader with a hand in the state's finances. In the committeemen's eyes Lewellen spoke treason when he denounced such men, even though his words were consistent with older understandings of Anglo-American liberty.

What other reason could they have had for threatening a person who was serving the state government as a justice of the peace and was answering militia musters? In 1777, criticizing members of the state governments or the Continental Congress or the American cause generally—even thinking bad thoughts—all of these could get a person in a lot of trouble. The list of political offenses had expanded relentlessly since 1775, and many points of view had become criminalized.

The confrontations changed things. Lewellen had seen or heard about suspected tories being interrogated, tortured, and imprisoned, their property seized and their families expelled from the new states. He knew exactly what to expect if the label "tory" stuck to him. Lewellen began denouncing James Mayo as being "very particular in atacting any that was thote to be enemies to the state." His phrasing again suggests he did not think of himself that way when he exchanged the angry words with Mayo.[7]

Within weeks Lewellen and a faction in the movement's leadership began to consider violence against the revolutionary leaders in the Albemarle region. Lewellen argued that James Mayo should be killed, and he tasked Peter Tyler and James Rawlings with this assassination. Feelings against Mayo became so intense that when James Rawlings heard gunfire in the third week of June, he erroneously believed someone had murdered Mayo. Nathan Mayo also became a target. Brethren leaders described him as a "very Busy Body," a "son of a bitch" who would get himself killed for spying on Lewellen and their movement.[8]

John Lewellen's angry logic pushed the leadership toward a tory position. Lewellen realized he could not just murder the Mayo brothers. They represented the region's revolutionary committees and the militias that supported them. In late May, Lewellen began to contemplate a decapitating strike against the southern Albemarle's revolutionary elite. Speaking to James Rawlings, he declared that "they could Destroy Whitmarsh Hill, Colonel William, Thom. Hunter, Nathan Mayo, Colonel Salter and one Talor," as well as James Mayo.[9]

These men controlled key revolutionary institutions in the Albemarle region. Nathan Mayo acted as a militia officer in Martin County and perhaps Pitt County as well; "Coloniel William" was probably Martin County militia colonel William Williams, who also served in the new state senate and may have been related by marriage to Nathan Mayo; Whitmel Hill acted as a Lieutenant Colonel of the Martin County militia and a member of the committee of safety; "one Talor" was William or Joseph Taylor, members of Hillsborough's committee of safety; and "Colonel Salter" was Robert or John Salter, militia officers in Pitt County, the former also acting as a member of the county's committee of safety. Martin County's Henry Culpeper reported that Lewellen "seem'd to be angry" after the exchange with James Mayo. He soon came to believe they needed to "kill all the heads of the County."[10]

What began with an unhappy conversation soon cascaded into plans to decapitate the state government. Lewellen's began discussing killing Governor Richard Caswell and the entire state elite. It seems that he again became caught in his own words. He couldn't just kill Mayo, he had to kill the regional elite as well. If he killed them, he had to kill the state elite. Lewellen advocated seizing the Halifax powder magazine and murdering the governor during a planned gubernatorial visit to the town sometime in June. The Brethren would eliminate with one thrust the state leaders who had embraced French-tainted popery *and* those who had threatened to arrest them.[11]

An element within the Brethren's leadership supported Lewellen's bloody plans. James Rawlings declared that "several others" approved Lewellen's views, though he failed to name them. Other depositions, though, suggest who they might have been. Daniel and Absalom Legate supported this would-be coup. The latter man spoke in a militant tone, and discussed the plan to "kill the gentlemen in the Night" if the state authorities tried to suppress the Brethren. According to Thomas Best, associator Isaac Barbree wanted to shoot James Mayo for the same reasons as Lewellen— he had been threatened by committeemen. Best also believed that Brethren Barbree, David Taylor (Tailer), Hardy Counsell, and James Rodgers had hostile intent toward Nathan Mayo, although whether that made them loyalists in their own eyes is unclear. The revolutionary committees' intimidation that began in 1774 and extended into the war had alienated many even as it had also solidified support for independence and revolution.[12]

By mid-June this Brethren faction began talking like the king's friends when they spoke to potential recruits. This change too took place over time and varied from person to person. When James Rawlings brought David Taylor into the movement in late May, he indicated that the associators opposed the state government because "the Congress had given up the Country to the French to be governed by them, and then Popery would come into the Country." He then went on to mention keeping their lands if royal authority was restored. But the central thrust remained fear of popery.[13]

Soon, though, some leaders began making militant proclamations of loyalty to the king and the empire. The threats against Lewellen and the state government's embrace of France and heresy drove this seemingly anomalous change. George III and his ministry now seemed less a threat than their own state leaders.

The effort to get John Clifton of Anson County to associate captures this transformation as it occurred. In mid- to late May 1777, Martin County's William Tyler and John Staten of Anson County approached Clifton. It was at the time when Lewellen and others became more violent in their plans and tory in their goals. Tyler introduced Clifton to James Rawlings, the group's spiritual leader, who tried to get him to swear to keep a secret. When Clifton refused to take the oath without knowing what the Brethren stood for, Rawlings told him "it was only to employ a reader," meaning a church reader or lay preacher. Clifton seemed agreeable to this effort to restore the religious life they had known in the provincial past.[14]

Clifton's meeting with John Lewellen a day later, though, brought a more troubling message. Lewellen still advocated "an agreement to employ a reader," and even provided a schedule to pay the reader. Then, though, he declared that the movement now existed to support "King George." Members, Lewellen insisted, had to be ready to join any royal forces that came to the Albemarle region and would receive munitions to do so. Lewellen went on to say "they would shoot any man who divulged the secret."

Clinton specifically stated that Lewellen *spoke* to him the part about supporting the king and imperial armies. He went out of his way to mention that he did not think it had been added to the constitution whose authors had advocated the defense of Protestantism and protecting community members drafted against their will. The prospect of fighting for the king made Clinton uneasy, and he neither recruited anyone else nor engaged in any actions with other associators, remaining silent about the whole matter until confessing to his brother weeks later.[15]

By the second half of June some senior wardens and wardens had stopped talking about anti-popery altogether or had deemphasized it. These senior wardens and wardens had become loyalists. The efforts to recruit John Hodge is evidence of this change. Lewellen read something to Hodge, probably the movement's constitution. But the conversation itself focused on protecting those who resisted drafts and "those called torys." Lewellen also told him to get powder and shot. The time for a violent action against the committees and militias seemed to be at hand.[16]

This shift toward a militant loyalism is also evident in Daniel Legate's conversations with several men in June and early July. Legate asked one of the Thomas Harrisons (there were several men with this name involved in what happened in 1777) to join with others to "support their religion." Legate, though, then told him they intended to seize the Halifax powder magazine, and that General Howe knew about their movement. Hearing this, Harrison, who sympathized with Legate, nonetheless feared that a "world of bloodshed" lay ahead.[17]

Their emerging loyalism still reflected values embedded in Protestant political culture. Faith sanctified resistance to a new state government that had embraced the ungodly and the popish. Some recruiters told would-be recruits that the state leaders had to be confronted because the state loyalty oath contained heretical ideas. When Richard Faggan tried to recruit Salvanas Buttrey, Faggan told him the oath was "very Bad and would ruin his Sole." John Lewellen denounced Richard Caswell as "an infidel" who "didn't believe in the Holy Trinity." In their worldview, anti-Christian authority could be justly resisted. This popular loyalism was not a betrayal but a defense of soul as well as political liberty. Indeed, the two could not be separated.[18]

By mid-June Lewellen and others who supported the loyalist turn actively began to consider inviting the king's forces into the state. Up to that point the associators had had no contact with the British army or royal authorities. The movement was spurred by the situation in the Albemarle, not by British machinations or gold. These leaders approached their compatriot James Sherrard for money to fund a trip by Lewellen and several others to the British stronghold of New York City to see "General How." But Sherrard, who had been cooperative with the movement's leaders, refused, saying he would provide no "money for that purpose."[19]

Can we really understand words uttered in anger on some forgotten rural trace as not only evidence of profound ideological change in revolutionary America, but cause of change as well? We must if we wish to understand ideological change in revolutionary America at all. Archival sources reveal the role individual confrontations, pushing and shoving, rumors and threats, mobbings and assaults, battle and war played in transforming the revolutionary generation's worldview. This is what happened in the Albemarle.

The threats made against Lewellen, and later other Brethren leaders, transformed the movement's political orientation. Ideologically, Protestant political culture remained at its base, but by mid-June these leaders were no longer trying to save the commonwealth or support what they thought of as a Protestant revolution. They felt driven to a point where the empire and British army looked more attractive as rulers than their own countryman.

This change in political orientation explains the strange divergence in understanding within the depositions taken when the movement came to be suppressed. Some depositions and petitions portray the Brethren as a spiritual-political movement focused on stopping popery and heresy, and others suggest a loyalist conspiracy and do not mention popery or even forced drafts, or mention them only in passing. Across the six or seven months of its existence, the Brethren lived a profound shift in the nature of liberty.

John Lewellen defended liberty as it had been understood in the Protestant empire, and the committeemen represented independence and the freedom professed to come with it. The former belief system, separated by rebellion from the binding constraints of imperial institutional expression, had reverted in the hands of the Brethren associators to its original Protestant-libertarian character, and was used by those associators as a tool to criticize established power that seemed poised to become popish and arbitrary. That this power was a republican representative government did not matter at all, for the revolutionary generation suspected all institutionalized power of having the potential to become tyrannical. After independence the revolutionary state had taken on characteristics incompatible with traditional ideas of Protestant liberty, especially in places like North Carolina, where some of those creating that state held unorthodox spiritual beliefs.

In the revolutionary context that existed after July 4, the independent republican state's leaders refused to embrace ancient Anglo-American ideas about liberty and faith, and yet could find no way to fully co-opt them. That the vast majority of Americans were Protestants did nothing to inhibit these enlightened men, despite their heading a rebellion in favor of popular sovereignty. Their prioritizing of this enlightened view of liberty threatened the Protestant revolution and in the Albemarle drove at least some of the leading Brethren toward loyalism.

The movement began to unravel with this turn toward a violent loyalist coup. An ideological gap opened among the associators as word of the movement's new direction spread. When the leaders started to talk like tories, rank-and-file associators began to go to the state authorities to tell them what they knew and denounce the bloody-minded plans for a tory coup. These yeomen remained committed to Protestant liberty and the defense of community members. But they did not equate these goals with allegiance to a corrupted empire.

While fears about the leaders' militant toryism drove these defections, Lewellen's choice of local allies sealed the Brethren's fate. In his anger, Lewellen planned to instigate a diversionary slave revolt to achieve his goal of murdering the state's leadership. He had gone too far.[20]

The Specter of Slave Rebellion

Early America had a line that could not be crossed by any man or woman, rich or poor, white or black or Native American: You did not incite a slave rebellion. If you did, you could expect to be whipped, tortured, burned alive, hanged, disemboweled, or left in a cage to starve. And yet despite this, as Lewellen created his blueprint for a bloody coup, he suggested the unthinkable—that the Protestant associators should spark a diversionary slave uprising during Governor Caswell's planned visit to the Albemarle in the summer of 1777. Amid the resulting confusion the Brethren would seize local armories and then assassinate the chief executive and his party.

Lewellen had touched a subject so volatile—race relations in the season of revolution—that it ended the only way it could end, with him in chains, sentenced to death, abandoned by the movement's rank and file, who defected rather than support a tory revolt linked to a slave uprising. This is how it always ended for those who threatened the racial order until the Civil War destroyed slavery.

Eighteenth-century slave owners had two overriding concerns in regard to their human property: how to exploit them, and how to control them. On these twin impulses rested a superstructure of law, justification, and sanctification, an intricate tower that kept the slave population in place. In peacetime, slave owners tried to imagine their slaves as grateful children in need of guidance. During the imperial wars that stretched intermittently from 1690 forward, though, the presence of hostile forces nearby forced masters to acknowledge that those they owned probably hated them. The white population often projected onto their human property both bloody intent and in some cases crypto-Catholicism, understanding them as willing to rebel in favor of Britain's foreign, Catholic enemies. Conspiracies real and imagined inevitably resulted in brutal crackdowns up and down the Eastern Seaboard.

It is little wonder, then, that concerns about the possibility of servile insurrection increased dramatically in 1774. Many white Americans came to believe their slaves to be natural imperial loyalists who would use the turmoil to rise against their masters, perhaps in conjuncture with an armed incursion by British forces. These fears echoed earlier anxieties that slaves would run away during the wars with France, Spain, and their Native allies.[21]

Fears about slave uprisings in the Crown's favor manifested themselves everywhere as the empire began to split up in 1774 and 1775. New York City's white population became convinced that the London authorities were encouraging their slaves to rise. The New Yorkers hanged "Two tory Negroes. . . . several others were to be tried for their lives, they having been detected in joining the tories, and engaging to murder" masters who supported liberty. Fear of an uprising in Ulster County, New York, in February 1775 led to a wide-ranging crackdown against slaves in the Hudson River Valley. Other northern colonies saw similar episodes throughout the 1774–1776 period.[22]

Understandably, though, these fears ran strongest in the slave-dependent colonies in the Chesapeake and the Carolinas. There, the actions of Virginia governor Lord Dunmore in 1775 created a rolling crisis in the slave system. Rumors about Dunmore's intentions in regard to the enslaved began to circulate as imperial governments in the different colonies began to collapse. Finally, in November 1775, with Virginia in rebellion and fighting raging in Massachusetts, Dunmore proclaimed that bondsmen who ran away from masters who were in rebellion and joined the British military would be emancipated. Thousands of slaves absconded, shattering the myth of slave loyalty to supposedly paternalistic owners.[23]

In 1775 anxiety about the slaves' political intentions gripped North Carolina's white population as well. Little wonder, since North Carolina had between 60,000 and 70,000 bonded Africans and African Americans out of a total population near 300,000. The North Carolina revolutionary leadership helped mightily to create this anxiety. On May 31, 1775, the New Bern committee published a circular letter denouncing the British actions near Boston that led to the fighting at Lexington and Concord. Without any sense of irony, they declared that the British minister intended to enslave white freeholders and warned that they feared that "in these Times of general Tumult and Confusion, that the slaves may be instigated. . . . by our inveterate Enemies to an Insurrection." Such a rising, they continued, might destroy North Carolina. The committeemen recommended reinforcing the slave patrol with newly formed militia companies.[24]

Carolinians' suspicions about royal officials' intentions in regard to the slaves intensified month after month. In June 1775 a North Carolina writer would tell a friend in New York that people in the colony expected the London government to spirit up the slaves "whose barbarity, if roused, the most dreadful consequences will follow." North Carolina's congressional delegates joined this slave-fearing chorus. In the same June 1775 they explained that the other colonies had already begun to raise troops to defeat a tyrannical ministry. "North Carolina," they complained, "alone remains an inactive Spectator." Would the British ministry, the delegates asked, hesitate "to raise the hand of the servant against the master?"[25]

The revolutionary leaders soon began to claim that the London authorities and their local minions were actually trying to provoke a slave uprising in North Carolina. In July 1775 the Wilmington committee of safety received a report that "John Collett Commander at Fort Johnston had given Encouragement to Negroes to Elope from their Masters" and declared Collett would encourage them to insurrection if the colonies went into open rebellion. Joseph Hewes, delegate to the Second Continental Congress, assured the Edenton jurist James Iredell that the ministry intended to set slave against master. John Stuart, imperial agent to the Native Americans in the southwest, reported to London that the rebel leaders told their followers that the British ministry intended to encourage the slaves to kill their owners.[26]

Specific rumors about the intentions of North Carolina's governor, Josiah Martin, intensified these fears. Martin noted that his whig opponents had fabricated a rumor that he had "formed a design of Arming the Negroes" and would proclaim free all who would rally to the king's standard in emulation of Governor Dunmore's supposed design. Martin declared it to be false, but it became widely believed anyway when his response to an inquiry by the New Bern committee of safety was construed as threatening to raise the slaves should the colony rebel. That committee described Martin's poorly chosen words "as an alarm to the people of this Province against the horrid and barbarous designs of the enemies." The committeemen maintained that Martin made this threat to control the growing rebellion.[27]

What can only be called revolutionary North Carolina's great slave fear grew in this rumor-filled environment, which was made more unstable by proclamations and circular letters. A contemporary wrote in June 1775 that "there was a great [ ] the People about Negros Rising." The committees of safety ordered intensified slave patrols, which began whipping slaves indiscriminately for "walking peaceably along the Road, or being at Home," as one concerned Quaker put it. The Pitt County committee empowered its slave patrol to shoot any armed slaves as well as any combination of four or more slaves found off their masters' plantations. The Provincial Congress instructed slave owners along Cape Fear River to move male slaves "capable of bearing arms, or otherwise assisting the enemy," away from the coast, where the British navy might operate.[28]

It seems inevitable that the white population would uncover a conspiracy regardless of whether one existed or not. And indeed they did. In that same unsettled July 1775, Richard Cogdell, writing from Chatham, reported "a discovery that was made in Beaufort County by Mr. Bayner & one of Capt. Robert's Negro men Unto Capt. Thomas Rispass [?]" of an intended slave insurrection that very evening. Authorities sent an express message to Beaufort, and the committee of safety arrested nearly forty slaves. The committees cracked down hard on those they detained. The committeemen found it a "Horrid Trajeck Plan" designed to destroy the entire white population. By "Negro evidence" the whigs learned "that Capt. Johnson of Whitehaven [apparently a white tory co-conspirator]" had conspired with "Merrick, A Negro man slave who formerly Belongd to Major Clark," and loaded his brig with some kind of armaments. The committee of safety ordered that five imprisoned slaves receive eighty lashes and have their ears cropped. Thereafter the white population routinely arrested and scourged slaves they believed dangerous.[29]

Now, less than two years after this fear swept the countryside, John Lewellen wanted to start a slave uprising in order to assassinate the state's leaders. In June 1777 he told James Rawlings that he believed the associators should "git some Body to diseffect the Negroes." He had with those words stepped outside their reality.[30]

Lewellen fixated on David Taylor to play this role for a good, if ironic, reason. Taylor served as "a Patroler over the Negroes in that Neighborhood," a member of the expanded slave patrol. Taylor could move around the servile population without raising questions. He would claim to carry a message from a benevolent king liberating the slaves, and would also be credible when he would appear at Halifax to "give out an oration of their [slaves] Rising" in order to draw soldiers away from the village. Then Lewellen and the others would seize the armaments magazine at Halifax and assassinate Governor Caswell. Caswell failed to visit at Halifax at that time, and Lewellen put the uprising on hold to await another opportunity to strike.[31]

The specter of a white-inspired slave uprising accelerated the movement's internal unraveling. Slave patroller David Taylor could not bring himself to be involved in a servile revolt and was one of the first to give evidence against the Brethren's leaders. Early in June, Taylor told his brother about Lewellen's plans, including the diversionary slave rebellion. Seeing the potential for his sibling to end up on the gallows, this brother convinced Taylor to go to the authorities. They revealed what they knew and learned that officials had already heard rumors about a plot against the state.[32]

Others began to reveal the planned loyalist coup to the state authorities in mid-June. Amid rampant rumors about a rising involving slaves, assassinations, and British troops, "many have come in and made all the discovery they know." The movement to protect Protestants and Protestant political culture had been transformed into something dangerous to white freeholders, and had lost their support as a consequence.[33]

In the second half of June the state authorities began arresting those believed to be associators. The detention of William Tyler and William May around June 15 marked a turning point. Tyler at least knew about the efforts to contact Lord Howe and assassinate Governor Caswell. Worse yet, Tyler had been "taken with all the papers in his pocket"—meaning, apparently, the constitution, the oaths, and his membership lists. If Tyler gave information about their plans, the movement's leaders would be arrested and quite possibly executed as rebels against the republican revolution.[34]

The Gourd Patch

With the revolutionary government closing in and followers beginning to defect, the Brethren's leadership finally tried to act. The crisis came in the third week of June. Lewellen ordered associators living in and near Pitt County to get powder and shot. On June 20 they met at a place "called the goard patch" near Tarborough, in Edgecombe County. They sought to free May and Tyler, who were being held by "Wm. Robinson & Mr. Salter, of Pitt County," the former a militia officer and the latter a member of that county's committee of safety. Lewellen told the Brethren at one point that if they could not free May and Tyler by intimidation, the Protestant associators would have to "kill some of them," meaning the local committeemen. The moment of truth had come.[35]

Bloodshed seemed inevitable. About thirty men gathered to rescue their imprisoned comrades. But when Lieutenant Colonel Henry Irwin, an officer in the state's Continental line and a member of the Edgecombe County committee of safety, made a spirited opposition to them with a roughly equal-sized force (some of whom may have been Continental troops), the associators hesitated. They apparently recoiled at the thought of actually killing people, or getting killed, and Irwin seized and disarmed them all. He further reported that he had made many take the dreaded state loyalty oath.[36]

The Brethren would not be transformed into an armed loyalist force. When confronted, the will to shed blood, if it ever truly existed for the rank and file, collapsed. Men who had associated to defend Protestantism and community members in chaotic times did not want to be drawn into assassinating the state's governor amid a servile uprising.

The movement's internal unwinding accelerated in this non-uprising's wake. The more serious Lewellen and the others got about their bloody plans, the more difficult it became to recruit new members or retain old ones. Horrified by talk of the Brethren's leaders inviting in British troops and the specter of a Brethren-inspired slave rebellion, would-be recruits turned on the movement. Thomas Stubbs, told by Thomas Harrison that General Howe might become involved and "Befriend them & know his friends from his foes," refused to associate and in fact actively sought to persuade Harrison to leave the movement. Stubbs believed disaster loomed for the associators, and on July 14 he told the state authorities what he knew.[37]

One after another of the potential recruits refused to cooperate. When Daniel Legate tried to get one of the several men named Benjamin Harrison in Tyrrell County to swear at the very least to defend those pressed unwillingly into the military—a recruiting tactic that had worked in the past—Harrison demurred. He testified that he had heard "that he General How had a hint of matters carrying on by the Association before that time." On July 16 he provided the state authorities with an affidavit about the Brethren.[38]

Other would-be Brethren also veered clear. Nathan Everett swore that when Daniel Legate offered Thomas Rogers a "commission for a solicitor," in early July, Rogers promptly refused it. By then the movement was failing on all fronts, its fate already becoming apparent.[39]

Those who had taken one or more oaths began to defect as the loyalist turn became more pronounced. Early in July, Samuel Black swore the oaths in the woods near a wheat field owned by one of Thomas Harrison Sr.'s sons. But when the constitution was read to him, he believed he detected "something that might mean Bad on it." Perhaps he meant the resistance to drafts; it is unclear what he objected to or why he became uneasy. But he told John Stewart he "had an intention to declare it," meaning to denounce or reveal the document to the state.[40]

Benjamin Harrison's relative William Harrison also became suspicious of the movement's new loyalist-tainted goals. He had sworn three oaths to the movement around the first of June. But when

Daniel Legate offered to tell him some secrets not contained in the three oaths—presumably concerning the now-planned loyalist coup—William Harrison declined to learn more. Having "observed something more than ordinary amongst his neighbors," he became frightened that Legate "was leading them into trouble."[41]

Like a number of other Protestant associators and would-be associators, William Harrison was, tellingly, still answering the republican state's incessant militia musters, and he heard even more disturbing news while at a muster on July 5. As they drilled, William learned that "some people up the country" had been jailed for their involvement with the Brethren. What he heard seemed to confirm his suspicions about Legate's true, traitorous intentions. Harrison then tried to rescue his neighbors "by breaking up the plot." He claimed, apparently truthfully, to have confronted Legate and other Brethren leaders involved in the coup talk and urged them to end it all, angering the militant Legate in the process. Nonetheless, Harrison and several members of his family persisted in arguing that the movement should now be disbanded.[42]

John Clifton, cautious in the extreme about joining when he had been approached by his old acquaintance William Tyler, had refused to take all the oaths. As the movement's loyalist turn became known, he finally decided to tell the state what he knew. Accompanied by his brother Peter for support, John Clifton revealed what he knew to Judge Thomas Pugh. "The said Clifton," he continued, speaking in the third person, "disapproving of their purpose [meaning the assassination of the governor], had a great desire to reveal it" even earlier. But having taken the first oath to keep the movement secret, he hesitated to do so. He claimed to have never "attempted to influence anyone" to join before he finally decided to expose the movement and its plan.[43]

Other yeomen who had been drawn in by wardens telling them that the state oath contained heretical ideas abandoned the Brethren when they discovered the oath's true contents. Warden James Sherrard had approached John Wheatly and "represented the state oath . . . in a very Dreadfull lights Contrary to what he now find it." Wheatly felt little loyalty once the movement's new trajectory became apparent and the state oath's actual content became known to him. Salvanas Buttrey also offered evidence once confronted with the movement's new, loyalist-tinged goals and the state oath's actual content, which bound men to the Revolution, not Satan.[44]

Fears about the fate of Protestantism had drawn them in, and the twin specters of a loyalist coup and a servile rebellion drove them away. Thomas Harrison swore that he had agreed to join to "support their religion," as long as there was "no harm in it." When it looked to become harmful, he left. Lemuel Hyman "voluntarily offered to depose on oath all he knew," though he had taken the secrecy oath. He claimed not to have understood the movement's ultimate goals and or what was meant by forcibly carrying men away from their wives and children (forced drafts).[45]

Some solicitors and wardens expressed what seemed to be real shock at the movement's change in direction. According to John Collins, he one day encountered a downtrodden James Sherrard. Collins believed Sherrard might be sick, but the latter man said no. Rather, it was "dreadful news which gave me . . . much uneasiness." Sherrard revealed that Lewellen and some other leaders among the Brethren intended "to make an End to all the heads of the County." Collins urged his downcast acquaintance "for God's sake Take off that Evil Intent, Quash it if you can." Sherrard told Collins that had he known of these evil plans he would have never associated. Collins went on to state that, as far as he knew, Sherrard had not, as some claimed, purchased gunpowder for the conspirators during a visit to the town of Windsor. Nor did he lend the Brethren leaders money so that they might travel to parley with Lord Howe. The court found Collins credible.[46]

Even the movement's lay preacher James Rawlings claimed to have developed deep doubts as planning for the coup expanded. He initially endorsed the idea of rising if British troops entered the state. Rawlings's views changed, though, when Lewellen suggested using the diversionary slave uprising to assassinate the governor and murder the county leaders. Rawlings claimed he resisted this militant turn and also refused orders to kill Lewellen's arch-nemesis, Captain James Mayo, in cold blood. When Rawlings objected to the idea of sparking a slave insurrection, Lewellen told him "if he Divulg'd anything, Death was the portion to him or any one else" who talked openly about the planned coup.[47]

More people went to the authorities as the conspiratorial rhetoric intensified. Tyrrell County residents Mary Walker and Elizabeth Ward gave evidence after hearing associator Stephen Burges say that he hoped the king's forces would "put us [meaning those who rebelled] all to the sword" for rebellion. Two days after Sampson Taylor heard James Haise [Hays] say "Good news . . . that ye Scotch and Tores ware Imbodying and that they Intended to have Governor Caswell's head" in three or four weeks. Taylor went before a state magistrate to report what he had heard.[48]

The information provided by the defectors allowed the state government to crush the movement. By July 31, dozens of Brethren had been arrested, and a "strong guard constantly kept up" secured the Edenton magazine and other military stores throughout the Albemarle. The Edenton militia was stretched so thin by those duties that authorities had trouble keeping a unit in place to guard the dilapidated jail as it came to be stuffed with the Protestant associators. The revolutionary leadership prepared for a Brethren-led loyalist uprising as threats against the republican state seemed to loom everywhere.[49]

In this last prediction, the state authorities could not have been more wrong. A centuries-long slumber awaited the Protestant associators, with them signaling their loyalty to one another and Protestant Christianity only in the largely forgotten depositions and petitions created as the state eradicated their movement.

Becoming Loyalist, Becoming Unknown

The process of defining people and beliefs to fit the emerging new order occurred in every state. Some who imagined themselves as non-offending citizens at times found themselves threatened or even expelled by committeemen determined to create a unified republican citizenry, a tendency that became exaggerated at times of military crisis. War on their own soil had channeled the revolutionary state's idealism into very specific paths.[50]

Many whose views are not easily reconciled with the categories of revolutionary allegiance through which we have understood the period ended up defined as enemies to the Revolution. When James Mayo and other state authorities labeled the Protestant associators loyalists and tories, they in essence refought, perhaps unintentionally, the battle the heretical Fourteen had waged and lost at the state convention in December 1776. In their interactions with the leading Brethren, the authorities had redefined those who connected liberty with Protestantism as enemies of the Revolution, and made it difficult for the Protestant associators and those like them to speak to us about the historical changes they lived and those they helped make. How they understood the Revolution and what they had pledged to do was lost, at least initially, on the state authorities.

It is entirely understandable on a human level. Confronted with threats against their lives, Richard Caswell and the others in the revolutionary government could not afford to examine the nuances of ideological positions. They needed to deal with the Brethren, and as they did, they began to actually build the republican state. Crushing the movement expressed in one locale the beginning of a decades-long process that eventually turned British Americans into—Americans.

8

THE SWORD
AND THE SCALE

DANIEL AUSTIN awoke on the third Monday in July 1777 to find
two visitors at his father's home. William Brimage, a major landholder and formerly a judge in the royal admiralty courts, had arrived unannounced, accompanied by a stranger "who afterwards
called himself Campbell." Young Austin did not know it yet, but
his two guests were trying to elude the growing dragnet deployed
by the state against the Brethren's leadership.[1]

Brimage had excellent reason to flee. He had accepted the title
of senior warden at the edge of a forgotten wheat field in the
southern Albemarle around July 1, despite having attended the Provincial Congress at Hillsborough in the late summer of 1775 as a
delegate for Bertie County and later accepting a judgeship in the
revolutionary republican state. He had sworn himself to the Brethren
at the very moment when it became a tory movement and begun to
fall apart. By that third week in July, the state had mobilized what
forces it had against the movement and members of the Brethren
leadership were running for their lives or going into hiding.[2]

Although it is unclear whether Brimage ever even recruited
anyone into the movement, state authorities had detained him as
soon as his name came into evidence. There is little question as to

why they did this. Many revolutionary officials erroneously believed that Brimage and/or some other great man had initiated the movement. Even with republicanism's anti-patriarchal tendencies, North Carolina's leadership still understood the world as operating on hierarchical principles. They believed that any serious political unrest had to be organized by a leading man or men. "It Doth not," as one of them put it, "Remain a Doubt with me But that there is some persons of note concerned in this Horrid Plan."[3]

Brimage fit perfectly the state leadership's image of what a loyalist conspiracy organizer would look like. He was wealthy and had served the empire not only as a judge but also as deputy attorney for the Crown in the New Bern District. The authorities didn't yet know the Brethren's origins or extent, or about the angry exchange between John Lewellen and James Mayo that had sparked the turn toward a violent loyalist coup. They did not know about Daniel Legate's tireless efforts to recruit Protestant associators and spread the Brethren's message. The state leaders as yet had no interest in the movement's finer points.

In July Brimage found himself hauled in for questioning, jailed at Halifax, placed on parole, and sent to (or perhaps he simply went to) what was called the "tory brig," a ship that was supposed to carry loyalists out of the state and then out of the United States. Parole was a common practice in a period when America had no true prisons or prisoner of war camps. Even the gentlemen among the Highlanders who rose in a failed armed rebellion against North Carolina's revolution early in 1776 received paroles.[4]

The onetime admiralty judge's situation deteriorated as each new detail about the would-be loyalist coup emerged. Governor Caswell had, by late July, become convinced that Brimage was "one of the powers of their diabolic plot." He ordered Dobbs militia major David Barrow to bring Brimage back from the tory brig, and to "apply to Col. Bryan ... & request he will send a party of the Cravan militia immediately to ... bring Mr. Brimage back" to New Bern.

If Colonel Bryan failed in his mission, the governor ordered Barrow to do it himself. Barrow soon reported that he had dispatched a Lieutenant Shedrick Fulcher with a party of men to go after Brimage, "with orders not to return without him." A man as dangerous as Brimage could not be left on the loose.[5]

Caswell soon learned to his dismay that Brimage had fled. A militia captain had removed him from the tory-laden ship and re-arrested him at Ocacock on the Outer Banks, but allowed him parole within the village. With more fingers pointing at him day by day, and his situation obviously dire, Brimage jumped that parole and tried to escape the state. He had become revolutionary North Carolina's fugitive number one by the time he arrived at the Austin home shortly thereafter. He asked Daniel Austin to transport himself and "Campbell" to Roanoke Island, to the north of Ocacock between Pamlico and Albemarle Sounds, which Austin offered to do for ten dollars.[6]

Brimage seems imprudently frugal given that he knew himself to be a wanted man believed to be the head of a murderous tory plot. He haggled, and offered eight dollars instead of ten. Austin finally agreed, and with his brother Cornelius acting as crew, they readied their father's boat, joined just before they departed by a third man, Bertie County blacksmith John Smith, who asked to join the group. They pushed away from shore and headed to Roanoke Island, three wanted men being taken across the sound by two innocent boys.[7]

Once afloat, the fugitives suddenly demanded to be taken to the New Inlet. This breach in the Outer Banks's ever-shifting wall of sands that guard Albemarle Sound from the Atlantic had appeared in the 1730s and become a local landmark. The travelers offered the Austin brothers the full ten dollars if they would take them there. "Brimage," the brothers' account recalled, "insisted to go to the New Inlet." After some discussion, the brothers agreed to their passengers' increasingly frantic requests and changed course.[8]

Crisis of the Militias

Force maintained the Revolution as the Brethren became known and their leaders sought to flee in midsummer 1777. This reality created intense consternation among the revolutionary leadership. War and the general upheaval made it impossible to normalize republican institutions even after the convention wrote the state's first constitution in December 1776. When the authorities confronted the Brethren's leaders in the summer of 1777, North Carolina's committees of safety and the militia units still acted as the Revolution's ultimate arbitrators on the local level. But the militia units in the state were becoming unstable by then. The state leadership realized ad hoc rule by force should not continue and sought to normalize civil institutions under the auspices of popular sovereignty. The movement's suppression became a key moment in the creation of a republican state in North Carolina when the revolutionary leadership chose to deal with the Protestant associators via the newly created civil court system.

Most Americans had believed that the committees and conventions that had seized control in 1774 and 1775 would subside with independence and the creation of new state constitutions. Liberty and property would again find protection in a settled constitutional order. But that had not happened; rule by committees and militias continued in 1777. It was troubling; rule by force was incompatible with free government and unsuitable for a free people. A revolution in favor of popular sovereignty fueled by a spectrum of antiauthoritarian beliefs could not remain legitimate if it rested on raw power.

By the summer of 1777 the ideological issues around rule by force had become linked to an immediate practical problem that threatened the entire Revolution. The chronic manpower shortages that had led to the forced drafts in late 1776 had begun to give way to a general crisis in the state's military formations by mid-1777. The county militias especially had begun to unravel under the pressure of constant mobilization. Although they were supposed to be called up for terms lasting no more than three months, with the war and Revolution one emergency followed another. Units tasked with enforcing the committees of safety's authority, protecting the state from British invasion, and guarding against slave rebellions were stretched to the point that their very existence and the Revolution's long term viability were in question. The ongoing crisis was testing the population's civic virtue, and North Carolinians increasingly were failing this examination.[9]

From the beginning of the war, North Carolina's revolutionary government had had problems getting units to accept their newly minted authority. In the summer of 1775 the New Hanover County militia refused to serve under certain officers. The men threatened to form independent ranger companies free from the Hillsborough Provincial Congress's control if they did not get the officers they wanted. By the summer of 1776 some people were ignoring militia musters altogether. Militiamen in the Hillsborough District refused a Council of Safety order to mobilize in response to renewed conflict with the Cherokees on Carolina's western border. These men "failed to attend the Muster" in their counties, and refused to march when drafted. The Council of Safety empowered militia officers to try these delinquents even while it remained unclear why they failed to muster.[10]

By mid-1777 the revolutionary government was gradually losing control over the militia units they had. The stress created by extended service and lack of pay for militia units and units in the state line was leading to open unrest in the formations that did muster. In July a militia commander named John Williams reported that a "mutiny that happened in camp last Saturday" had almost become general. The problem? Units resented being on constant alert, with orders "to hold themselves in readiness to march over the river." The situation remained volatile and Williams promised to "do my best" to prevent "mutiny & desertion." But he sounded desperate. Another militia commander in Wilmington reported that his company had so few men they could not guard munitions stored in his area.[11]

Desertion from military formations became widespread as the frequent mobilizations continued. Serving without pay, or facing the prospect of fighting away from North Carolina, men felt entitled or compelled to go home. Lt. Colonel Mebane of the state's Seventh Battalion added, "We have numbers of deserters, who I think it will be impossible ever to have brought in. . . . as they generally live too obscure for proclamations or any other offered clemency to reach them." Some officers, he continued, had begun to disobey orders and begged to resign.[12]

Even those officers holding their formations together faced unnerving problems rooted in a lack of pay and equipment. In the summer of 1777, Captain John Vance, in command at Fort Foster, wrote to Governor Richard Caswell and declared his unit's morale strong, despite the lack of a paymaster, doctor, and officers. He claimed that had he not arrived when he did, "the Company would have been totally broke up." A militia officer named Bradley told Governor Caswell that his men complained daily "for want of their money" and were deserting. Only the company's sergeants held the unit together, and they had not been paid, either. "Without their money," he warned, "they will not stay." Bradley stopped the mutiny, but he feared for his unit's stability.[13]

If the militias failed, the institutional structures left in the revolutionary counties might fall apart. In July, Colonel David Smith of Cross Creek in Cumberland County declared it "absolutely necessary that an armed Company should be maintained in this county." Smith believed that the county might disintegrate without the militia in place. Many residents, he believed, were "already become insolent" in regard to the new order. In mid-1777 the units seemed to be at the point of disintegration. The state could not survive without the militias, but the way the leadership used them threatened to unravel the Revolution itself.[14]

The state leaders recognized that the units had become overextended. They wanted to rule through the new republican civil institutions authorized by the December 1776 state constitution; it would take some of the pressure off the militia units and legitimate their new regime. But in 1777 the power vacuum in civil life created when imperial institutions collapsed remained. In April 1777, Governor Caswell complained that the legislature had failed to erect new republican institutions and in fact had "done little more than Settle the decorum to be Observed between each House & the method of doing Business." The assemblymen's tentativeness is understandable given the tensions over the new constitution evident just months before. And Caswell's scathing reaction to their timidity is hardly surprising given that a brutal war raged on American soil.[15]

Those who refused to muster exposed the state's lack of legitimacy at its birth. They passively threatened the Revolution itself. It is indeed ironic, and telling, that some Protestant associators continued to answer militia musters in the summer of 1777 when others refused to. It speaks to a political position that defies categorization using the terms and languages that have shaped our understanding for 240 years. Like many others who continued to muster, they increasingly found the state oppressive and even tyrannical. As the disruptions intensified, they brought reactions; the Brethren can be seen as part of this reaction. The Revolution was going to fail if rule by committee and militia could not be ended, whatever the verdict on the battlefield.

A new normal had to be established under republican auspices to stabilize the state, and the Brethren movement's suppression ultimately became a means to that end. The revelation of the plot against the governor and the state leaders amid the militia crisis created an intense imperative to establish working civil institutions. This new civil legal system would legitimize the Revolution itself in North Carolina.

Authority that seems normal—this is the true goal, or truly the endpoint, of all revolutions. When revolutionary innovation no longer seemed novel as encountered in day-to-day society, the Revolution would have succeeded. State authorities knew this, but they confronted one difficulty after another as they tried to create a working republican judiciary. And yet they had no choice. North Carolina was adrift in that moment, at sea with no easy course to salvation.

At Sea

William Brimage and his two companions were literally at sea. And the Austin brothers were becoming very uneasy about their three passengers as the voyagers made their way across the sound. Landing at a beach with the fugitives, the two boys suddenly found themselves being held at gunpoint. "Campbell," it turned out, was really a Royal Navy lieutenant now determined to escape North Carolina. He "took out a Handkerchief with two Pistols in it," and walked "after this deponent [Daniel Austin], who turned and . . . asked him if he intended to hurt him."[16]

A British officer among the Brethren's leadership! Brimage had become at the moment of the movement's collapse a true traitor to the Revolution. It's unclear how he came to know this man, or whether the other Brethren leaders knew about the British officer. He may have been on the tory brig with Brimage, but there is no mention of him. Brimage's actions, along with those of Lewellen and some of the other leaders, revealed them now as active loyalists, a position rejected by many in the movement's rank and file.

The conspirators' flight began to fall apart as the conversation at gunpoint continued on the beach. Campbell told the frightened Austin brothers he intended to take their boat and make his escape, presumably to rendezvous with one of the British warships operating off Virginia and North Carolina's Outer Banks. And he seemed to be actively considering killing these two young men. Brimage and Smith then intervened and swore they would die before they allowed Campbell to harm the unoffending brothers. Cornelius Austin then tried to turn Smith against the British officer, asking him to help subdue "Campbell," which Smith refused to do, as "the Lieutenant was a blooded minded Fellow and was afraid he would kill some of them."[17]

This unhappy band of faux-Argonauts then sailed to the nearby Currituck inlet. The fugitives promised the boys money and their freedom to take them there, even as they continued to hold the Austins against their will. When they landed, Daniel Austin summoned up the courage to ask his kidnapper-passengers why they had fled. Brimage and Smith replied that "they had done no harm, but being suspected Tories, had come away, as they would not take the oath [of loyalty to the state]." For Brimage, this was a self-serving understatement. He had taken a position as a judge in the new state, only then to become involved with the Brethren at the moment the movement turned toward an active loyalist coup. He had then somehow contacted a British naval officer and was trying to flee the state with him. It was a good way to get himself hanged.[18]

What had become a tiny nautical opera continued, irresistibly, toward its third act. Forced to set sail yet again, a squall soon enveloped the sound, and led the Austins to land the boat near a place called Dolbey's Point. The brothers planned their escape as the summer sky pelted the voyagers. Daniel whispered to his brother to get the boat and go, and that he would run, "which accordingly they did," leaving their captors alone on the windswept beach.[19]

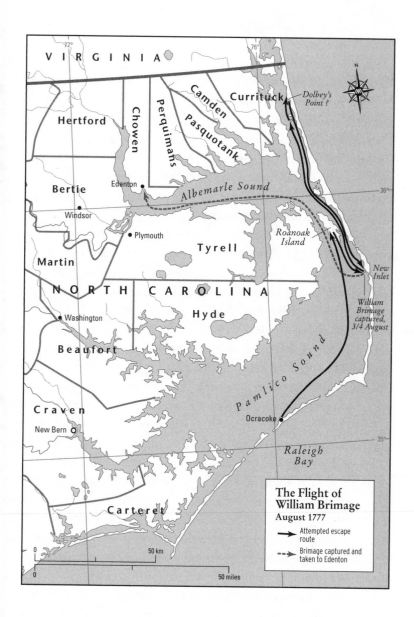

V I R G I N I A

Hertford

Chowen

Perquimans

Camden

Pasquotank

Currituck

Dolbey's
Point ?

Edenton

Bertie

Windsor

Albemarle Sound

Plymouth

Tyrell

Roanoak
Island

New
Inlet

Martin

N O R T H   C A R O L I N A

Hyde

William
Brimage
captured,
3/4 August

Washington

B e a u f o r t

Pamlico Sound

C r a v e n

New Bern

Ocracoke

Raleigh
Bay

C a r t e r e t

0   50 km

0   50 miles

The Flight of
William Brimage
August 1777

→ Attempted escape
route

⤍ Brimage captured and
taken to Edenton

The Scale

The law's time came again with the efforts to crush the Brethren. As Protestant associators began to fill the jails around the sound in late July, Governor Caswell and the other state leaders made a crucial decision. A new republican civil legal system would determine the associators' fate, not vigilantes or ad hoc meetings of committees or militiamen. It was a bold but necessary step. If the Brethren could be dealt with by civil courts, "the state of North Carolina" would become more than a phrase. Dealing with the associators via a republican judiciary became a vehicle to create a working legal order in revolutionary North Carolina.

Such a legal order would be something of a novelty. There had been chronic problems in the late provincial North Carolina's legal system. Legal procedures had been reformed in 1762 at the order of London under the direction of then-speaker of the provincial assembly: Richard Caswell. Under Caswell's guidance, legal procedures were generally Anglicized, becoming more like those in England, with Caswell also trying to make some allowance for local conditions and customs. Each county in North Carolina could establish courts of sessions as well as courts of pleas, and incorporated towns and hamlets could appoint justices of the peace.[20]

Provincial politics kept it from working well, and the reforms began years of political conflict over control of the legal system. Royal governors had the appointing power in this tiny legal structure, a power coveted by the provincial assembly. London's persistent unwillingness to accept some local legal practices that Caswell had protected in 1762 eventually allowed the legislature to challenge the royal governors for control of court patronage. Bitter disputes over the courts continued throughout the 1760s and 1770s, exacerbated by the Regulator crisis (1766–1771) in North Carolina's interior, which grew in large part because of the belief that self-interested lawyers controlled the courts. The legal system collapsed in those western counties in the late 1760s and could not be reestablished until late in 1771.[21]

In that same year, the newly arrived royal governor Josiah Martin and the assembly became locked in bitter conflict again over the 1762 legal reform acts. Martin came with instructions to suspend the courts if they did not discontinue the practices allowed by Caswell during the reforms in 1762 that were seen from London as being inconsistent with English law. The resulting clashes led court bills to be shelved, superior courts to be suspended, and inferior courts to be allowed to continue only by the assembly's leave. The issue of when to seize the property of insolvent debtors became intertwined with these conflicts. The London government demanded that the colony's debtor laws conform to those of the metropole.[22]

The whole legal system then fell into disarray. The Reverend Mr. Reed, Anglican cleric at Edenton in the 1770s, reported in January 1774 that the "Assembly & Administration cannot agree about the mode for establishing Courts of Indicature." The lack of working courts had thrown the province "in a great confusion for a year past," even as the terminal crisis of empire manifested itself around them. The system, in other words, did not function properly before the crisis in 1774 and 1775. In the latter year, the assembly went as far as to claim that the imperial turmoil itself, and the collapse of imperial control in North Carolina, grew from the royal instructions that inhibited Martin "from giving your assent to the laws for establishing Superior and inferior courts."[23]

The endless debates in the royal assembly about the Superior Court Bill continued even as the empire came down around them. As the imperial crisis spread in 1775, jurymen refused to sit in royally sanctioned local courts, and many legal functionaries either refused to serve under a royal appointment, or, conversely were loyal to the British king and would not recognize the popular convention's authority. In Pitt County, for example, "Magistrates . . .

refused to Qualify, for motives laudable to themselves"—in other words, because they would not serve under royal appointment. When the third Provincial Congress gave the committees of safety effective control over the courts in September 1775, the royal legal system withered away.[24]

The Chowan County Superior Court records suggest the collapse's depth. At Edenton, jurists held inferior courts of pleas and sessions under royal auspices in March and June 1776, trying a nail-stealer in the former session and a few men for assault in the latter before adjourning—forever. No superior court meetings occurred in that county between 1775 and the fall of 1777, and those legal proceedings that were held were irregular and unrecorded. Beginning in 1775, the courts, and the idea of law and legal process, temporarily disappeared. The committees of safety administered what law they had, acting as judge, jury, and perhaps executioner as well.[25]

The inability to establish a working legal system weighed heavily on the new state's leadership in the months after independence. The county and oyer and terminer courts (courts with jurisdiction over crimes punishable by death, as well as other criminal acts), which had been so central to maintaining local society in British America had either ceased functioning or were meeting under committee control. In late March 1777, for example, Governor Caswell received word that "no Court of Oyer & Terminer was held at the time appointed at Hillsborough," although he had tried to get one to sit. The failure to meet caused him "real concern." No courts meant no order, no rites that visualized authority, no real civil society, and no court processes to try the imprisoned.[26]

The longer the courts failed to function, or functioned irregularly, the stronger the need for them became. And each day that passed without a working civil legal order indicted republican government. This failure made the leadership more dependent on militia units whose stability could no longer be depended on.

The legislature created by the Fifth Congress in December 1776 refused to address the legal crisis. When the state senate met in April 1777, a bill introduced for establishing six legal districts in the state, each with "a Superior Court of Justice" and "quarter Sessions in the several Counties," was soundly defeated. Abner Nash wrote that "it is my full belief that the Assembly will not open Courts nor even make a Ct. Law this session," as most members believed the state was too disordered to hold civil courts. Writing to Thomas Burke in May 1777, Governor Caswell explained that Nash's prophecy had indeed been fulfilled. The April meeting of the legislature had accomplished nothing. The worthies, he complained, had "adjourned to the 3rd November next ... no Courts of Law are established, County Courts & Courts of Oyer Continued upon the late plan Struck out by Congress"—in other words, temporary measures allowed the inferior courts to meet. The idea that establishing courts might bring the disorder to an end seemed to escape many in the legislature.[27]

By then the flight of a significant portion of the state's trained legal cadre had further complicated efforts to establish a republican judiciary. There had been about forty-five lawyers in late imperial North Carolina. But a portion of the bar had disappeared amid the political turmoil. Some held other offices in the new regime, or served as military officers with the Continental forces fighting for their lives in the north. And some favored the empire and had fled the state. As late as January 1778, New Bern had no notary to record basic legal transactions, and a correspondent reported "there is not any lawyer resident in the town."[28]

How could they run a legitimate legal system without lawyers? How could they try dozens, or even potentially hundreds, of associators accused of treason or other crimes against the Revolution without learned judges? In the early summer of 1777 the conservative North Carolina revolutionary jurist Samuel Johnson complained that those recommended "as Judges of the Court of Oyer and

Terminer" were unqualified "to Execute the most inconsiderable office in the State." They knew nothing of court procedures or a working legal system.[29]

These problems could not be easily resolved. Governor Caswell, upon investigating, reported that it was the lack of trained judges that had kept the oyer & terminer courts from meeting at Hillsborough in March 1777. The judge he appointed, J. Kinchin, by his own admission was "consciousness of my inexperience & want of abilities to discharge the . . . arduous duty of a judge." He felt unable to hold the court himself, and the judge appointed to assist him failed to appear.[30]

Others deemed qualified to judge, like Edenton's Charles Bonafield, refused to take judicial positions. "I cannot," as he put it, be "prevailed upon to qualify to the Commission of Oyer & Terminer" being planned for Edenton to deal with, among other things, the arrested Brethren awaiting trial in the Edenton jail. It may have been political, or he may not have wanted to condemn those threatened with the death penalty. Or he may have indeed felt unqualified, writing that he hoped that "some capable person may . . . accept the Commission."[31]

The lack of a trained legal cadre had even more disagreeable implications for those accused of crimes, including the Protestant associators. In the early spring of 1777 Governor Caswell reported that people were petitioning him from jail, "complaining of the length of time they have been imprisoned." With legal processes in collapse, people in jail were being left to rot. Robert Smith of Edenton expressed displeasure that, with the Protestant associator treason trials approaching, a suitable judge had not materialized despite several desperate months of searching. "We shall," Smith wrote to Caswell, "have many unhappy devils to take their trial for their life next Oyer court," and yet they had received no new commission naming a judge. The state leaders would be placing associators on trial for capital crimes without trained judges and with a general population in violent turmoil—"an exasperated Jury and a Lay Judge, my God!" as Smith so dramatically put it.[32]

The state's leadership realized that independence itself had also created another set of problems in regard to procedures and precedent that might inhibit a new republican legal order from addressing serious legal issues in the civil law. The procedures from the past remained familiar, at least to some, but questions soon arose: Could they be used in a system based on popular sovereignty rather than royal authority? How would judicial procedures work in a society whose legal mentality grew from a precedent-based legal tradition, at the very moment when provincial legal culture and the past generally were being denied?

Efforts to establish admiralty courts that governed trade, prizes taken at sea, and other maritime matters demonstrated these difficulties. In April 1777, John Ancrum, appointed admiralty judge for the port of Wilmington, North Carolina, by the Continental Congress, wrote to Governor Caswell about an "intricate affair appearing before me now, in consequence of a Prise libeled in said court." Ancrum explained that he knew nothing of "the resolves of the Continental Congress, of the mode of proceeding in the Court of Admiralty for the United States." Were they the same as they had been under the empire? Or republicanized? He asked Caswell to rush him "the mode & rules of trial. . . . by the first opportunity." Lacking appropriate procedural knowledge, Ancrum adjourned "said court until further notice."[33]

A related issue became more disturbing and potentially dangerous to the society: Could crimes committed under the empire be judged under a new republican political contract based on popular sovereignty? A manslaughter case in the Hillsborough District involving William Jackson brought the question to the surface. The oyer and terminer court that sat in September 1777 found Jackson guilty of manslaughter. But his attorney challenged the verdict by claiming that the court had no jurisdiction on a crime that occurred before July 1776. "The fact," the lawyer wrote in regard to the crime, having "been committed before the Declaration of this State the Court having no power to Judge." In essence he argued that the crime had been committed under a different political contract, not against the new state's laws or republican constitution. And at least some agreed. The group being divided, they put the entire matter off until they could determine whether the state's sovereign power extended back in time into the empire.[34]

The rule of law did not really exist in North Carolina or anywhere in America early in the Revolution. Its absence can be seen on a certain level as defining the Revolution's early period. The Brethren's fate would be decided at the dawn of a new era where the laws of empire began to give way to those of the new regime, and where English rights and American freedom were reconsidered and reconstituted.

The Desolate Shore

Abandoned by the Austin brothers on the Outer Banks, Brimage, Smith and "Campbell" stood on the rain-swept beach, unable to conquer even two frightened boys, let alone a state or a nation. Perhaps in that moment they imagined themselves condemned to death, sent swinging for treason by Brimage's former neighbors, transfigured in their imaginations into wild-eyed, French-loving deist-republicans determined to shed blood. The three had become fugitives on a desolate shore with no sure path ahead.

Their pathetic flight quickly devolved into an episode of every man for himself. The violence-minded "Campbell" abandoned his companions, stole another boat and escaped, never to be seen again. Brimage and Smith continued their desperate journey, but a local named John Mann recognized the well-known Brimage and apprehended the fugitives near the New Inlet. Militiamen then transported the fugitives to new accommodations: the Edenton jail.[35]

Like some provincial Lucifer hurled from the imperial heavens, the once-powerful Brimage now found himself imprisoned among North Carolina's dregs. Committed to what he called "a poisonous and noisome dungeon," Brimage begged Governor Caswell for parole. Having seen Brimage jump bail once, the governor refused him. Brimage continued on in his pandemonium, locked away with social inferiors in a dank cell, at times chained to the floor, awaiting a treason trial and perhaps the death penalty. Caswell even denied the imprisoned man his "Portmanteau"—his baggage—despite the prisoner's pathetic pleading for his personal effects. He was still asking for his bags in October 1777 when he had apparently been again paroled and sent to his home, Westbrook, in Bertie County to await his fate.[36]

Doubt's dark shadow descended everywhere in this moment of retribution. The committeemen and militia units still loyal to the state government fanned out, arresting leaders as well as any rank-and-file Protestant associators they could find. Hundreds of people who had sworn themselves to the movement or kept its existence a secret found their futures in doubt as the state leaders hunted anyone the movement touched.[37]

Those believed to be involved in planning the turn toward a tory coup received special attention. At some point the authorities came to recognized John Lewellen's central role in the whole movement. Like Brimage, Lewellen ran for his life. Nonetheless, he soon found himself jailed, his angry defiance of the new order at an end. Having plotted to raise the slaves and kill the governor, he knew what to expect. Dozens could bear witness to his impassioned words against the state leaders. The gallows loomed for him and the others who pushed for the coup and the diversionary slave rebellion.[38]

James Rawlings also ran. The movement's lay preacher later testified that it was Lewellen who persuaded him "to not be taken" when state officials uncovered the movement. Aware now of the gravity of his situation, Rawlings fled by boat on July 5. But it was to no avail. He was soon intercepted at sea by Hyde County's Abram Jones, who recounted to the state courts his own miniature naval triumph against the Brethren and their bloody tory design. After receiving word that Rawlings, "one of the Heads amongst the Tories," might sail by his home at Mattamuskeet, Jones resolved to capture him if possible. On a Saturday in that North Carolina August, Jones "Spied a small sail off in the Sound." He gathered four men and intercepted the craft, finding Rawlings and his family huddled in the little boat's hull. Jones then triumphantly carried his prisoner to a magistrate. Rawlings surely saw the death penalty ahead as he was interrogated, charged with high treason, and then jailed in Craven County.[39]

On August 13 the state jailed senior warden Daniel Legate at Edenton. Legate denied advocating bloodshed, but his story fell on deaf ears. Too many had heard him support the violent turn and speak of General Howe having knowledge of their movement. Legate found himself detained among a crowd of familiar faces, many extremely lucky to have been charged only with misprision of treason—the aiding or hiding knowledge of a treasonous plot—rather than treason itself. Legate's father, Absalom, was likewise indicted, charged that he did "maliciously and advisedly endeavor to excite a great number of People to resist the government of the said state." Formally accused of misprision of treason on September 16, 1777, Absalom too found himself in jail.[40]

Martin County planter and Protestant associator William Tyler also faced the scales of justice. Having been involved in Lewellen's efforts to contact the British in New York, the state accused him of having attempted to give information to the enemy. The state authorities believed he had agreed to travel in "company with two other Persons to General Howe, commander in chief of the Forces of the King of Great Britain in America" in order to given him intelligence about the situation in North Carolina. He was fortunate in the extreme to have been indicted only for misprision of treason.[41]

Even those who had associated conditionally, or had sworn only the secrecy oath, found themselves in legal jeopardy. The authorities forced "William Skiles [Skyles], William Buskill, Robert Knox," as well as "P Carters and John Johnston of the said County," meaning Bertie, to give twenty-pound bonds for their appearance at the courts to "give evidence against Absalom Leggett" in regard to his role among the Brethren. Some of these men may have been associators, but none had been involved in the turn toward loyalism. Indeed, Skyles claimed "great uneasiness" when he learned what the leaders intended to do. Nonetheless, the authorities arrested, closely questioned, deposed, and then either bailed or held them.[42]

Many in the rank and file did not believe they had done anything wrong. They had acted to defend Protestantism and save North Carolina from a popish conspiracy and / or heresy. They remained unaware of the planned coup, and provided whatever information was requested by the state government that they did not know they were in rebellion against. They generally expressed their willingness to obey the new state's magistrates and accepted the oath of allegiance once authorities actually read it to them. The judges and sheriffs built a legal case as they questioned these forlorn men and, inadvertently, probed the revolutionary countryside's mind immediately after independence, revealing ideas and attitudes prevalent in those months after July 4, 1776.[43]

Republican Justice

On the morning of September 16, 1777, twenty-six-year-old James Iredell left his Edenton home and headed toward the Chowan

County courthouse. He was to start his career as a republican jurist by acting as the prosecuting attorney for the state as it tried a group of men from the southern Albemarle who had planned to raise the slaves and embrace the king. His steps that day began a journey not only through the small town on the Albemarle Sound, but through the Revolution itself. This immigrant from Britain would be appointed attorney general for North Carolina, become intimate with the American cause's great leaders, and end up as an associate justice of the United States Supreme Court.

Iredell could not foresee any of that on that September morning. What he did know was that the charges against the accused were of the most serious nature. If found guilty, these men might be fined, expelled from the state, or hanged. They had rebelled against the future and now must suffer their fate. At the courthouse Iredell found at least eighteen men awaiting trial. With the Honorable John Baptist Beasley acting as presiding judge and Iredell acting as prosecuting attorney, several leading associators were charged with treason or misprision of treason. The court charged those they deemed the rank-and-file associators with misprision of treason.[44]

The need to deal with these rebels had provided the state's leadership with the motivation to rebuild the oyer and terminer courts in the eastern counties under republican auspices. Some eastern counties used the standard three judges, whereas others could find only two who were qualified and willing to sit. For the Brethren, the time of judgment had come.

The evidence against John Lewellen was overwhelming. One after another, men related to the Brethren's leader by blood or marriage, as well as those who he had long known or helped to recruit into the movement, gave evidence. John Carter, Henry Culpepper, William Wallace, James Council, and Thomas Best mounted the stand and bore witness against him. There was no real defense, though at one point Lewellen declared he acted because he believed

Governor Caswell a heretic. The jury quickly found Lewellen guilty of high treason and the court sentenced him to death.[45]

Even more men bore witness against Daniel Legate. Ten men, including four members of the heavily involved Harrison family, took the stand to describe Legate's actions in building the Protestant association. The jury found Legate guilty of misprision of treason. Given his embrace of loyalism, it seems strange indeed that he was not tried and convicted of treason. But there had been a prolonged and intense debate in the assembly the previous April over the differences between treason and misprision of treason, and the results of that debate led the prosecution to try him for the latter crime.[46]

One by one the Protestant associators answered to the people's law. The September court meeting either tried them or bound them over for trial at the next court meeting. Absalom Legate, William Tyler, Peter Tyler, James Hayes, John Garrett, John Everett, Daniel Bunting, Christian Savage, Sterling Savage, James Rogers, Malachi Manning, Willoughby Wells, John Everitt, James Harrison, William Lewellen, and Francis Winsom all remained jailed or were forced to give large bonds.

The trials and legal proceedings continued through September and into that October. At least five others—William Skyles, William Burket, Robert Knox, Peter Carter, and John Johnston, all of Bertie—stood before Judge John Baptist Beasley on September 20 at Edenton and gave bond to appear in October to testify against John Lewellen's son William. The court forced the younger Lewellen, accused of misprision of treason, to give a 1,000-pound bond in October 1777. The same court demanded that Thomas Hunter and John Everitt each give bond of 500 pounds to remain out of jail. Courts held in Bertie, Tyrrell, and Pitt Counties deposed and tried other associators, and by the new year the movement had been dealt with via civil legal process.[47]

In the trials' immediate aftermath, many state officials argued strongly that John Lewellen's sentence should be carried out immediately. Ingrate, tory slave inciter, found guilty at a trial—surely he was worthy of death. The state assembly put it in a message to the governor "that . . . it doth not appear that there were any mitigating circumstances" that could excuse his behavior. Hanging him would discourage anyone who would challenge the government. The assembly leaders urged the death sentence against Lewellen "to be put immediately into execution." They further asked Governor Caswell to place a strong guard over Lewellen lest he try to escape.[48]

Some of the state leaders advocated for a more extensive bloodletting. Allen Jones, anticipating guilty verdicts, advocated "hanging, about a dozen," which, he believed, would "have exceedingly good effect, in this state, and give stability to our new government." He had accepted due process, but he wanted a show of force to punctuate it. Others thought the same: suppressing the Brethren legally gave state civil processes legitimacy, but also offered the opportunity to turn the state's enemies into a lasting example.[49]

The trials marked a turning point. That the state refused to simply execute or beat their enemy into submission in a summary fashion seems, from a distance of two and a half centuries, a kind of miracle. The bloody revolutionary justice handed out by committees, militias, and mobs beginning in 1774 continued into the war, and indeed after it. But in 1777 a civil legal system based on popular sovereignty came into being and proved in the end enduring.

The process of creating a normalized civil society based on a new legal order would not be completed during the effort to crush this movement. But the civil law's return in 1777 marked a turning point in the Revolution's course in the state. That fall, regular court meetings began to be held, including in the Albemarle region; James Iredell and John Johnston were involved in legal proceedings in the Bertie County courts in late October.[50]

The state's second assembly, sitting in that same fall of 1777, moved to establish superior courts, and those who were appointed the superior court's judges, including Edenton attorney James Iredell, began riding a superior court circuit. The heretical Wylie Jones brought in an assembly bill to normalize republican civil courts when the assembly met in November 15, 1777, and in April 1778 a bill was introduced calling for the establishment of "a Court of Chancery." It is clear that the trials of the Protestant associators helped initiate the process of creating a working republican legal order.[51]

Nothing—no army, no police, and no amount of gold—is as important to the working of governing institutions as the sense that their authority is regular, uniform, and timeless. The rule of law must seem simply a part of civil life, and justice should have force but not seem arbitrary. North Carolina's new leadership knew this. Timelessness, the sense that republican institutions were normal and could not be dispensed with, could not be achieved during the lives of those who lived through the Revolution and created these institutions. That would be the work of a later generation—but the other factors that buttressed normalized authority could be established. The courts, rather than the militias and committees, had dealt with the Protestant associators.

With the trials over, the Brethren awaited punishment and historical oblivion. Execution, expulsion, or proscription: What would be the penalty for their transgressions? To answer these questions, society ultimately turned to its governor and leading men. The fathers' time had come again.

9

The Return
of the Father

"Relying upon your Mercy & goodness," wrote a repentant Daniel Legate to Governor Richard Caswell and his council late in 1777, "I send this paper as an humble advocate to plead in Some Measure that So it May abate the Severity of your Just Dispeasure & Appease that Stroke of Justice that I have incurred upon Myself by My horrid transgression." Legate's aggressive militancy was gone. He was now just a poor yeoman from the southern Albemarle with a hundred acres who had committed a serious political sin. He returned to the fold a "prodigal, a true and unfeigned penitent" who hoped to find "Mercy . . . at your hands." He reminded Caswell that the Almighty "promised A blessedness to the Merciful." Legate desired nothing more now than "to be Number'd with your subjects." The Brethren were gone; only punishment lay ahead for those who began trying to save the Protestant revolution and ended plotting a massacre.[1]

Legate's rambling plea reveals two central things about the Protestant associators' plight. Governor Richard Caswell, the man their leaders had wanted to kill, had the last word about the associators' fate. Whatever punishment the court ordered, the governor might override the decision by granting clemency, issuing a pardon, or commuting the sentence. And mercy, as Legate somehow realized, was possible because mercy might have broader meaning in the society's tumultuous revolutionary politics. Mercy could legitimate the new state. Mercy was about power. And mercy was of the father.

These factors helped the Brethren escape the gallows. Governor Caswell saw in mercy a way to assert the republican governor's prerogative power. The successful exercise of these powers would restore aspects of the political patriarchy weakened by revolutionary idealism and expressed as hostility to all forms of patriarchy and to all executive authority. Caswell's strategic use of mercy for those who had so egregiously transgressed enabled the father's return to the political order. The assertion of such powers wasn't counterrevolution, but it did express retrenchment in a revolution by then entering its fourth year.

Caswell's efforts to restore patriarchal authority in the political order by extending mercy to the Protestant associators helped mark the end of the Revolution's beginning in North Carolina. Significant elements in the revolutionary leadership wanted an order based on political fathers, albeit republican ones whose authority would be resituated in a regime of popular sovereignty. These broader issues around the role of governors as political patriarchs drove the strange turn of events that saw the Brethren's leadership delivered from execution.

Richard Caswell and the Paradox of Revolutionary Patriarchy

The new states' citizenry institutionalized hostility to governing fathers when their delegates wrote the first state constitutions that did away with sole executives and/or weakened the executive office and other positions of patriarchal authority. New Hampshire and Massachusetts did away with the governor's office, for seventeen years in the former state. Pennsylvania's revolutionary convention famously replaced the single executive with a plural executive council, and North Carolina had considered doing the same. Every state that kept sole governors saw some restrictions placed on the executive office and all went to annual elections except New York, which empowered the executive the most and elected them every three years. But even New York's chief magistrates still had far less power than an imperial governor. The constitutions had fundamentally altered governors' roles.[2]

The North Carolina constitution of December 1776 had followed this broad pattern. The state retained a single executive but confined the governor to a largely ceremonial role. The executive had no veto, could not dissolve the assembly, or even select his own executive council. The document did away with the governor's prerogative over other appointments as well. The constitution restrained the governor's military control in peace and tempered it even during wartime. Worse yet, there were term limits: governors had to stand for election every year, and could only hold office for three consecutive years. The political patriarchs so normal in the British Empire seemed set to disappear in the emerging republican utopias on the Atlantic's western shore.[3]

It was in this situation that Richard Caswell found himself elected independent North Carolina's first governor. Like so many others, he had come to North Carolina as a migrant from the north. Born in 1729 to a prominent family in Harford County, Maryland, he arrived in North Carolina in the late 1740s hoping to establish a career as a surveyor and land speculator. He quickly became a substantial property owner, holding more than 15,000 acres by 1760. Over time he purchased a large number of slaves to work this land.

Financial success and an advantageous marriage translated into political prominence. Caswell held a succession of progressively more important offices in the empire. In 1754 he became an assemblyman for Johnston County. In 1758, after his first wife's death, the governor-to-be married Sarah Heritage, whose father, William, served as the General Assembly's clerk. Caswell read law with his father-in-law, gained admittance to the bar in 1759, and with his father-in-law's assistance was soon appointed deputy attorney general for the province. He became speaker of the [lower] house in 1770 amid the tumultuous North Carolina Regulation, and won imperial favor by fighting beside Governor William Tryon at the 1771 Battle of the Alamance River that ended the turmoil in the province's western reaches. Governor Tryon's successor, Josiah Martin, appointed Caswell an oyer and terminer judge in 1771.[4]

Despite his close relationships with these imperial governors, Caswell supported the protests against the London ministry, and then the Revolution itself. He became a prominent leader in the provisional North Carolina government and was appointed to the Second Continental Congress. He returned to North Carolina to lead the nascent state's forces at the Battle of Moore's Bridge that crushed a growing Scottish Highlander-led tory rebellion early in 1776. He then became chief executive of North Carolina's Fifth Provincial Congress, and that body, which wrote the first state constitution, elected him acting governor in December 1776.[5]

Those who would have maintained the fathers' rule in some form could not limit the Revolution's anti-patriarchal impulses during the revolutionary surge in 1775–1776. A republican utopia free of tyrannical fathers seemed at hand as images of a corrupted father-king crashed down at independence. But the fears created by the war and the near anarchy after July 4, 1776, forced even those revolutionaries with the most radical social-leveling notions to acknowledge a brutal, hulking reality: society needed to be governed. Not every issue could be debated at length and the legislature could not remain in permanent session.

This reality would eventually allow Caswell to reassert himself as the political father. In April 1777 the state assembly voted to make him the state's first republican governor. By then Caswell, like John Adams and others, thought that the anti-patriarchal impulses in the state constitutions had created a dangerous constitutional imbalance by overly constraining the executive office. He believed the executive power in North Carolina had become severely "cramped." Caswell and others were soon working for the return of a strong but paternal executive. He accepted that political patriarchy had to be republicanized, but still saw real executive power used by a governor as necessary for the appropriate working of a mixed and balanced constitution.[6]

Caswell used the few true executive powers that remained—the ability to grant temporary reprieves and stays of execution, legal clemency, and pardons—as part of a broader effort to reassume the governor's symbolic power as patriarch. This was what was at work when he settled the Protestant associators' fate. Caswell considered the state's entire political and constitutional situation as he weighed what to do. He, or someone he trusted, may well have read the depositions taken in July and August and realized that many associators believed they were saving the state from heresy and popery rather than conquering it for the king.

Clearly, though, Caswell and those around him soon fixed on a central question of politics and justice. Should they end the Brethren with a wave of executions to demonstrate the new state's power . . . or should they find mercy?

Sometime in the fall of 1777 the governor came to think that the key to dealing with the movement was not bloodshed. Restraint would help normalize state power based on popular sovereignty, and demonstrate the benevolence of that power. On a certain level, what happened to the Protestant associators boiled down to a calculation about the meaning of public benevolence. By wielding mercy shrewdly, Caswell helped create patriarchal republicanism as the new order's norm.[7]

The Politics of Mercy

In the early modern period, political leaders and legal officials would occasionally assist the unfortunate or pardon a criminal after hearing pleas for assistance or leniency. These rulers wanted to be understood as shield for the weak and the corrector of the wayward in a manner that celebrated their paternal authority rather than asserting domination by force. Such acts connected the administration of justice to the Christian benevolence that was supposed to inform the actions of Protestant Christian rulers.

A considerable tradition of benevolent intervention had been inherited from the imperial past in North Carolina. Royal governors had granted pardons or commuted sentences from time to time to demonstrate their paternal power and their restraint. Perhaps most famously, in 1771 Governor Tryon had pardoned or encouraged royal authorities to pardon six of the Regulators sentenced to death after the Battle of the Alamance River.[8]

Efforts to secure leniency often became small morality plays designed to demonstrate that those convicted or awaiting trial understood who had legitimate power. These performances involved immature or dependent subordinates begging their political fathers for leniency for wayward relatives in a manner that portrayed the governor or magistrate as a benevolent ruler. Downtrodden women and children were seen as especially deserving of assistance by these rulers. Consequently, wives and children frequently carried petitions trying to save their husbands, brothers, sons, or fathers, or were invoked by male petitioners as reasons to grant clemency or a pardon.

One such episode unfolded in Bladen County in 1773. People in that county asked for mercy for convicted murderer Reynold Mc-Dugal. The petitioners described McDugal, age eighteen, as "so diminutive that he does not wear the least appearance of manhood." Further, they claimed he was the sole support for "an infirm old widowed mother, with four helpless, miserable orphans," a family that had already been reduced to poverty. Governor Josiah Martin stayed the execution pending advice from London, demonstrating to the people of the county his sensitivity to the weak and helpless.[9]

The ad hoc revolutionary government heard similar pleas for mercy even before the crisis in the Albemarle broke. In the "Declaration" issued by the Halifax Congress in late April 1776, the revolutionary proto-government declared that they "war not with the helpless females which they left behind," in regard to the wives and daughters of those enemies of the people arrested or expelled in 1775 and 1776. "We sympathize in their sorrow," the Declaration's authors' wrote, "and wish to pour the balm of pity" into the wounds caused by the separations. These women, the writers continued, deserved mercy; such sympathy fitted republicanism notions of compassion while also being interpretable as acts of benevolent Christian charity.[10]

Women and children associated with loyalists did not always receive compassion. There were ugly incidents of political and ethnic cleansing throughout the war in North Carolina and everywhere else. But extending sympathy to those perceived as helpless at times solidified the legitimacy of institutions whose life span could be measured in months, not years. Edgecombe County's Elizabeth Pope explained the "Distresses" she suffered without a man to provide for her, and begged via a petition to the legislature that her husband, Jacob, imprisoned as an enemy of the people, be released. The assemblymen resolved to return him to his home as long as he took "the oath to the State" and gave 500 pounds for good behavior.[11]

In the late summer of 1777 Richard Caswell weighed the political value of mercy as the jails filled with the Protestant associators. The basic logic he used is evident in a letter he received from Edenton lawyer Robert Smith on July 31, 1777. "Law," he wrote in regard to the looming trials, "should be strictly attended to," and "severity exercised" against those that threatened the state. Nonetheless, he thought that "the doors of mercy should never be shut." Should a "good Lawyer," he believed, "act at this time, I am convinced it would be a great means of giving dignity to Courts, strength to the Law," and would restore "union to this distracted Country." The wise republican lawgiver, a true political father, might in this construction provide legitimacy to the infant republican legal system with a balance of justice and restraint.[12]

Caswell followed this advice. He knew that mercy had power in the Anglo-American world. Mercy expressed control, and demonstrated that the leadership remained restrained and balanced, as Anglo-American political theory taught magistrate-fathers should be. Mercy might win more support among an already war-weary population whose political and social beliefs were fragmented. New blood debts could be avoided by applying the father's benevolent hand to erring political children. Such mercy would not bring an end to the struggle to restore executive power or revive society's patriarchal structuring. That struggle waxed and waned in the state, and re-erupted into public view when the British invaded the south later in the war. Indeed, the struggle over patriarchal authority would continue to rage across American politics and society even after the federal constitution established the presidency.[13]

Certainly Caswell could have executed John Lewellen without causing a crisis. The Albemarle planter had plotted to encourage slaves to rebel in order to kill the state's governor. Even in fragmented revolutionary North Carolina, no one would have questioned Lewellen's execution. Lewellen's former friends had nothing to say on his behalf other than that he had, until his angry exchanges with James Mayo and the committee of safety, been understood as a solid citizen not in conflict with the new order, or the old for that matter. Lewellen's own bloody-minded words had condemned him.[14]

This leading Brethren seemed headed for an unlamented end until Caswell allowed himself to be persuaded to hear pleas for mercy. Sometime in September, Caswell, after consulting with his council, issued a temporary reprieve of Lewellen's death sentence, "till the meeting of the next General Assembly." He then issued similar reprieves for a number of others found guilty of misprision of treason. He used that breathing space to allow those who would plead for mercy to come to him and make their case, assuming as he did so the mantle of republican political father. In so doing Caswell revealed how the century's gender norms played into establishing patriarchal power via miniature political dramas.[15]

The petitioners who pleaded for John Lewellen's life portrayed Governor Caswell as a protector of women and children as they made their case. John Beasly, who apparently knew both Lewellen and Caswell before this crisis, invoked the "distressed circumstances of Mary Lewellen." Beasly told Caswell that no male could head the household if the state executed the condemned man, a plea made even though Lewellen had a grown son, William, also under indictment. Beasly begged Caswell for "Mercy which as it is a darling attribute of the deity [I] hope it will prevail." Beasly continued that, unhappily, he had "nothing [more] to plead in his behalf but Mercy," as Lewellen's offense deserved the death penalty.[16]

Thomas Hall made a more detailed plea for Lewellen using the same tropes. Hall explained that the episode was "his [Lewellen's] first Deviation from Rectitude and Virtue, and the almost exemplary fairness of his former Character." He had been in good standing with his peers in the old elite before the war, and with the revolutionary authorities at independence, in part because he held substantial landed property, and in part because he had shared their views. Indeed, up until the Brethren's formation, Lewellen had taken the state's part. He had accepted the position of justice of the peace in the new order and answered militia musters after independence.[17]

Like Beasly, Hall pleaded the distressed circumstances of Lewellen's wife and family. He insisted that "Disgrace and penury must remain entailed on his family consisting almost entirely of the softer Sex, and chiefly arrived to Womanhood." How would these innocents survive without a man to support and protect them? He appealed to the true and better angels of Caswell's conscience "for Mercy" for the condemned man. Hall cast Caswell as republican-ized version of the patriarchal protector of women and children. He invoked in his plea "the Knowledge which I and all the World have of the more than Ordinary tenderness of your Disposition." Only Caswell, Hall maintained, could calm the "Tears of the Widow and the Orphan" who needed help in times of crisis. In this construction, the tender republican governor became the new order's benevolent patriarch.[18]

Caswell finally agreed to meet Mary Lewellen. While her ef-forts to save her husband's life followed a well-trodden pattern in the early modern world, her assistant in her desperate journey to the governor was nothing short of extraordinary given what had happen in that summer of 1777. Hall explained that "a Gentleman, one Mr. Mayo who will be able to inform your Excellency of the Character of the subscribers to a Label which will be delivered with the Petition" would accompany her. This was Nathan Mayo, James Mayo's brother! His shocking appearance reveals a second factor at work that resulted in mercy in this case: the contending parties in this crisis knew each other. In fact, it was Mayo, joined by Wil-liam Williams, another man whom Lewellen intended to kill, who made the appeal for the reprieve that allowed Mary Lewellen to take her case to the governor.[19]

The Mayo brothers: James and Nathan. Their threatening words had encouraged the now-condemned Lewellen to try to transform the Brethren from a defense of Protestantism to a loyalist uprising against the state. Lewellen and other associators had threatened to kill both Mayo brothers in response to those threats. Now, just months later, Nathan Mayo sought to keep Lewellen from the noose. Hall went on to add, "The most considerable Men in Martin County . . . very earnestly wish the success of Mrs. Lewellen's Petition." Some of these might have flirted with the movement themselves, but others would surely have suffered had the Brethren succeeded. Now they sought to save the leader-neighbor who had planned a bloodbath.[20]

The plea for mercy by the Martin County elite seems the strangest twist indeed in this story from the revolutionary country-side. And yet perhaps it reveals something very central about the Revolution. On the local level, it was personal. The Mayo family and the Lewellen families knew each other before the war. Such familiarity complicated the Revolution, leading to intense, angry outbursts, deep remorse and regret, severing some social ties forever, and renewing and reshaping others. Familiarity complicated the questions of revolutionary allegiance, ideology, and identity in a manner that makes understanding them difficult. Prewar connections help explain many of these seemingly strange twists and turns in this crisis and many other aspects of the Revolution.

As this drama around Lewellen unfolded, other Brethren leaders or their families began to beg for leniency from the political father they had planned to kill. It became high theater, as those trying to avoid the rope outdid one another in confessing their sins. They promised political penance if only the governor-father would forgive them.

It was at this juncture that Daniel Legate began to plead desperately for his life. Initially rebuffed, Legate continued to seek a reconciliation with the state. In a last-ditch measure, he sent the petition of December 4 begging for a pardon. He had ample reason to be nervous; as a man of common origins who played a central role among the Brethren and had encouraged the turn toward a tory coup, he might have been seen as excellent material to be made an example of. He had no important friends to protect him.[21]

The movement's spiritual leader, James Rawlings, also begged for mercy. Imprisoned in Craven County since having been intercepted on the waters of the Albemarle Sound, Rawlings told the state authorities all he knew. He testified that he had fallen out with

Lewellen when the leaders planned to raise the slaves and attack the governor, and broken with him when Lewellen insisted on Rawlings assassinating James Mayo. Rawlings swore he had risked death at Lewellen's hands by refusing to kill, and now "humbly Crave pardon for having had any hand in sd plot or scheme."[22]

Eventually his fears overcame his remorse. By early September Rawlings saw the noose ahead. Despite giving an extensive account of his activities to the authorities, he still lay under threat of penalty of death should he be convicted. Whatever prayers this lay minister offered did nothing to calm his troubled soul. Shortly before the trials, Rawlings, "a noted villain ... one of the principles in the late conspiracy against the state," broke jail and fled along with two common criminals.

It is worth noting that the movement's spiritual leader was under indictment for high treason, when so many others who seem as involved or more so were charge with lesser crimes. He had made himself noteworthy by providing spiritual justification and a Protestant language of resistance to state authority. Or it may have been that his position as a lay reader made him seem especially dangerous. The jail keeper offered a reward of ten pounds for Rawlings, whom he described as forty years old, with a dark complexion and a wound on his cheek. He remained on the run at the year's end.[23]

Mercy, or a show of strength? Should the state government hang a dozen of these bloody-minded associators to make an example of them? The eighteen men tried at Edenton in September provided excellent material for a display of judicial power. It might stabilize the state by cowing any real or potential internal enemies. Or would state-sanctioned bloodshed only create more resentment and more potential enemies?[24]

Before Caswell had finally answered this question, the pleas for mercy sparked a constitutional confrontation that spoke directly to the issue of the executive's power and the nature of political patriarchy. At issue was the governor's power to pardon or grant clemency. The members of both houses concurred in the "opinion that as it doth not appear that there were mitigating circumstances" in the matter. How could people who tried to incite the slaves to rebellion be spared?[25]

The legislature now challenged the executive's power to pardon in these circumstances by claiming it violated the separation of powers in the new constitution. The verdict and sentence, the legislature argued, had been "certified by the Judge who presided at his trial," and the sentence should have been "carried into execution without delay." The state constitution, they lectured, "hath invested your Excellency with full powers" to do so; there was no need to consult with the legislature, and the law required that he act. They wanted Lewellen dead, but they did not want to have their hands on it. The legislators went on to assert that the constitution established "that the Legislative, Judicial and Executive powers of Government ought to be forever separate and distinct from each other," implying that Caswell's consideration of mercy violated judicial prerogative and breached the separation of powers by infringing on judicial powers.[26]

In the end Caswell successfully asserted the governor's prerogative in regard to mercy, and thus strengthened the executive office. He, joined by some others in the state elite, essentially let them all go. Astoundingly, Caswell even let Lewellen go. Lewellen was eventually allowed to return home on parole; his lands, which had been seized or taken as bond for good behavior in 1777, were returned to him by the state in 1778. He remained a local landholder of extensive property and a slave master in the Albemarle region after the war, dying in 1794.[27]

Many of the others who had been brought before the oyer and terminer courts in the Albemarle counties were also placed on a type of parole. This included those convicted of aiding or having knowledge of the movement. These people too went home, and afterward mostly remained in the Albemarle watershed, without any overt loss of status, although those involved in planning the slave uprising and governor's murder must have carried a stigma to their graves.

The disorder within the legal system probably worked in the associators' favor. The state's jurists had not even fully worked out what constituted treason and misprision of treason in a republican order when they placed the associators on trial, and nor had anyone determined what the penalties for these crimes would be. This troubled Richard Caswell and others, and in December the assembly heard a bill to rectify the situation. Whitmel Hill advocated strongly for the legislation; perhaps he believed the Protestant associators had escaped too lightly amid the legal chaos.[28]

The appeals for clemency or pardons acknowledged Richard Caswell as the new order's political patriarch, and his assertion of that power reclaimed it for the executive branch. The efforts to curtail the governorship or eliminate it entirely in the revolutionary turmoil in 1775–1776 had now met the realities of running a state involved in a desperate war. But why did the rest of the government accept this leniency? They may have well feared that executing gentry members threatened further instability; some knew the guilty before the crisis. It is unclear, as none commented on their views about this outcome.

Strangely, though, a few people ended up feeling the law more than the key leadership had. It is unclear why mercy was not extended to them. They were sent into exile, a fate common to loyalists but avoided by the other Protestant associators. Why they suffered this fate is a mystery not easily unraveled.

The Expelled

Expulsions, first used by the ad hoc committees to deal with their perceived enemies and later adopted by local and state governments, became a common punishment for political crimes throughout revolutionary America. In one locale after another, individuals and families believed to be enemies of the people were driven into exile from their home towns or states. Many then fled America entirely, severed from family, friends, and community for a time or forever. Such persecutions foreshadowed the mass expulsions of Loyalists at the war's end, when tens of thousands took ship for Canada, the British isles, the British West Indies, West Africa, or beyond.

Why did the North Carolina government use such targeted expulsions against a few associators? As the trials ran on in September, the state expelled Thomas Clark, Richard Jones, and the shipmaster Thomas Bogg (Bog, Boggs), all known as associators or sympathizers. The Bertie County court ordered that Bogg, Jones, and Clark "depart this State" as soon as possible. The three men begged Governor Caswell for a passport to leave, with the caveat that they be allowed to sail on the "Sloop Free Mason thirty tons . . . Thomas Bog master." Caswell apparently granted this request, and they quickly left the state.[29]

It is unclear why the state expelled these three men and let others seemingly so much more involved stay and keep their property. The names of these three appear only rarely in the numerous depositions about the Brethren; their role is still somehow misunderstood. North Carolina and other states were expelling tories, but it is difficult to understand why officials singled out these three but left so many other associators unpunished. It may have been the specific dynamic within the Bertie County trials, which ran parallel to those at Edenton, but from which no record survives. Different judges, different outcomes. It is also possible that Bogg, as a sea captain, was seen as a major threat to spread ideas antithetical to the government. Or it may be that the three were not seen as regular community members, and had no intermediaries to plead for mercy for them. Bogg, though, did own land in Bertie County in 1774, near the homesteads of other associators.[30]

William Brimage also found himself effectively expelled from North Carolina. Although tried for both treason and misprision of treason, he miraculously escaped conviction. His actions in regard to the Brethren had occurred so late in the unrest, and had been so limited in scope, that the prosecution could not gather enough evidence to convict him. But Brimage had become a marked man, refusing to swear the state's loyalty oath, jumping bail, fleeing with a British officer no less—these things ended him as a North Carolinian.

The state government ordered him into exile in the late fall of 1777. He left his wife and children behind in the hope that the belief in mercy for women and children would allow them to continue in the family home in Bertie County. Brimage went first to the British stronghold at New York, and then eventually to Bermuda, where he was appointed attorney general. He ended up in England at the war's end, where he filed a compensation claim with the Crown for his losses in North Carolina.[31]

The Brethren had failed. The oaths, the three-notched sticks, the hand signals and B-E-T-R-U-E: all for naught. They had failed to keep their secret, to defend Protestantism, to help those oppressed by drafts, or protect North Carolina from insidious French intrigue and heretical officials. Their leaders' efforts to turn the movement into a loyalist uprising had unraveled it all. With their suppression, the government they so feared began to gain force. Now historical oblivion awaited, for what the Brethren did would be forgotten at best, and misremembered at worst.

10

AFTERMATHS

"THE GUARD," wrote Richard Caswell to the Edenton militia commander in January 1778, "of militia over the Magazine & Goal," which had been so essential just months before when a bloody putsch seem imminent, was now no longer needed. He ordered the officer "to disband the same immediately." The crisis in the Albemarle passed into oblivion almost as quickly as it had developed. The Protestant associators had been crushed, arrested, imprisoned, forced to repent, pardoned, or expelled. The rites, the organization's constitution—all of it would soon be forgotten as the war went on and on and on.[1]

But the changes that led to the movement's formation, drove its transformation, and sparked its suppression reveal things critical to understanding the revolutionary era. Both the American revolutionary leadership and the London government failed to fully mobilize the yeomanry during the war because the beliefs espoused by these leaders were partially or fully incongruent with the values of the mass of free people. The rise and fall of the Brethren reflected this failure of ideology. And it helps explains something that has long been downplayed or ignored about the revolutionary yeomanry: people fought for no one, walked away from military units, or changed allegiances, often without apparently feeling any sense of ideological discontinuity in their actions. Sources hint that received beliefs from the imperial past—translatable to either side fighting the war, or no side at all—enabled such behaviors. Certainly such behaviors undermine the viability of the political identities and historical categories through which we have tended to examine the revolutionary era.

For certain, there were firm patriots and loyalists. But many people fought for one side and then another, refused to muster with their militia units, resisted the state's forced drafts, and ignored royal proclamations calling them to rally to the royal standard. It suggests a less ordered Revolution than has generally been accepted, and it suggests that people could potentially serve king, congress, both or none without violating an underlying value system rooted in a past, shared Anglo-American Protestant political culture.

Whig, tory, neutral, patriot, traitor—British and American authorities created these frameworks to define who supported them, and who opposed them. In the years after the war, writers tightly define whig and loyalist to make coherent and historically serviceable the tortured rupture in the Anglo-American world we call the American Revolution. If we accept these received categories as having existed before independence, and to have been tightly defined early in the war, we lose the chance to see how real human beings lived their beliefs during the Revolution, what those beliefs were, why they accepted or rejected new ideas, and how forces beyond individual control changed them all.

To Serve None

By January 1778 the Brethren had been crushed. The war, though, continued on relentlessly, and with it the endless pressure for troops and supplies. The new state governments continued to struggle with individuals and groups that resisted drafts and requisitions but otherwise accepted the new order. What were they to make of them, how should they be categorized, and above all what beliefs drove their refusals? Even when the fighting came in earnest to the southern states in 1779, some North Carolinians avoided mobilizing with their militia units, while refusing to proclaim themselves otherwise in rebellion against the state.

Such behavior bedeviled the state authorities that tried to politically categorize it. Officials sometime saw those who avoided service as more threatening than those in arms for the enemy, precisely because these avoiders remained in the American political community. An enemy could be defined, and then killed, exiled, or rehabilitated. Those who would not turn out for military service, on the other hand, seemed to indict the republican state from within. These avoiders understood their beliefs and interests as compatible with the Revolution or at least with citizenship in the state, but they refused to acknowledge the state government's authority in all matters.

Such people have remained out of our grasp historically. This is true even though they may have been representative of the views of many yeomen, perhaps the majority. Several episodes in North Carolina suggest that elements of the older Protestant political culture shaped the apathetic responses to drafts, mobilizations, and forced levees. The power of this received framework remained even as its relationship to institutional power became ambiguous and contested.

Those who wielded authority purportedly based on libertarian beliefs inevitably had difficulties coercing those who would live professed values limiting governmental authority. The actions of most resisters seemed consistent with the revolutionary opposition to standing armies and government coercion. But such actions simultaneously expressed a contempt of civic virtue, of serving the republican state in arms for the common good. Such an ideological contradiction could not be easily reconciled.[2]

Throughout the second half of 1777 and in 1778, North Carolina officials sought to uncover exactly what drove these resisters. County magistrates indicted those like Solomon Daughoty who "in Opposition to a draught did on the 12th Inst. Express himself in a manner Discouraging the people to turn out" and, it was charged, tried "to git men to Join with him to prevent a Draught." He, in short, actively encouraged draft resistance, by mob violence if necessary. But the courts did not label him a tory, though he had criminally defied state authority.[3]

Others thought as Solomon Daughoty did about the endless state drafts and militia mobilizations. These avoiders did not proclaim themselves loyalists, nor did the state authorities labeled them as such in state records. The authorities repeatedly complained about those like the "evil minded persons" in Anson, Cumberland, Bladen, and Guilford Counties who "openly . . . obstruct the recruiting service" that was desperately trying to fill quotas for the Continental and state lines as well as the local militias. Hostility to a standing army and drafts and mobilization still did not make those who expressed such views tories, at least not tories like the Scottish Highlanders, who repeatedly rebelled against the North Carolina government during the war, or the Brethren leaders who sought to kill the governor.[4]

They did not want to go, and they did not want their neighbors to have to go. Consider Craven County laborer John Bryan, who in May 1778 "traitorously discourage[d] the people from enlisting into the Service of this State and the United States" by speaking "seditious and treasonable Words, to wit 'that the (meaning him the said John) would use his Endeavours to send those in Nomination [those selected for the draft] and discourage others enlisting in their room, they (meaning the people) are damned fools if they did inlist." Bryan apparently never proclaimed for the king, or the empire, or toasted George over the water. He did not want to serve the state in the most essential role of citizen soldier, and he encouraged neighbors to evade service as well. He acted seditiously, he lacked civic virtue, but he was not a loyalist as we understand the term.[5]

The possibility that beliefs received from Protestant political culture encouraged draft resistance appears in some accounts of unrest related to impressment. The French alliance and the presence of actual French soldiers in North Carolina led to more Francophobic outbursts. In April 1778, for instance, with France newly entered into the war, the state assembly approved another levee of 2,000 troops, to be used in the state and Continental lines. At the same time a number of Frenchmen stranded in North Carolina began to travel the state, seeking recruits to form a military company to fight for the American cause.

A new draft and some armed alien Frenchmen wandering the state trying to create an armed band: What could possibly go wrong? In May 1778 a mob of sailors and local people in Craven County led by James Davis Esq. and his sons demanded the return of one of his son's apprentices, who had apparently been taken by or had offered to work for the French volunteers. Insulted by a French sergeant, Davis demanded that the local justices call out the militia to recover the apprentice. "This being objected to, by the Justices," the affidavit continued, "as unnecessary, he & his sons swore that if justice was not done him, they would take it themselves." The enraged Davis declared, "The Liberty we had been fighting for so long was about to be taken from us by the damned French, desired the mob in the street to stand by him."[6]

This mob's leaders understood themselves as something other than tories, engaged in something other than sedition. They rioted in defense of the liberty they had been fighting for in what had already become a long war. Like the Brethren, they too feared the ancient enemy's clutches, and saw the Revolution as defending a traditional, nonuniversalist, Anglo-American liberty that in part defined itself against French people.

The arrival of powerful British forces in Georgia and South Carolina in 1779 did little to change the behavior of those who saw the endless drafts and militia mobilizations as illegitimate. The tendency arose to describe their behavior as a product of war fatigue or laziness. One revolutionary leader declared in February 1779 in regard to the pending British invasion that he believed the state assembly "will exert itself on this occasion, but of the people I have my doubts; they seem tired of the business of war" and the militia might well refuse an order to march south.[7]

County leaders again and again commented on the problem. John Egan, the Chowan militia commander, complained bitterly that despite the British threat, the local militia remained "lazy Raskalls that hate to leave the fire side." Despite the looming invasion, the Chowan County militia refused direct orders to mobilize. The state could not furnish its quota of men, even after promising a generous rate of pay. By July they had raised only 500 of the quota of 2,000 new troops for the state line to meet the crisis. Governor Caswell turned to forced "drafts from the Militia" once again.[8]

Labeling the many men who tried to avoid service as the war in the south intensified as weary, lazy, or afraid does not help us understand them. In the summer of 1779, the governor's council became aware of a new group in Edgecombe and adjoining counties abutting the western Albemarle that had "assembled together and Assigned Articles of Association or Inlistment" to prevent local militias from being drafted into the state line. These new associators had defied the authority of local magistrates and militia officers, and had assisted a deserter or deserters from the Continental Army. The state ordered this new movement crushed, but the council did not label them tories or accuse them of treason, at least in their recorded deliberation on the matter.[9]

Suggesting that this new combination in the eastern North Carolina countryside might be evidence of toryism was left to the state's governor: Richard Caswell. He believed it possible that their "wicked and pernicious" attempts to avoid the draft might be part of a "traitorous" plot. But he wasn't sure. He asked the militia commander in the afflicted region to determine "these peoples' designs." Caswell was trying yet again to avoid the "spilling of human blood" if he could, and it is clear he was not sure of the meaning of these people's behavior. The only thing he knew for certain was they did not want to go to war.[10]

Amazingly, at least one man believed that his having first eagerly associated in 1777, and then denounced the Brethren's leadership, would be a suitable excuse to avoid drafts in 1779. As the crisis in the southern theater intensified, Albemarle planter William Berkett asked to be excused from military service with his militia unit, which had been mobilized to march to the south. His logic? He had in the recent past chosen to "Voluntarily declare & make known unto a member of the Committee a conspiracy that was forming & indeed putting into execution." Since that service to the state he had suffered "threats of many that was concerned in this sd Conspiracy . . . he goes in Continual Dangers of this life." He failed to mention at this juncture that he had been one of the few Protestant associators in 1777 who actually asked, and indeed insisted, on being allowed to join, as opposed to being asked to join. He also withheld that, after joining, he promptly turned on the movement, perhaps because of the leaders' conspiratorial loyalism, or perhaps not. He now asked that the state give him consideration "for so Meritorious a Service rendered to the county," and allow him to be excused from the militia. In other words, he asked to be exempt from military service because he had previously joined and then informed on a movement based on resistance to the draft that eventually became treasonous.[11]

The yeomanry's subsequent failure to rally to the king's standard when royal armies invaded North Carolina undermines the idea that the resisters should be considered latent loyalists. When Lord Cornwallis and his army arrived in 1781 and raised the king's standard, most Carolinians actively avoided service with the British army. Cornwallis repeatedly complained to Sir Henry Clinton that despite the population's supposed imperial sympathies, the country failed to rally to him. He issued a proclamation calling the loyal to join the imperial cause after he bested the American forces at the bloody Battle of Guilford Court House. Few came, and those who did offered nothing but a warm hello. "Many of the inhabitants," Cornwallis wrote bitterly to Clinton in the battle's aftermath, "rode into camp, shook me by the hand, said they were glad to see us, and to hear that we had beat Greene, and then rode home."[12]

Cornwallis tried again to rally the supposedly loyal when he reached Cross Creek, North Carolina in the same campaign. He called for the king's friends to bring in supplies for his increasingly beleaguered army. No one appeared. Many farmers refused even to sell the British army food and other necessities, let alone donate supplies, perhaps out of fear of the committees of safety, perhaps for other reasons. Locals, Cornwallis noted, avoided committing themselves to either side.[13]

What Cornwallis did not add is that his view of what the "sides" were did not fit these Carolinians, or their worldview. His experiences argue just as strongly against a latent loyalism among those who tried to avoid service as did state officials' frustrated efforts to recruit belie any raging patriotism. And even though some of these Carolinians may well have been "a sett of lazy Raskalls," as one American officer had so eloquently put it, there has to be more to it. People would not come to the war, and their reasoning extended beyond not wanting to get shot. A strong part of it was the need to attend to their farms; but again, there was more to it than this.

These North Carolinians wanted to be citizens without embracing the martial standard of civic virtue exemplified by the ancient Greek hoplite and the Roman Republic's legionary, a standard nominally embraced by the new order's neoclassical, enlightened leaders. Yet these resisters did not fit easily into the self-interested, individualistic, capitalistic model of citizenship seen by many as the Revolution's end product. Some resisters saw the state as oppressive and opposed to the Revolution's professed values; others held values more consistent with the imperial past's Protestant libertarianism; others could or would not leave farms and communities, seeing themselves as having little vested in the great crisis of their times; and still others clung to religious convictions inconsistent with military service. They thus have remained largely invisible historically, defying easy political categorization as defiantly as they did the endless drafts and mobilizations.[14]

Those who did serve seem equally mysterious. For they could fight for one cause, and then another, and then none, without any sense of discontinuity. How was that possible?

To Serve All

What is often startling when reading loyalist, whig, and British commentators is not how distinctly different these Anglo-American voices sound ideologically and politically, but instead how much they all shared. It makes sense that they should. The contending parties' beliefs were closely interrelated, rooted in an inherited British libertarian Protestant political culture. The shared Anglophone language of liberty and rights, coupled to the shared history of struggle against popish tyranny, helps explain how some could move between the contending parties, serving in different armies or assisting them in turn, without causing emotional or perceptual dislocation. Many people held core beliefs that they saw as being compatible simultaneously with independence, empire, or neutrality. And some treason-tainted Protestant associators demonstrated this flexibility, again revealing just how problematic political categorization was and is historically.

The case of Bertie County associator James Knott illustrates an aspect of this phenomenon. Though named during the suppression as a Brethren in 1777, Knott was neither deposed nor arrested. He disappeared for some time, and then reappeared to give bond to be loyal to the state in 1779. Then he disappeared from the Albemarle again without a trace. Cornwallis's army had already stacked its arms at Yorktown in October 1781 when the legal system finally caught up with Knott. He was accused of being part of a treasonous plot, meaning the Brethren. The state seemed to have assumed he was a tory on the run, but the opposite proved true.

"He was," it came to be revealed, "in Charles Town [South Carolina] during a good Time of the siege . . . by Cornwallis's army in 1780]," fighting with American forces. His actions won the approval of his officers, and he behaved in such a manner "as to acquit him of the least Degree of Suspicion of being an enemy of his country or to Toryism." Falling ill, Knott had been sent home to Bertie County shortly before General Lincoln's army at Charleston surrendered in the spring of 1780. On his return to North Carolina, Knott learned the authorities had been seeking him for questioning about the events in 1777. The former associator then failed to go to the court, believing (essentially correctly) that the North Carolina judiciary had again collapsed in 1780 due to the ongoing military crisis.

It wasn't over even then. Knott prepared once again to answer for his actions with the Brethren at the May 1781 court sitting, but that court then failed to meet when Cornwallis invaded the state. Knott declared, with no sense of irony, given the movement's turn to loyalism, that he had twice been drafted into the American forces, and had served without "Blame or Censure." The court released him, and he retained his property. Like many other Brethren, he saw no contradiction between association and defending the Revolution as he understood it, even though to do so nominally put him on different "sides" of the conflict.[15]

As the court officers well knew, others moved among political allegiances or military commitments. In December 1779, Martin County's John Buttery, also involved in with the Brethren movement to some degree, marched south with his county's militia during the extended crisis caused by the appearance of British forces in Georgia and South Carolina. He apparently served without issue.[16]

In the dark moments of 1780 and 1781, when the American cause hung in the balance in a way it had not since the autumn of 1776, the state government tacitly acknowledged how permeable allegiances were. Desperate for manpower for the state's Continental line, the state offered complete amnesty to those who had avoided the draft or been accused of loyalism if they would now join the American cause. Governor Alexander Martin repeatedly "issue[d] this my proclamation of pardon to such of the above persons [loyalists] . . . on this express condition, that they immediately enlist in the Continental battalions." If they served faithfully for a year, they would "be restored to the privileges of citizens."[17]

It was not just in North Carolina, and it was not just among yeomen. Certainly, it was true in South Carolina during the British invasion of 1779 and 1780. Early in 1780 the secretary to the British peace commissioners who had been sent to try to reconcile with the colonies reported that "both [Henry?] Laurens and [Edward] Rutledge [a signer of the Declaration of Independence] had taken measures which indicated their wishes to be received with forgiveness." These men, two of the most important leaders in revolutionary South Carolina, were frightened that the slaves would rebel when the British entered the state. Also apprehensive about radicals in the white population, the two men considered defecting into a kind of pro-British neutrality. But the rapidly changing context yanked this opportunity for the British to split the rebel leadership. These two leaders remained in the American camp even after Charleston fell. But they were not entirely consistent in their loyalties.[18]

Throughout the war, people in all parts of America changed sides—or, perhaps more accurately, obscured what side they were on, if any—surprisingly frequently. They slid from patriot to loyalist and back, in turn becoming pacifist neutrals, or even armed neutrals. Some of these changes have a surreal quality to them from our distant perspective.

Take, for instance, the ceremony celebrating the nation's independence in 1777 in Philadelphia. Wanting musical entertainment, and lacking their own band, officials turned to the only band available, "the Hessian band of Music, taken in Trenton the 26th of December last [when Washington successively counterattacked imperial forces], attended and heightened the festivity with some fine performances suited to the joyous occasion." This would seem a strange choice for musical entertainment, given that the rebel state's entire political leadership, and many Continental congressmen, joined them. As the bemused North Carolina congressional delegate Doctor Thomas Burke noted to Governor Caswell, the Hessians "performed very delightfully," the pleasure of the moment "not a little heightened by the reflection that they were hired by the British Court for purposes very different from those to which they were applied." Very different indeed.[19]

It was not nearly as odd, though, as the choice of soldiers to demonstrate close-order drill before the gathered worthies. These men, "a corps of British deserters, taken into the service of the continent by the State of Georgia," were saluted for filling "up the intervals with feux de joie." It did not seem strange at all, apparently, to entertain the gathered worthies with performances by armed (presumably with unloaded guns) soldiers who, shortly before, had been in the imperial army. Throughout the war, people were impressed or hired into one army after another; some deserted one army to serve in another, or not at all; prisoners changed sides to avoid incarceration; seamen were impressed into the British navy—and the awareness of this defeats the idea of rigidly defined identities more decisively than Washington bested Cornwallis at Yorktown. [20]

Changes in allegiance could be quite calculated, and intentionally temporary. As the Massachusetts writer "Spectator" noted about his own supposedly overwhelmingly whig region, "that many of you who are now Whigs, or Tories, according to the various successes of a battle, having no principle whereon to stand, but being solicitous only for your personal security . . . Tories when Howe prevails, and Whigs when Washington is crowned with success." Such calculation is a very human constant, and the slings and arrows of a long, cruel, grinding war frequently saw people move politically, depending on the outcome of battle. At that level, below the rage of war and factions, there were just different perspectives and different immediate situations. [21]

Yet there would have been no Revolution without those truly committed to their respective causes. People did indeed take sides, and with that came bloodshed, not only between armies or even the rival groups of loyalists and patriots that famously ravaged the Carolinas in the period between 1779 and 1783, but among neighbors and friends. John Lewellen was hardly the only one to think harmful thoughts about those around him.

The Price of Allegiance

On August 22, 1777, with the Brethren's trials approaching, one of their arch-nemeses, Nathan Mayo, ran into his neighbor, Thomas Clark, near their lands in Pitt County. They began to talk casually about troubled times, and the ongoing war with Great Britain. Until that day they had always "lived in Peace as neighbors." They were both drunk, and friendly conversation soon gave way to angry words about politics. Clarke declared he would "stand up for King George, and that no Person who would not support him was fit to live." It escalated. Mayo replied "that any Person who would not stand by and defend his Country ought to be taken up," presumably by the local committee of safety.[22]

Mayo had seen how his brother's angry words had helped destabilize the entire Albemarle region. Yet such was his zeal for independence that he had refused to learn. Clark became enraged, and according to Mayo, the drunken tory "leveled a loaded gun . . . and snapt her at him, and upon . . . missing fire" then tried twice more to shoot. Understandably alarmed, Mayo went and got his own gun. He shot Clark in the side, and watched as the wounded man suffered in agony for about half an hour before expiring steps from his killer's home. Mayo insisted that he believed "that Clarke would otherwise have killed him."[23]

How are we to understand the kind of rage Nathan Mayo and his unlucky neighbor felt? It was politics at the most primordial—personal, heart politics, driven by lived experience. For certain, imperial political culture shaped it, as did participation in the committees of safety and militias, or being targeted by the same committees; these were conduits. Such episodes reveal how real the internalization of politics was for some.

Mayo's alcohol-fueled anger at those who still grasped the imperial father's hand had fatally boiled over. His neighbor had died because of a few words in favor of a king becoming more distant every day. Mayo soon found himself on trial for his life in the state whose independence he too vehemently upheld, filled with remorse and sadly maintaining that he "bore him [Clark] no malices" until their fateful encounter. He was acquitted. It was perhaps this trauma that led him to assist John Lewellen's wife in her plea for mercy that autumn. He had come to a more profound understanding of just how fraught the times were.[24]

The Revolution among neighbors has remained beyond our grasp despite scholars' best efforts to reveal the revolutionary up-heaval "from below." Talk about complexity and ambiguity in allegiance should not mask the fact that in revolutionary America people took sides—vehemently, emotionally, firmly, violently. They were willing to fight and die for their beliefs. Although we have understood this on a macro-, ocean-spanning scale, and seen it in clashing armies and bold political proclamations, the way it worked itself out in lives, in a rural countryside among neighbors, has too often been lost.

In North Carolina, familiars with different political views remained in tight physical proximity until public incidents, often enabled by alcohol, led them to act against one another. This began even before independence, as the committees and militias began their efforts to police the countryside and create revolutionary unity by force and intimidation. In March 1776, for example, William Bourk, believing himself among friends, declared that "we should all be subdued by . . . May by the King's Troops" and went on to denounce General Gage for being too soft on the colonials in Boston. Within twenty-four hours his friends had turned him in to the Provincial Council, who arrested him and confined him at Halifax as an enemy of the people. The Revolution had redefined even the most basic human bonds; even friendship became political in nature as the boundary between public and private collapsed.[25]

North Carolina's records stand witness to these alterations in the nature of friendship caused by the Revolution. In Surry County, James Douhet got himself accused of treason. He had drunk to "Damnation to the States & good health to George over the water" in a public setting, and been turned in by his drinking companions. Some of these companions must have had questions about his loyalties before, but until this public display, they had let it ride. When it became a public issue, they turned on him.[26]

Thomas Butcher's unsolicited and inaccurate military commentary in the New Bern District in 1778 got him dragged into court for speaking treasonous words. He, apparently without prompting, informed those around him that the British general Sir William Howe had captured General Washington's artillery train, and that while Washington had lost battle after battle, "Genl. Howe had never Attempted to git to any Place but that he had done it." In an environment where what we call rumors and facts were often indistinguishable, such statements were interpreted as efforts to undermine the state. "P Robertson," and others within earshot of this proclamation reported it to the state authorities, which is how Butcher ended up in the legal system. For his friends to let it go was to potentially indict oneself alongside the guilty party.[27]

It went on this way, neighbors turning in friends, until at least the war's end. In 1779 another forced draft led Theophilus Mann "in the presence of divers Persons did speak . . . several seditious and inflammatory words following, to wit 'Good luck to George our King. . . . that if he must fight, he would be damned if he did not fight against the continent,' to the evil example of all others." He was different from those associators who had sworn to defend Protestantism and rejected the turn to empire that destroyed the movement, as he was clearly a type of loyalist, one emotionally attached to the king. But it only became a public issue when Mann made it so. He was indicted when someone reported him.[28]

In some circumstances, would-be loyalists had to go far to get themselves punished, even by passing strangers, though in the end many managed it. Consider the determined, if oblivious, Richmond (Virginia) shoemaker who cried out "Hurrah for King George!" as a party of North Carolina soldiers march by his door headed toward the fighting in the north early in the war. Ordered by their general to ignore him, the troops marched on to camp outside the town. Rather than thanking divine providence for his miraculous deliverance from retribution, the shoemaker pursued the party "and began again to hurrah for King George." When the general and his aides "mounted and started, he still followed them, hurrahing for King George."

Finally, the officers lost their patience. The general ordered "him to be taken back to the river and ducked," one of the traditional punishments of the early modern period, a kind of folk water-boarding in which people were repeatedly plunged underwater. The troops grabbed a long rope, tied it "round his middle, and seesawed him backwards and forwards until we had him nearly drowned." But every time "he got his head above water he would cry for King George."[29]

This shoemaker was loyal. Even after spending time underwater, he continued to cheer for his king. The general finally "ordered him to be tarred and feathered." His wife and children beseeched him to be quiet, but he would not stop cheering for a monarch he would never see. "We tore the [man's own feather bed] open," continued the account, and "plunged him headlong" into a tar barrel. He was then "rolled in the feathers until he was a sight," but still he "would hurra for King George." He was finally drummed out of town, and told they would shoot him if he continued.[30]

Historians have barely uncovered this brutal subscript, neighbors killing or torturing or denouncing neighbors because of a loose word. The sparse records that examine such actions convey the human essence of that time better than virtually anything that has survived from then until now. This low-level violence, the pushing and shoving, the blood and the guts and the alcohol, may in sum tell us as much about change in the revolutionary generation as all we have accomplished in the last fifty years as a community of scholars.

This is especially true for places like the Carolinas and the Mid-Atlantic, with populations so ethnically and linguistically jumbled. And without a doubt, it will reveal both the usefulness and the very real limits of the frameworks we use to understand those who lived through the turmoil in the 1770s and 1780s. The period's political ambiguities and contradictions expose the limits of these frameworks.

Whatever their beliefs, or political positions, people knew they lived in a world where a wrong word between neighbors could get you killed. North Carolina, the South Carolina interior, Georgia, parts of the eastern shore, and the entire Mid-Atlantic: during the war, and perhaps until 1786 or 1787, they prove that Thomas Hobbes had a point, again, again and again. The extent of bloody conflicts between rival ethnic and religious groups, or within them, has become increasingly clear over the last generation as scholars have investigated strife in different regions during the war. But the Revolution between neighbors has remained just beyond our grasp.

Reading primary sources will enable this particular brand of history from below. There in the archives, and increasingly on our digital screens, authentic voices await to explain the death of one society, and the birth of another, on a human scale and in active relationship with their past. For them, the Revolution was neither myth, nor founding, nor historical problem. It engulfed them all, forcing them to find a new understanding of themselves and, in so doing, to reshape their world.

Postcript: A Funeral and Two Weddings

The great war ended shortly after Cornwallis's 1781 North Carolina sojourn. A Franco-American force trapped the British at Yorktown and captured their entire army. In the aftermath, the British population lost the will to fight on and negotiations began that would lead to the Treaty of Paris. The London ministry withdrew imperial forces from the rebel states and acknowledged American independence. The battles had ended for kings and diplomats, but for those who had lived the fratricide in the American countryside, the struggle to rebuild and to reconcile—if possible—had just begun.

For John Lewellen that new struggle, to reconcile himself to his neighbors and to a republicanizing society, began when he returned home after escaping the hangman in 1777. Lewellen left no diary, no searing letters, and no depositions that traced this part of his revolutionary journey. But the records that do exist tell a remarkable story about him and those around him, former enemies living in close proximity. For them, the path to reconciliation went through a funeral and two weddings.

The first leg of Lewellen's journey into this new republican world had begun with discord and ended with plans for a bloodletting. But he had escaped proscription. During and after the war he received several distributions of property and purchased land. More land encouraged Lewellen to buy more people to grow the crops and harvest timber: by the time of the Census of 1790, John Lewellen owned twenty human beings in Martin County.[31]

That census revealed something else. In 1790 Lewellen continued to live in close proximity to parties involved in the 1777 unrest, including his arch-nemesis-turned-savior, Nathan Mayo. By 1790 Mayo had, like Lewellen, become a major landowner himself and held fifteen people in slavery.[32]

It would be easy to imagine Lewellen and Mayo having a troubled relationship, but the opposite proved true. For when John Lewellen began to plan for his death in the early 1790s, he went to the person he believed he could trust the most to act as the will's executor: Nathan Mayo, a man he had tried to kill in 1777. It is a remarkable turn, as strange as when Mayo escorted Lewellen's wife to see Governor Caswell so that they might plead for Lewellen's life in the fall of 1777.

Lewellen's death in 1794 and Mayo's subsequent administration of his will should have ended their revolutionary existence together on North Carolina's coastal plain. But it did not, for love would indeed conquer all in the southern Albemarle, even the bitterness spawned in the American Revolution. Lewellen's daughter Sussanah, like so many people at that time, sought her marriage partners close to home, from those of similar status and beliefs. And with those imperatives in mind, living in close proximity to the Mayo family, she would go on to marry one of Nathan Mayo's sons, Fredrick, after her first husband died. They were married in the Baptist Church, the denomination embraced by Nathan Mayo in 1776 as the Church of England collapsed around him. Their son John Lewellen Mayo carried both family names, the genes of loyalist and committeemen intertwined within him, waiting to be read in some future generation. Sussanah was accepted into the family and the church, and became so beloved by her father-in-law that he would eventually treat her as he did his own children in his will.[33]

And when Fredrick died in 1802, the already twice-widowed Sussanah turned again to what she knew: she quickly married her brother-in-law, Nathan Mayo Jr. It was Romeo and Juliet in the forgotten southern countryside, rewritten with a new and infinitely more hopeful ending. For a funeral and two marriages announced the true end of the fratricidal conflict that had rendered the Albemarle at the Revolution's opening, and laid to rest whatever hate the memories of it encouraged. The families that had come to the brink of deadly blows in 1777 had become united by blood, joined as one in their new Baptist faith and the new republic, and in that embrace they would continue, linked also by their paradoxical shared history that ran back through the Gourd Patch Conspiracy. Their story became part of a larger saga—of civil war, convulsion, expulsion, and for some, redemption and forgiveness—the story of the human face of the American Revolution.

CONCLUSION

A Great Change of Seasons

IT IS DIFFICULT IN A WAY to accept that the Revolution began with the belief that a beloved Protestant empire's core had been corrupted by popery and infiltrated by Rome's tyrannical minions. Such views express neither the sophistication nor the enlightened promise nor the purity of purpose that our society would like to find at its moment of origin. And yet it is undeniable that this ever-spreading perception became the primary motivation for revolutionary mobilization in British America and destroyed imperial authority within eighteen months.

The revolutionary era's most momentous ideological shift has hidden this reality from us. After independence the Francophobic and anti-Catholic beliefs that had defined the empire's Protestant liberty and then been turned against imperial authority, along with those related beliefs that indicted standing armies as a threat to liberty, became inconvenient. A revolutionary elite needing a French alliance and a standing army to win a desperate war could not speak in the traditional language of Protestant liberty. When the revolutionary leaders abandoned that language, they created a fundamental gulf between themselves and the many who would still define liberty as somehow Protestant. The gulf that opened then has continued in American culture in different guises from that time to our own.

In detaching the language that linked liberty to Protestantism in the new republican order, revolutionary leaders created for those who were opposed to their policies a potent and historically legitimate idiom of political criticism that might be directed against them, the new states, or even the revolutionary project itself. What happened in North Carolina in 1777 illustrates this alteration in the political location of Protestant libertarian idioms, and how they could be seen as a threat to a frail revolutionary republican order. That those who used the language may have initially thought themselves defending liberty and an independent Protestant commonwealth became immaterial amid the ongoing revolutionary crisis.

That some loyalists used these Protestant idioms to define themselves politically only served to further obscure what had happened. Loyalism as an ideological construct was not solely a product of the revolutionary leadership's abandonment of Protestant political culture. Loyalism was complex, regionally and chronologically varied, and ever-changing ideologically. But the process of deinstitutionalizing Protestant political beliefs in the new order did provide those who would oppose the republican state, including imperial adherents but not restricted to them, with a powerful, and historically legitimate, language of criticism that eventually became prevalent in loyalist publications.

A writer in the *Royal Gazette,* a loyalist paper published in British-occupied New York, traced the great arch of what had happened in the American camp to the traditional understanding of Britain, Protestantism, and liberty. He asked why Americans would want "a final separation from Britain, the ancient and chief support of the protestant religion in the world." That tie had always secured their "secular and religious freedom." He noted that the Continental Congress had once accepted the connection between

Protestantism and liberty. After the Quebec Act passed in 1774, "the bare toleration of the Roman Catholic Religion in Canada . . . was treated as a wicked attempt" to establish a faith that "'had for ages filled the world with blood and slaughter."

By 1778, though, Congress had "altered their tone." American leaders willingly embraced Catholic France, "the most powerful . . . enemies of the reformation." The alliance threatened "the universal re-establishment of Popery thro all Christendom." He also denounced the French for "a general infidelity," a code word for heretical enlightened beliefs, and claimed such infidelity led ultimately back to the Church of Rome and political popery.[1]

These became common tropes of loyalist writings after 1778. Even Benedict Arnold sought to legitimate his betrayal of the American cause using Francophobic and anti-Catholic idioms. Their origins in Protestant libertarianism, and their use to attack the Congress and their French friends as tyrannical—in other words, as a libertarian indictment of republicanism and republican government—has been misunderstood or ignored by scholars, but is very real. And the persistence of this language in all of the period's political communities has been similarly ignored.[2]

The Brethren's story is an account of this revolutionary transformation as lived by people in one place. In North Carolina the combination of military necessity and enlightened learning led revolutionary leaders—the Fourteen and others—to discard older Protestant-centered idioms of freedom and to attack Protestant political practices long believed central to a free state's legitimacy. The relationship that had long been believed to exist between faith and freedom had been altered even as that relationship remained critical to how most Americans understood their liberty.

It is easy to see all these changes as a triumph for toleration. Scholars have done so for two centuries. Dissenters in the south, Anglicans in the north, and the enlightened everywhere benefited from disestablishments in the different states, and the muffling of anti-Catholicism no doubted eased the path for the waves of Catholics who would arrive in America in the nineteenth century. This spiritual liberation is so central to our national identity, it is hard to imagine that identity without it. It has become a cornerstone in the foundation of our national greatness.

By shedding bigoted views, the elite of the revolutionary generation ostensibly freed the society's formal processes and political language from ancient hatreds. But the ruptures with older ideas of liberty and good government based in Protestantism created in the process an unescapable dilemma of political order in an immediate sense, and an instability between governing legitimacy, public morality, and spiritual identity that explains much about what happened in the five decades after 1776, and, in a sense, until today.

These early efforts to separate the spiritual from the political set off the fifty years of turmoil that defined the revolutionary era. Protestant political culture continued to provide the primary framework through which the yeoman mass viewed politics and the world, albeit with many denominational variations. Christianity continued to hold a place in formal political processes after institutional structures were separated. Article 32 of the North Carolina constitution of 1776 is one example of this. It assured that officeholders would swear to Christ's divinity and the Bible's divine origins in that state. Formal support for spiritual institutions gradually ended, but political language remained spiritually infused, especially among those lower in the social order.

The resulting tensions would not end until a new spiritual-political church-state establishment, rhetorical rather than formalized in law, embodied in the term "American democracy," emerged in 1820s. Even then, open splits between groups of educated elites with nontraditional spiritual views, on the one hand, and a Protestant Christian majority, on the other, often moved to the center of American political life.

Conflicts along this fracture have again and again made it evident that Americans often do not share enough cultural terrain to allow institutional practice or public policy to express commonly held values. The implosion of the early nineteenth century's rhetorical church-state settlement in the late twentieth century has gradually crippled the society's ability to express any shared values and morals in the political culture or in policy. The efforts to turn democracy itself into a moral as well as a political system to compensate has, ironically, helped concentrate rather than spread power in a rapidly changing society. As a result, a shared understanding of democracy itself has eroded to an alarming extent.

This story from the Albemarle has awaited us patiently for over two centuries. It is compelling precisely because it makes visible some of the thinking at the nation's dawn that has remained hidden—its ambiguity, its complexity, its connection to the past and an unknown future. The rise and fall of the Brethren reveal how people lived the great ideological inversion of Protestant political culture and Protestant liberty in the months after independence. What happened in North Carolina in 1776 and 1777 allows us to reconsider what we know about the Revolution itself.

NOTES

NOTE ON SOURCES

ACKNOWLEDGMENTS

INDEX

NOTES

INTRODUCTION

1. John Gray Blount to His Excellency Governor Richard Caswell, Contentney July 5, 1777, Governor Richard Caswell Correspondence, July 5–6, Governors Papers, vol. 1, 53–54, State Archives of North Carolina (SANC).

2. This movement lasted perhaps six months, and for this reason most scholars have ignored it. Jeffrey J. Crow's short, thoughtful 1978 piece in the *North Carolina Historical Review* is the only article devoted solely to this movement. Crow's piece is well drawn, and based on a careful, measured reading of the primary sources. But we diverge on some essential points—that the movement was primarily a loyalist plot, and that it was driven by the desire to save the Church of England—as well as with regard to what sparked the movement, and in regard to its broader meaning. Jeffrey J. Crow, "Tory Plots and Anglican Loyalty: The Llewelyn Conspiracy of 1777," *North Carolina Historical Review* [*NCHR*] 55 (January 1978): 1–17.

The Crow article grew from an unexpected development. Early in 1972, unknown persons from the area around Greensboro, North Carolina, sent a box of documents related to the conspiracy to the State Archives of North Carolina in Raleigh, primarily the depositions taken from those involved in the unrest. Some of these had been published in the *North Carolina Historical and Genealogical Register* early in the twentieth century. These documents' pleasantly mysterious reemergence led to the publication of the Crow article. "Rec'd 1-12-72, sender unknown, Mailed from Greensboro area of North Carolina." From the Card in the SANC card catalogue, "Court Records CCR-DCR."

Another well-thought-through local study is Gerald W. Thomas, *Rebels and King's Men: Bertie County in the Revolutionary War* (Raleigh, 2013), 67–88. Thomas parallels Crow's central points about the conspiracy. Although I disagree with them about important points, both of these studies are scholarly, based on primary sources, and aim to show how the Revolution played out on the local level. They are the sorts of quality local studies that have become, unfortunately, increasingly uncommon as publishing has contracted and historical journals have faced financial retrenchment or even extinction.

3. For use of the term "Brethren," see the Deposition of Michael Ward, Bertie County, July 9, 1777, Edenton District Superior Court, Depositions from persons in Bertie, Chowan, Hyde, Martin and Tyrrell counties relative to charges against John Lewelling and others for treason, 1777, Beaufort, Bertie, Carteret, Chowan, Davidson, Davie, Edenton District, Forsyth, Guilford, Lenoir, Madison, and Pasquotank Counties, Misc. Records, 1699–1865, CRX box 4, SANC.

4. J. R. B. Hathaway, ed., *North Carolina Historical and Genealogical Register* (Edenton, 1901), 2:209–210.

5. Brendan McConville, *The King's Three Faces: The Rise and Fall of Royal America* (Chapel Hill, 2006), examines this culture. Francis Cogliano, Alfred Young, Gary Nash, and Peter Shaw have all examined Pope's Day's place in the political culture of eighteenth-century America. See especially Gary Nash, *The Unknown Revolution: The Unruly Birth of Democracy and the Struggle to Create America* (New York, 2005), 47, 52, 58; Peter Shaw, *American Patriots and the Rituals of Revolution* (Cambridge, MA, 1981), 11, 15–18, 69, 104–105, 142, 178–180, 186, 198–199, 202–203, 204–208, 216–217, 220–221, 231. Francis D. Cogliano, *No King, No Popery: Anti-Catholicism in Revolutionary New England* (Westport, 1995), was the first major study to take the rhetoric of anti-popery in revolutionary America seriously. Mary Ray's earlier study, *American Opinion of Roman Catholicism in the Eighteenth Century* (New York, 1936), began this process, although it receives scant attention today. The closest anyone has come to giving fear of popery causal primacy in bringing on the revolutionary crisis is Stephen J. Stein, "An Apocalyptic Rationale for the American Revolution," *Early American Literature* 9 (Winter 1975): 211–225. See also Vernon P. Creviston, writing in "'No King unless It Be a Constitutional King': Rethinking the Place of the Quebec Act in the Coming of the American Revolution," *Historian* 73, no. 3 (2011): 463–479. Other important works in this vein include Nathan Hatch, *The Sacred Cause of Liberty* (New Haven, 1977); Stephen Marini, *The Radical Sects of Revolutionary New England* (Cambridge, MA, 1982); Ruth Bloch, *Visionary Republic: Millennial Themes in American Thought, 1756–1800* (Cambridge, 1988); Thomas Kidd, *God of Liberty: A Religious History of the American Revolution* (New York, 2010).

6. See Gordon S. Wood, *The Creation of the American Republic* (Williamsburg, 1998), esp. 46–90; Wood, *The Radicalism of the American Revolution* (New York, 1993), esp. 95–228; Bernard Bailyn, *The Ideological Origins of the American Revolution* (Cambridge, MA, 1968); J. G. A. Pocock, *The Machiavellian Moment: Florentine Political Thought and the Atlantic Republican Tradition* (Princeton, 1975); Pocock, *Barbarism and Religion*, 6 vols. (Cambridge, 2001–2015); Robert E. Shalhope, "Toward a Republican Synthesis: The Emergence of an Understanding of Republicanism in American Historiography," *William and Mary Quarterly* 29, no. 1 (January 1972): 49–80; Caroline Winterer, *The Culture of Classicism: Ancient Greece and Rome in American Intellectual Life, 1780–1910* (Baltimore, 2002). The books and articles related to this strain of thinking run into the hundreds of titles.

7. The role of tensions between evangelicals and the enlightened in creating revolutionary conditions in America has been studied since at least since the publication of Alan Heimert's *Religion and the American Mind: From the Great Awakening to the*

Revolution (Cambridge, MA, 1966). Rhys Isaac's famous study *The Transformation of Virginia, 1740–1790* (Williamsburg, 1999) examines the role of evangelicals in challenging the Tidewater elite's social hegemony in the decades before the imperial crisis. Gordon Mailer has taken up aspects of this question in his biography of John Witherspoon, *John Witherspoon's American Revolution: Enlightenment and Religion from the Creation of Britain to the Founding of the United States* (Williamsburg, 2017).

8. Historical literature on loyalism began to appear at the end of the eighteenth century and continues to appear today. Lorenzo Sabine, *The American Loyalists: Or Biographical Sketches of Adherents to the British Crown in the War of the Revolution* (Boston, 1847), marked a turning point in those early considerations despite its now-visible limitations; Claude Van Tyne, *The Loyalists in the American Revolution* (New York, 1902). Modern consideration of the phenomenon as a whole began with William H. Nelson, *The American Tory* (Oxford, 1961); Wallace Brown, *The King's Friends* (Providence, 1965); Brown, *The Good Americans: The Loyalists in the American Revolution* (New York, 1969); Mary Beth Norton, *The British Americans: The Loyalist Exiles in England, 1774–1789* (Boston 1972); Paul Smith, *Loyalists and Redcoats: A Study in British Revolutionary Policy* (New York, 1972); Robert Calhoon, *The Loyalists in Revolutionary America, 1760–1781* (New York, 1971); Sheila L. Skemp, *William Franklin: Son of a Patriot, Servant of a King* (Oxford, 1990); Robert Calhoon, Timothy Barnes, and Robert S. Davis, *Tory Insurgents: The Loyalist Perception and Other Essays* (Columbia, 2010); Thomas B. Allen, *Tories: Fighting for the King in America's First Civil War* (New York, 2011).

Five recent studies about dissent against the Revolution have tried to straddle scholarly and popular audiences. These are Nathaniel Philbrick's *Valiant Ambition: George Washington, Benedict Arnold, and the Fate of the American Revolution* (New York, 2017); Stephen Brumwell's *Turncoat: Benedict Arnold and the Crisis of American Liberty* (New Haven, 2018); and Joyce Lee Malcolm's *The Tragedy of Benedict Arnold* (New York, 2018). Richard Godbeer has recently published *World of Trouble: A Philadelphia Quaker Family's Journey through the American Revolution* (New Haven, 2019). Maya Jasanoff, *Liberty's Exiles: American Loyalists in the Revolutionary World* (New York, 2011), examines the global dispersal of loyalists.

For efforts to examine non-elite, obscure loyalists, see the essays in Joseph S. Tiedemann, Eugene R. Fingerhut, and Robert W. Venables, eds., *The Other Loyalists: Ordinary People, Royalism, and the Revolution in the Middle Colonies, 1763–1787* (Albany, 2009); the piece by Eugene R. Fingerhut, "From Revolutionary to Traitor: The American Career of Herman Zedtwitz," speaks to some of the same themes I explore here. Also pertinent are John B. Frantz and William Pencak, eds., *Beyond Philadelphia: The American Revolution in the Pennsylvania Hinterland* (University Park, PA, 1998); Joseph S. Tiedemann and Eugene R. Fingerhut, eds., *The Other New York: The American Revolution beyond New York City, 1763–1787* (Albany, 2005); Jerry Bannister and Liam Riordan, eds., *The Loyal Atlantic: Remaking the British Atlantic in the Revolutionary Era* (Toronto, 2012); John Shy, "Armed Loyalism: The Case of the Lower Hudson Valley," in Shy, *A People Numerous and Armed: Reflections on the Military Struggle for American Independence* (Oxford, 1976), 181–192.

Research on conspiratorial political movements has tended to reflect, directly and indirectly, the influence of Richard Hofstadter's *Anti-Intellectualism in American Life* (New York, 1963) and his *The Paranoid Style in American Politics* (New York, 1964). Recent studies of racial conflict and fears of slave conspiracy have tended to study the mentality of the enslaved. This study builds on the approaches in those studies to examine the unrest in North Carolina.

1. ALONG THE SOUND

1. William L. Saunders, ed., *The Colonial Records of North Carolina* (Raleigh, 1886–1890), 1:20–33; Samuel Ashe, *History of North Carolina*, vol. 1: *1584–1783* (repr., Raleigh, 1971), 68, 217–220. For the charter of 1663, see Mattie Erma Edwards Parker, ed., *The Colonial Records of North Carolina: North Carolina Charters and Constitutions, 1578–1698* (Raleigh, 1963), 74–89, and see 90–104 for the Charter of 1665, which altered and clarified the boundaries of the grant.

2. Ashe, *History of North Carolina*, 1:98–104. "The Fundamental Constitution of Carolina, March 1, 1669," The Avalon Project, Documents in Law, History, Diplomacy, Yale University Law School.

3. Ashe, *History of North Carolina*, 1:88–93; William E. Nelson, "Politicizing the Courts and Undermining the Law: A Legal History of Colonial North Carolina, 1660–1775," *North Carolina Law Review* 88, no. 6 (2010): 2136; Parker, *Colonial Records*, 107; Noeleen McIlvenna, *A Very Mutinous People: The Struggle for North Carolina, 1660–1713* (Chapel Hill, 2009), 31.

4. For the split in colonial North Carolina between tobacco- and rice-growing regions, see Lawrence F. London, "The Representation Controversy in Colonial North Carolina," *North Carolina Historical Review* [*NCHR*] 11 (October 1934): 255–270; Ashe, *History of North Carolina*, 1:88–178, remains the central discussion of the period institutionally.

5. Archibald Henderson, *North Carolina: The Old North State and the New*, vol. 1 (Chicago, 1941), 41–74; Ashe, *History of North Carolina*, 1:85–87, 94–97; Michael J. Crawford, *The Having of Negroes Is Become a Burden: The Quaker Struggle to Free Slaves in Revolutionary North Carolina* (Gainesville, 2010), 69. McIlvenna, *A Very Mutinous People*, describes a power struggle in a diverse society eventually won by tobacco planters, merchants, and members of the proprietary government.

6. Ashe, *History of North Carolina*, 1:110, 113–120. For the efforts to both promote and regulate tobacco production in the seventeenth-century English Atlantic and in the Albemarle region, see Harleian Manuscripts, Papers Relating to Tobacco, folios 1–62, British Library, microfilm, State Archives of North Carolina (SANC). For Maryland's efforts to get Albemarle planters to restrain tobacco planting in 1666 due to market conditions, see Saunders, *Colonial Records*, 1:139–140, 152–153. See also McIlvenna, *A Very Mutinous People*, 31–32.

7. A number of studies of Virginia, Maryland, and the Chesapeake generally have focused on tobacco and the region's culture and character. See Jacob M. Price, "The

Rise of Glasgow in the Chesapeake Tobacco Trade, 1707–1775," *William and Mary Quarterly* 11, no. 2 (April 1954): 179–199; Price, "The Economic Growth of the Chesapeake and the European Market, 1697–1775," *Journal of Economic History* 24 (1964): 496–511; Edmund Morgan, *American Slavery, American Freedom* (New York, 2003); Allan Kulikoff, *Tobacco and Slaves: The Development of Southern Cultures in the Chesapeake, 1680–1800* (Chapel Hill, 1986); Lois G. Carr and Russell Menard, *Robert Cole's World: Agriculture and Society in Early Maryland* (Chapel Hill, 1991); Philip Morgan, *Slave Counterpoint: Black Culture in the Eighteenth-Century Chesapeake and Low Country* (Chapel Hill, 1998); Charles Wetherell, "Boom and Bust in the Colonial Chesapeake Economy," *Journal of Interdisciplinary History* 50 (1984): 185–210. For tobacco in the general economy, see John J. McCusker and Russell Menard, *The Economy of British America, 1607–1789* (Chapel Hill, 1991), and Ronald Hoffman, John McCusker, Russell Menard, and Peter Alberts, eds., *The Economy of Early America: The Revolutionary Period, 1763–1790* (Charlottesville, 1988).

Two excellent studies probe tobacco's role in shaping revolutionary consciousness in Virginia. See T. H. Breen, *Tobacco Culture: The Mentality of the Great Tidewater Planters on the Eve of Revolution* (Princeton, 2001), and Rhys Isaac, *The Transformation of Virginia* (Chapel Hill, 1999). See also Paul Clemens, *The Atlantic Economy and Colonial Maryland's Eastern Shore: From Tobacco to Grain* (Ithaca, 1980); Walter E. Minchinton, "The Seaborne Slave Trade of North Carolina," *NCHR* 71, no.1 (January 1994): 1–61; Alan Watson, *Bertie County: A Brief History* (Raleigh, 1982), 46. The taverns were apparently used for a time as the Bertie County courthouse. See Saunders, *Colonial Records*, 9:804–806. An 1802 visitor to the western Albemarle watershed noted that people continued to live in dispersed homesteads. See W. C. Allen, *History of Halifax County* (Boston, 1918), 64.

8. Alan D. Watson, *Tyrrell County: A Brief History* (Raleigh, 2010), 27.

9. See Tax List, Bertie County, 1774, General Assembly Papers, G.A. 11.1, SANC. Alan D. Watson, "Society and Economy in Colonial Edgecombe County," *NCHR* 50, no. 3 (July 1973): 247; Watson, *Bertie County*, 67, addresses William Brimage's status before the war, and his landholdings are described at the Bertie County, NC Genproject website, "Loyalists," https://sites.rootsweb.com/~ncbertie/loyalist.htm. See also Tax List, Bertie County, 1774, General Assembly Papers, G.A. 11.1, SANC. For the role of Freemasonry in establishing status, see Steven C. Bullock, *Revolutionary Brotherhood: Freemasonry and the Transformation of the American Social Order, 1730–1840* (Chapel Hill, 1998).

10. See Tax List, Bertie County, 1774, General Assembly Papers, G.A. 11.1, SANC. Laurel Horton, "Looking for Polly Armistead: Intimations of a Mortality and Identity in a Late Eighteenth-Century Needlework," *Journal of Early Southern Decorative Arts* 29 (2018).

11. Ashe, *History of North Carolina*, vol. 1, 377–395, describes the development of this gentry and their social order, and the various groups in the elite. Don Higginbotham, ed., *The Papers of James Iredell*, vol. 1 (Raleigh, 1976), xxxviii–liv, describes the Albemarle gentry's lives at Edenton and in the region generally; see also Tax List, Bertie County, 1774, General Assembly Papers, G.A. 11.1, SANC.

12. See Tax List, Bertie County, 1774, General Assembly Papers, G.A. 11.1, SANC. Watson, "Society and Economy," 247. For the wooden houses, see Hugh Talmage Lefler, ed., *North Carolina History Told by Contemporaries* (Chapel Hill, 1965), 63.

13. Marvin L. Michael Kay and Lorin Lee Cary, *Slavery in North Carolina, 1748–1775* (Chapel Hill, 1995), 2, 19, 22, 15; Thomas L. Purvis, ed., *Revolutionary America, 1763–1800* (New York, 1995), 183, table 5.65; Kay and Cary, *Slavery in North Carolina*, 19, 22, 15, 221, 226–227. Francis Grave Morris and Phyllis Mary Morris, "Economic Conditions in North Carolina about 1780, Part II, Ownership of Town Lots, Slaves, and Cattle," *NCHR* 16 (July 1939): 310–311; map 1 shows that the northern Albemarle's counties, and nearby counties with historical ties to Virginia, had the most slaves. In the counties around Albemarle Sound, slaves composed 25 to 50 percent of the population. Documents that record slave ownership in Tyrrell County reveal that this same pattern of distribution of wealth survived independence. Around 1780 there were 651 slaves living in the county; persons who owned large numbers of slaves were a tiny fraction of the total population. Watson, *Tyrrell County*, 27; Morris and Morris, "Economic Conditions," pt. 2, 296–327, and see 305, 308, 309, for charts on slave ownership.

14. Marvin L. Michael Kay and Lorin Lee Cary, "Slave Runaways in Colonial North Carolina, 1748–1775," *NCHR* 63, no.1 (January 1986): 1–39, examines slave resistance via flight. See also R. H. Taylor, "Slave Conspiracies in North Carolina" *NCHR* 5 (January 1928): 20–34; Ernest James Clark Jr., "Aspects of the North Carolina Slave Code, 1715–1860," *NCHR* 39 (April 1962): 148–164; Alan Watson, "North Carolina Slave Courts, 1715–1785," *NCHR* 60 (January 1983): 24–36.

15. William Byrd, *The History of the Dividing Line betwixt Virginia and North Carolina* (Petersburg, 1841), 30; Robert Cain, ed., *The Colonial Records of North Carolina*, 2nd ser., vol. 10: *The Church of England in North Carolina: Documents, 1699–1741* (Raleigh, 1999), 470n.

16. Catherine W. Bishir and Michael T. Southern, *A Guide to the Historic Architecture of Eastern North Carolina* (Chapel Hill, 1996), 136. For pictures, see "Edenton Courthouse, Built 1767 and Renovated 2004," *This Day in North Carolina History* (blog), North Carolina Department of Natural and Cultural Resources, October 8, https://www .ncdcr.gov/blog/2014/10/08/edenton-courthouse-built-1767-and-renovated-2004; Robert Cain, ed., *The Colonial Records of North Carolina*, 2nd ser., vol. 10: *The Church of England in North Carolina: Documents, 1699–1741* (Raleigh, 1999), 383 for efforts to finish St. Paul's Church at Edenton in 1738. Ashe, *History of North Carolina*, 1:377–378, gives an account of Edenton. Harry Roy Merrens, *Colonial North Carolina in the Eighteenth Century* (Chapel Hill, 2012), 36, 37–38, 46, 87. For the number of homes, see Julia Cherry Spruill, "Virginia and Carolina Homes before the Revolution," *NCHR* 12 (October 1935): 332. Watson, *Tyrrell County*, 20–21. They imported British goods and exported tobacco, timber, and naval products. See "1751. The Revd Henry Calbeck to R. Cocke," and "Account of Sales of the Estate of Rev. D Mr. Calbeck, 1752," both in folder 2, box 1, Edenton Papers, Wilson Special Collections, University of North Carolina, Chapel Hill.

17. Hugh Buckner Johnston, "The Journal of Ebenezer Hazard in North Carolina, 1777 and 1778," *NCHR* 36 (July 1959): 365.

18. Saunders, *Colonial Records*, 6:1029; Watson, "Society and Economy," 243, 244–245, 248.

19. For the transformation from tobacco to wheat in the colonies to the north, the best study remains Clemens, *The Atlantic Economy*. Also extremely useful is Jacob M. Price, *Capital and Credit in British Overseas Trade: The View from the Chesapeake, 1700–1776* (Cambridge, MA, 1980), and Price, "The Rise of Glasgow," 179–199, and Price, "Glasgow, the Tobacco Trade, and the Scottish Customs, 1707–1730: Some Commercial, Administrative and Political Implications of the Union," *Scottish Historical Review* 63 (1984): 1–36. See also T. M. Devine, *The Tobacco Lords: A Study of the Tobacco Merchants of Glasgow and Their Trading Activities* (Edinburgh, 1975). Breen, *Tobacco Culture*, esp. 160–211, addresses the impact of the decline of tobacco and the spread of wheat culture.

20. Saunders, *Colonial Records*, 6:1029. For the boom–bust cycle in tobacco in the Chesapeake, see Earle, *Evolution of a Tidewater Settlement System*, 215–219; Wetherell, "Boom and Bust," 185–210; Breen, *Tobacco Culture*, 124–128. Both the primary sources and the secondary literature created by or devoted to the Virginia planters later labeled as founding fathers give often-extensive accounting of the impacts of both boom and bust. Extremely useful in regard to price pressure is Price, *Capital and Credit*, the articles by Price on the tobacco trade written between the 1950s and the 1970s, and Breen, *Tobacco Culture*, esp. 160–211 discusses the relationship between wheat growing and the adoption of republicanism.

21. Merrens, *Colonial North Carolina*, 36, 37–38, 46, 87; Watson, "Society and Economy," 243, 244–245, 248. A Spanish traveler in 1783 saw fields "planted chiefly corn, barley, wheat and potatoes" south of the Albemarle. J. Fred Rippy, "A View of the Carolinas in 1783," *NCHR* 6 (October 1929): 364. For this shift in the Virginia Tidewater and eastern shore, and the increase in wheat and grain production, see John J. McCusker and Russell R. Menard, *The Economy of British America, 1607–1789* (Chapel Hill, 1991), 130, table 6.1, 132, table 6.2, and see 130–134 for a general overview. Walter Clark, ed., *Colonial and State Records of North Carolina*, vol. 25: *Acts of the North Carolina General Assembly* (Raleigh, 1906), 255.

22. Saunders, *Colonial Records*, 6:1030. An 1802 visitor to Halifax noted that a strong shift toward growing cereals and grains had occurred, although he notes that tobacco was still being planted. See Allen, *History of Halifax County*, 64; Saunders, *Colonial Records*, 9:621; W. Neil Franklin, "Agriculture in Colonial North Carolina," *NCHR* 3 (October 1926): 555.

23. Saunders, *Colonial Records*, 9:621, 669; "By His Excellency Josiah Martin, Esquire.... A Proclamation," August 28, 1772, Colonial Governors Papers, vol. 8, Governor Josiah Martin, 1771–1775, SANC. For wheat cultivation in the northern Albemarle, see Edmund Berkeley and Dorothy S. Berkeley, eds., "'The Manner of Living of the North Carolinians,' by Francis Veale, December 19, 1730," *NCHR* 41 (April 1964): 242.

24. See https://web.viu.ca/davies/h320/population.colonies.htm for population figures. Tax List, Bertie County, 1774, General Assembly Papers, G.A. 11.1, SANC. Francis Grave Morris and Phyllis Mary Morris, "Economic Conditions in North Carolina about 1780, Part 1, Landholdings," *NCHR* 16 (April 1939): 120.

25. Merrens, *Colonial North Carolina*, 36, 37–38, 46, 87; Watson, "Society and Economy," 243, 244–245, 248.

26. For early economic diversification, see McIlvenna, *A Very Mutinous People*, 20–23, 91, 133, 199; Ashe, *History of North Carolina*, 1:377; William S. Powell, ed., "Tryon's 'Book' on North Carolina," *NCHR* 34, no. 3 (July 1957): 411; Merrens, *Colonial North Carolina*, 36, 37–38, 46, 87; Watson, "Society and Economy," 243, 244–245, 248. In 1753 the colony exported 84,000 barrels of pitch, tar, and turpentine. Herring and shad worked their way into the economy, and the diet, of those living on the Albemarle's southern shores. For North Carolina's wood product production between 1768–1774, see Purvis, *Revolutionary America*, 73, 74, 75, 76. For a mention of the export from Edenton of tar, a key export in the marine industry, see Higginbotham, *Papers of James Iredell*, 1:276; Virginia B. Platt, "Tar, Staves, and New England Rum: The Trade of Aaron Lopez of Newport, Rhode Island with Colonial North Carolina," *NCHR* (January 1971): 1–22. For tar and turpentine export in 1753, see "Industry and Invention," website of the North Carolina Museum of History, https://www.NCmuseumofhistory.org. For cattle, see Morris and Morris, "Economic Conditions," pt. 2, 316 and 317, table 11. For tobacco rebounding in Edgecombe in the 1770s, see Watson, "Society and Economy," 246. The enforcement of nonimportation allows for a significant view of what had been flowing in and out of the Albemarle in the late imperial period. See Alice Barnswell Keith, ed., *The John Gray Blount Papers*, vol. 1 (Raleigh, 1952), 4–5; "1751. The Revd Henry Calbeck to R. Cocke," and "Account of Sales of the Estate of Rev. D Mr. Calbeck, 1752. For fisheries in North Carolina, see, for example, [William? Johnston?], 1772? folder 1.69, Johnston Family Series, Hayes Collection, Wilson Library, University of North Carolina, Chapel Hill. For corn, hogs, and whaling, as well as tobacco planting, in the 1660s and 1670s, see William S. Powell, ed., *Ye Countie of Albemarle in Carolina* (Raleigh, 1958), esp. 62–63. For Governor Martin's comment on the effort to establish indigo and rice in parts of southeastern North Carolina, see Saunders, *Colonial Records*, 9:687. For indigo, also see Keith, *John Gray Blount Papers*, 1:4–5.

27. J. R. B. Hathaway, ed., *North Carolina Historical and Genealogical Register* (Edenton, 1900–1903) (hereafter cited as *NCHGR*), 2:209–211, 212, 213, 214–215, 567. For Harrison Sr., see also the deposition of Thomas Harrison Sr., Tyrrell County, July 14, 1777, Edenton District Superior Court, Depositions from Persons in Bertie, Chowan, Hyde, Martin and Tyrrell Counties relative to charges against John Lewellen . . . and others for Treason, 1777, Misc. Records, 1699–1865, CRX box 4, Court Records, SANC. Armel Holles reported he was "reaping" when he was approached. Deposition of Armel Holles, Tyrrell County, July 15, 1777, Oyer and Terminer, Edenton District, September 1777, Lewellen Treason Trial, Edenton District, Records of the Superior Court, 1774–1779, SANC. Thomas Harrison, son of John, reported he was approached "in his Cornfield." *NCHGR*, 2:211. James Harrison was approached in Thomas Harrison's cornfield; Testimony of James Harrison, Tyrrell County, July 15, 1777, Edenton District Superior Court, Depositions from persons in Bertie, Chowan, Hyde, Martin and Tyrrell Counties relative to charges against John Lewelling and others for treason, 1777, Beaufort, Bertie, Carteret, Chowan, Davidson, Davie, Edenton District, Forsyth,

Guilford, Lenoir, Madison, and Pasquotank Counties, Misc. Records, 1699–1865, CRX box 4, SANC.

28. Claiborne T. Smith Jr., "John Lewelling," NCpedia, https://www.ncpedia.org /biography/lewelling-john. He was apparently a communicant at a country chapel at Hamilton, Martin County. For Lewellen as a Tyrrell County JP, see Robert Cain, ed., *The Colonial Records of North Carolina,* 2nd ser., vol. 9: *Records of the Executive Council, 1755–1775* (Raleigh, 1994), 274.

29. Billy Mayo, "Captain John William Lewellyn: North Carolina Tories in the Revolutionary War," *North Carolina's Lost Souls in the Revolutionary War Project,* http:// ncrevwar.lostsoulsgenealogy.com/tories/johnwilliamllewellynar.htm.

2. PROTESTANTS

1. Deposition of James Rawlings Martin County, August 10, 1777, Oyer and Terminer, Edenton District, September 1777, Edenton District Records of the Superior Court, 1774–1779, State Archives of North Carolina (SANC). When he was later arrested, Rawlings claimed this was the March 1777 muster. For a variety of reasons, I believe it was the December 1776 muster, right after the state constitutional convention.

2. For the roots of the Church of England in North Carolina, see Sarah McCulloh Lemmon, "The Genesis of the Protestant Episcopal Diocese of North Carolina, 1701–1823," *North Carolina Historical Review [NCHR]* 23 (October 1951): 426–462. The work of John Murrin has defined understanding of the processes of Anglicization. The establishment of the Church of England is representative of this process, which had a variety of aspects.

3. Among the most important of recent works on the Glorious Revolution are John Miller, *James II* (New Haven, 2000); Tim Harris, *Revolution: The Great Crisis of the British Monarchy, 1685–1720* (London, 2007); Steve Pincus, *1688: The First Modern Revolution* (New Haven, 2011). Somewhat earlier works vital to understanding the period after the Glorious Revolution include Linda Colley, *Britons: Forging the Nation, 1707–1837* (New Haven, 1992); and John Brewer, *The Sinews of Power: War, Finance, and the English State, 1688–1783* (New York, 1989). For the American colonies, see David Lovejoy's *The Glorious Revolution in America* (New York, 1972) remains a central study. More recently, Owen Stanwood, *The Empire Reformed: English America in the Age of the Glorious Revolution* (Philadelphia, 2013), has revised significant aspects of our understanding. My understanding has also been shaped by a number of essays by John Murrin concerning the Glorious Revolution in America.

4. For the Hanoverian's genealogical connection to James I, see Jeremy Black, *The Hanoverians: The History of a Dynasty* (New York, 2004), 1–2, 55–58.

5. After 1688, England's political history was rewritten as a genealogy of the ongoing providential battle waged by Protestants against popery, Catholic powers, and Catholics generally. For early America, see Brendan McConville, *The King's Three Faces: The Rise and Fall of Royal America* (Chapel Hill, 2006), 49–144.

6. Robert J. Cain, ed., *The Colonial Records of North Carolina*, 2nd ser., vol. 10: *The Church of England in North Carolina: Documents, 1699–1741* (Raleigh, 1999), 8. For a solid discussion of the Seven Years War in North Carolina, see John R. Maass, *The French and Indian War in North Carolina* (Charleston, SC, 2013); and the older study, Samuel Ashe, *History of North Carolina*, vol. 1: *1584–1783* (repr., Raleigh, 1971), 280–309.

7. Cain, *Colonial Records,* 10:8; Ashe, *History of North Carolina*, 1:301–302. See also Thomas Kidd, *The Protestant Interest: New England after Puritanism* (New Haven, 2013).

8. The area received missionary visits from the Quaker leader George Fox and others. See Haskell Monroe, "Religious Toleration and Politics in Early North Carolina," *NCHR* 39, no. 3 (July 1962): 269–271; William L. Saunders, ed., *The Colonial Records of North Carolina* (Raleigh, 1886–1890), 1:xvii–xix, 215–216, 216–218, 226–227; Ashe, *History of North Carolina,*1: 109, 158–159, 165–168.

9. Ashe, *History of North Carolina*, 1:196–197. In Europe, Queen Anne's War is known, of course, as the War of the Spanish Succession. Noeleen McIlvenna, *A Very Mutinous People: The Struggle for North Carolina, 1660–1713* (Chapel Hill, 2009), 95–111, describes the tensions caused by the efforts to establish the Church. Ashe, *History of North Carolina,* 1: 158–159, 165–168, 196–197. For the Fundamental Constitution of 1698, see Mattie Erma Edwards Parker, ed., *The Colonial Records of North Carolina: North Carolina Charters and Constitutions, 1578–1698* (Raleigh, 1963), 238.

10. Saunders, *Colonial Records,* 1:520, 544–545, 571–573; Ashe, *History of North Carolina,* 1: 169–178.

11. Saunders, *Colonial Records,* 1:572–573. Cain, *Colonial Records,* 10:22, and see 58 for a similar description. William Byrd, *The History of the Dividing Line betwixt Virginia and North Carolina* (Petersburg, 1841), 29; Cain, *Colonial Records,* 10:29.

12. Cain, *Colonial Records,* 10:217. For a similar, earlier account of a Church minister refusing to go to North Carolina, see Cain, *Colonial Records,* 10:24. Sarah McCulloh Lemmon, "The Genesis of the Protestant Episcopal Diocese of North Carolina, 1701–1823," *NCHR* 28, no. 4 (October 1951): 438, discusses the dearth of Church of England clergymen in the 1720s.

13. Governor Sir Richard Everhard to the Bishop of London, January 25, 1725, reel Z.5.191, 217–218, microfilm, SANC, filmed from Fulham Papers, General Correspondence, Continental Colonies, Lambeth Palace Library, London (hereafter cited as Fulham Papers). J. R. B. Hathaway, ed., *North Carolina Historical and Genealogical Register* (Edenton, 1900–1903) (hereafter cited as *NCHGR*), 2:132–133. For Bret, see Cain, *Colonial Records,* 10:15. For another example of this sort of clergyman, see the accounts of the behavior of the Reverend John Urmston in Cain, *Colonial Records,* 10:80, 93–94, 103, 115–121, 139, 158, 170–171, 272–273; and Lemmon, "The Genesis," 435.

14. Byrd, *History of the Dividing Line,* 29.

15. See Saunders, *Colonial Records,* 3:339; for Whitefield's letter, see Cain, *Colonial Records,*10:423–424.

16. For the introduction of more clergy, see William S. Powell, ed., "Tryon's 'Book' on North Carolina," *NCHR* 34, no. 3 (July 1957): 409. I parallel here, to some degree, Paul Conklin, "The Church Establishment in North Carolina, 1765–1776," *NCHR* 32, no. 1 (January, 1955): 9–11, who focused on the two governors' role.

17. Saunders, *Colonial Records*, 6:1026. Governor Arthur Dobbs to the Board of Trade, London, March 29, 1764, reel Z.5.191, 300–301, microfilm, SANC, filmed from Fulham Papers. See also Saunders, *Colonial Records*, 6:1039–1040, for Dobbs's account of the Church of England. For the Orthodox Clergy Act, see Conklin, "The Church Establishment," 5. Glebe lands were lands tasked specifically to support ministers or for the minister's use.

18. Saunders, *Colonial Records*, 7:102. Governor William Tryon to SPG, Report on the State of Religion in North Carolina, reel Z.5.191, 306–307, microfilm, SANC, filmed from Fulham Papers; Conklin, "The Church Establishment," 5.

19. Governor William Tryon to SPG. Tryon push to get Church of England clergy began in a sense when his predecessor, Governor Dobbs, was buried without a clergyman in 1764; "the Funeral Service was performed by a Majestrate of Peace." R. W. D. Connor, *History of North Carolina*, vol. 1: *The Colonial and Revolutionary Periods, 1584–1783* (New York, 1919), 192. Saunders, *Colonial Records*, 7:102, 103, 490; for the number of parishes and ministers, see 103; for Tryon's efforts to seduce clergymen from other colonies in 1769, see 8:45. Ashe, *History of North Carolina*, 1:302, 386–387, 389, 390. See Paul David Nelson, *William Tryon and the Course of Empire: A Life in British Imperial Service* (Chapel Hill, 1990), 16–17, 25; for an extended discussion of Tryon's efforts to reinforce the Church, see 16–31. Paul Conkin, "The Church Establishment in North Carolina, 1765–1776," *NCHR* 32, no. 1 (January 1955): 2, 4. Conklin discusses the tensions over establishment, and over local versus central control in the Church of England between 1750 and 1776. See also the *North Carolina Gazette and Wilmington Weekly Post-Boy*, July 10, 1765, 4. For the efforts to reinforce the Church's position in the 1770s, see Saunders, *Colonial Records*, 9:888, 889.

20. See Rhys Isaac, *The Transformation of Virginia, 1740–1790* (Williamsburg, 1999). Isaac discusses at length the Church of England's position and character in Virginia. See also Dell Upton, *Holy Things and Profane: Anglican Parish Churches in Colonial Virginia* (New Haven, 1997); John K. Nelson, *A Blessed Company: Parish, Parsons and Parishioners in Anglican Virginia* (Chapel Hill, 2002); Lauren F. Winner, *A Cheerful and Comfortable Faith: Anglican Religious Practice in Elite Households of Eighteenth-Century Virginia* (New Haven, 2010). For an example of their ongoing tensions in North Carolina, see the Rev. Mr. Taylor's letter to the SPG extracted in Saunders, *Colonial Records*, 9:1003. Cain, ed., *Colonial Records*, 10:407.

21. There are mentions of chapels early in the eighteenth century. Reverend James Adams told the SPG that he preached at "a Church and two Chappels of ease the Precinct being of two great an extent to meet all at one or two places." List of the Clergy in North Carolina, July 1770, Society for the Propagation of the Gospel Letters, ser. B, 5–6, 1761–1782, microfilm, SANC. Cain, *Colonial Records*, 10:64–65. For other early examples of this circuit riding, see Cain, *Colonial Records*, 10:12, 282–283, 284; and see Reverend John Urmston to the SPG in Cain, *Colonial Records*, 10:243–257, 263–265, 267–268, 270–271. The Rev. Thomas Baylye to the Bishop of London, May 12, 1726, claimed to be ministering to half of North Carolina, though his reputation was so poor it is impossible to know whether this is true. Reel Z.5.191, 220–221, microfilm, SANC, filmed from Fulham Papers. See also John E. Tyler, "The Church of England in Colonial

Bertie County" (typescript, SANC), 1–2; See Saunders, *Colonial Records,* 1:765, for a circuit-chapel structure in the early eighteenth century. The Tyrrell County Court that met in September 1751 ordered a road constructed "to the Chappel and back [to Mrs. Carketts] landing" in a county whose population would become involved in the unrest in 1776 and 1777. The reconstruction of the locations of the Halifax chapels can be found in Graebner, *Anglican Church Buildings,* 3. Norris, "Church of England." September 1751 meeting of the Court of Pleas and Quarter Sessions, Meeting of the Tyrrell County, North Carolina Minutes Court of Pleas and Quarter Sessions, 1735 thru 1754, 104 (transcript, 1981, Betty Fagan Burr, transcriber), SANC; Tyler, "The Church of England," 14, 5–6. For the circuit and preaching of James Moir in 1764, see Saunders, *Colonial Records,* 6:1051–1053. For St. Paul's chapels, see Saunders, *Colonial Records,* 10:496, and Bennett H. Wall, "Charles Pettigrew, First Bishop-Elect of the North Carolina Episcopal Church," *NCHR* 28 (January 1951): 18. Bertie County, NC Genproject website, "Loyalists," https://sites.rootsweb.com/~ncbertie/loyalist.htm.

22. The Reverend N. Brooks Graebner, *Anglican Church Buildings in North Carolina, 1701–1776: A Study in Frustration* (2011), https://www.episdionc.org/uploads/files/Anglican_Church_Building_Graebner.pdf. Daniel Earl, who served as rector at St. Paul's at Edenton, also visited chapels in the Albemarle countryside. Quote as in David A. Norris, "Church of England," NCpedia, https://www.ncpedia.org/church-england; Don Higginbotham, ed., *The Papers of James Iredell,* vol. 1 (Raleigh, 1970), 218n12.

23. Saunders, *Colonial Records,* 4:924, 925.

24. A portion of the first quote in this paragraph is cited in James R. Caldwell Jr., "The Churches of Granville County, North Carolina, in the Eighteenth Century," in J. Carlyle Sitterson, ed., *The James Sprunt Studies in History and Political Science,* vol. 39: *Studies in Southern History* (Chapel Hill, 1957), 2. Robert J. Cain and Jan-Michael Poff, eds., *The Colonial Records of North Carolina,* 2nd ser., vol. 11: *The Church of England in North Carolina: Documents, 1742–1763* (Raleigh, 2007); Cain, *Colonial Records,* 9:111. For Moir's circuit, see Cain and Poff, *Colonial Records,* 11:347–348, and Saunders, *Colonial Records,* 6:1051–1053. The practice of circuit riding continued right up to the Revolution due to the lack of ministers. See, for example, "A Letter from the Revd. Mr. Earle, Miss., in North Carolina, May 15, 1775, At a General Meeting of the Society for the Propagating the Gospel in Foreign Parts Held September 15th, 1775," microfilm, SPG Journals 1775, SANC. Earle bemoaned the fact that his illness prevented him from riding the circuit of what he called "destitute parishes," meaning parishes without ministers. Saunders, *Colonial Records,* 7:458.

25. Saunders, *Colonial Records,* 6:1052.

26. Graebner, *Anglican Church Buildings,* 3. Norris, "Church of England." For committees of trustees at chapels in the early 1770s, see Saunders, *Colonial Records,* 9:639. Governor Arthur Dobbs to the Bishop of London, January 31, 1756, reel Z.5.192, 306–307, microfilm, SANC, filmed from Ordination Papers, Fulham Papers. Saunders, *Colonial Records,* 7:103. Tyler, "The Church of England," 5–6. September 1751 meeting of the Court of Pleas and Quarter Sessions, Meeting of the Tyrrell County, North

Carolina Minutes Court of Pleas and Quarter Sessions, 1735 thru 1754, 104 (transcript, 1981, Betty Fagan Burr, transcriber), SANC.

27. Edmund and Dorothy S. Berkeley, eds., "'The Manner of Living of the North Carolinians,' by Francis Veale, December 19, 1730," *NCHR* 41 (April 1964): 242.

28. Chancel Book of Common Prayer, published in London in 1760. The inscription in the book reads "Gift of the Society for Propagation of the Gospel in Foreign Parts; for the use of the Chapels in North Carolina." Inscribed as "The Gift of His Excellency William Tryon for the use of Society Parish in Bertie County, North Carolina" (London, England, 1760). Accession no. P.T.P. 1964.010.001, Collection of Tryon Palace Museum and Historical Site. I would note here the assistance of Lindy Cummings, Tryon Palace site historian, in retrieving and photographing images from this volume for me.

29. For the volume from the northern Albemarle, see *Small Book of Common Prayer with "New Version of the Psalms"* (Edinboro, Scotland, 1768) Accession no. P.T.P. 1960.024.001, Collection of the North Carolina Museum of History. This latter volume was owned by a household in Hertford County, North Carolina. It is possible that this latter volume was acquired by that household after 1777, but it seems unlikely and I have included it here as suggestive of what was available to the chapel readers. For examples of prayers for the king becoming a political issue late in the crisis, see Rev. L. C. Vass, *History of the Presbyterian Church of New Bern, N.C., with Resume of Early Ecclesiastical Affairs in Eastern North Carolina and Sketch of the Early Days of New Bern, N.C.* (Richmond, VA, 1886), 77–78, 87–88; see Saunders, *Colonial Records*, 10:153, for the related issue of refusing to preach on a fast day ordered by the revolutionary government.

30. Cain, *Colonial Records*, 10:410.

31. *North Carolina Gazette*, April 15, 1757, 3–4.

32. Saunders, *Colonial Records*, 6:521. For a royal governor's entrance in New Bern, see *The North Carolina Magazine; Universal Intelligencer*, December 28, 1764, 1–2, and see 2 for drinking to the King's health. Given the high level of practical illiteracy among the Protestant associators, the role that print culture played in shaping their worldview is unclear.

33. Richard J. Hooker, ed., *The Carolina Backcountry on the Eve of the Revolution: The Journal and Other Writings of Charles Woodmason, Anglican Itinerant* (Chapel Hill, 1953), 39.

34. The role of other Protestant sects in what happened in 1777 is unclear. At independence, dissenters heavily outnumbered the Church of England congregants in the colony as a whole, though in 1776 dissenters remained a minority in the Albemarle region. Thomas L. Purvis, ed., *Revolutionary America, 1763–1800* (New York, 1995), 198, table 7.4. For Baptists in the region during the Revolution, see Billy Mayo, "Captain John William Lewellyn: North Carolina Tories in the Revolutionary War," *North Carolina's Lost Souls in the Revolutionary War Project*, http://ncrevwar.lostsoulsgenealogy .com/tories/johnwilliamllewellynar.htm. "13th December 1774," Martin County, Records of Deeds, Deed Book A, p. 6, 1774–1787, SANC. In the chapters that follow,

I examine Rawlings's central role in the Association. Crow speculates that the Gourd Patch incident reflected a conflict between evangelicals and the Church of England, because Nathan Mayo, central to the whole affair as a persecutor of John Lewellen, was a recent Baptist convert. But the Protestant associators never used anti-evangelical idioms, instead focusing on heretical strains in the state leadership's thinking and the threat posed by a Catholic-tainted conspiracy in the state. For the Baptists on the sound's north shore, see *NCHGR,* 2:195, and Governor Sir Richard Everard to the Bishop of London, October 12, 1729, reel Z.5.191, 228–229, microfilm, SANC, filmed from Fulham Papers. The Baptists, Moravians, Presbyterians, and others became prevalent in central and western North Carolina. For a general discussion, see Saunders, *Colonial Records,* 5:1144–1228; also see 5:1163–1164 for the early presence of Baptists, 5:1164–1165 for those who migrated from Virginia to Halifax County, 5:1163 for the number of General Baptist settlements, and 5:1193–1194 for the Presbyterian presence.

Examination of Peleg Belote in the County Court of Bertie at the Court begun and held for the said County August 12, 1777, Edenton District Superior Court, Depositions from Persons in Bertie, Chowan, Hyde, Martin and Tyrrell Counties relative to charges against John Lewellen . . . and others for Treason, 1777, Misc. Records, 1699–1865, CRX box 4, Court Records, SANC.

35. Cain, *Colonial Records,* 10:27–29, describes the logic of the circuits as explained by the Reverend Mr. Blair in 1704.

3. Revolution

1. Robert J. Cain, ed., *The Colonial Records of North Carolina,* 2nd ser., vol. 9: *Records of the Executive Council, 1755–1775* (Raleigh, 1994), 332.

2. Periodically, scholars have acknowledged the intensity of violence during the American Revolution. For two recent studies, see Holger Hoock, *Scars of Independence: America's Violent Birth* (New York, 2017), and Alan Taylor, *American Revolutions: A Continental History* (New York, 2017).

3. Crucial to my thinking here in a general conceptual sense is John M. Murrin, "The Great Inversion, or Court versus Country: A Comparison of the Revolution Settlements in England (1688–1721) and America (1776–1816)," in J. G. A. Pocock, ed., *Three British Revolutions: 1641, 1688, 1776* (Princeton, 1980), 368–453.

4. *North Carolina Gazette,* November 20, 1765, 1. Robert M. Weir, "North Carolina's Reaction to the Currency Act of 1764," *North Carolina Historical Review* [*NCHR*] 40 (April 1963): 183–199; Lawrence Lee, "Days of Defiance: Resistance to the Stamp Act in the Lower Cape Fear," *NCHR* 43 (April 1966): 186–202; William L. Saunders, ed., *The Colonial Records of North Carolina* (Raleigh, 1886–1890), 7:123; Samuel Ashe, *History of North Carolina,* vol. 1: *1584–1783* (repr., Raleigh, 1971), 315–317, 323; Marshall Delancey Haywood, *Governor William Tryon and His Administration in the Province of North Carolina, 1765–1771* (Raleigh, 1903), 38. See also Jack P. Greene and Henry McCulloh, "'A Dress of Horror': Henry McCulloh's Objections to the Stamp Act," *Huntington Library Quarterly* 26 (May 1963): 253–262.

5. *North Carolina Gazette,* September 2, 1774, 2.

6. Ruth Blackwelder, "The Attitude of North Carolina Moravians toward the American Revolution," *NCHR* 9, no. 1 (January 1932): 6–7, quotes at 7. For literacy, see Thomas L. Purvis, *Revolutionary America, 1763 to 1800* (New York, 1995), 274–275.

7. The literature on anti-popery in the British tradition is massive. See Carol Z. Wiener, "The Beleaguered Isle: A Study of Elizabethan and Early Jacobean Anti-Catholicism," *Past and Present* 51 (May 1971): 27–62; Robin Clifton, "Popular Fear of Catholics during the English Revolution," *Past and Present* 53 (May 1971): 23–55; Robin Clifton, "The Fear of Popery," in Conrad Russell, ed., *The Origins of the English Civil War* (London, 1973), 144–167; Caroline Hibbard, *Charles I and the Popish Plot* (Chapel Hill, 1983); John Miller, *Popery and Politics in England, 1660–1688* (Cambridge, 1973); Stephen A. Kent, "The Papist Charges against the Interregnum Quakers," *Journal of Religious History* 12 (1982–1983): 180–190; Ian Y. Thackray, "Zion Undermined: The Protestant Belief in a Popish Plot during the English Interregnum," *History Workshop Journal* 18 (1984): 28–52; Tim Harris, *London Crowds in the Reign of Charles II* (Cambridge, 1987); Peter Lake, "Anti-Popery: The Structure of a Prejudice," in Richard Cust and Ann Hughes, eds., *Conflict in Early Stuart England: Studies in Religion and Politics, 1603–1642* (Harlow, 1989), 72–106; David Cressy, *Bonfires and Bells: National Memory and the Protestant Calendar in Elizabethan and Stuart England* (London, 1989); Arthur F. Marotti, ed., *Catholicism and Anti-Catholicism in Early Modern English Texts* (Basingstoke, 1999); Alexandra Walsham, "'The Fatall Vesper': Providentialism and Anti-Popery in Late Jacobean London," *Past and Present* 144 (August 1994): 36–87; Jacqueline Rose, "Robert Brady's Intellectual History and Royalist Antipopery in Restoration England," *English Historical Review* 122, no. 499 (2007): 1287–1317; Jeffrey Collins, "Restoration Anti-Catholicism: A Prejudice in Motion," in Charles W. A. Prior and Glenn Burgess, eds., *England's Wars of Religion, Revisited* (Farnham, 2011), 281–306.

8. More scholarship on the 1774–1776 period has recently appeared. Among these works are Mary Beth Norton, *1774: The Long Year of Revolution* (New York, 2020); Richard Beeman, *Our Lives, Our Fortunes and Our Sacred Honor: The Forging of American Independence, 1774–1776* (New York, 2013); Joseph Ellis, *Revolutionary Summer: The Birth of American Independence* (New York, 2013); T. H. Breen, *American Insurgents, American Patriots: The Revolution of the People* (New York, 2011); Woody Holton, *Forced Founders: Indians, Debtors, Slaves and the Making of the American Revolution in Virginia* (Williamsburg, 1999); David Ammerman, *In the Common Cause: American Response to the Coercive Acts* (New York, 1975).

9. The classical study of the Tea Party and its aftermath remains Benjamin Larabee, *The Boston Tea Party* (Boston, 1979).

10. Bernard Bailyn's *The Ideological Origins of the American Revolution* and Gordon S. Wood's "Conspiracy and the Paranoid Style: Causality and Deceit in the Eighteenth Century," *William and Mary Quarterly* 39 (July 1982): 410–441, played a central role in bringing the conceptualization of conspiracy into the early American field. See also Frank Cogliano, *No King, No Popery: Anti-Catholicism in Revolutionary New England* (Westport, CT, 1995), 63–64; Thomas Bernard, *An Appeal to the Public, Stating and Considering the Objections to the Quebec Bill* (London, 1774). Vernon P. Creviston,

"'No King unless It Be a Constitutional King': Rethinking the Place of the Quebec Act in the Coming of the American Revolution," *Historian* 73, no. 3 (Fall 2011): 463–479, lays out the central issues.

11. Cogliano, *No King, No Popery*, 46–52, 53, 62–64, 79; Jeffrey J. Crow, "Tory Plots and Anglican Loyalty: The Llewelyn Conspiracy of 1777," *NCHR* 55 (January 1978): 1–17, suggests that the outburst against popery in 1774 shaped the Protestant associators use of anti-popery. I believe, though, that it is more logical to think that both that reaction during the imperial collapse and the unrest that led to the Association expressed a deeply embedded framework created by the empire itself and carried into the countryside via the chapels and preaching circuits, knowledge of royal rites in the towns, and print culture.

12. Alexander Elusley to Samuel Johnston, London, March 24, 1774, folder 1.78, Johnston Family Series, Hayes Collection, Wilson Library, University of North Carolina, Chapel Hill (hereafter cited as Johnston Family Series); for Johnston on the Intolerable Acts, the quote is as in R. D. W. Conner, *Revolutionary Leaders of North Carolina* (Chapel Hill, 1916), 113.

13. Don Higginbotham, ed., *The Papers of James Iredell*, vol. 1 (Raleigh, 1976), xxiii, liii–liv, 226, 235–237.

14. Higginbotham, *Papers of James Iredell*, 1:336.

15. Higginbotham, *Papers of James Iredell*, 1:397–398, 251–268, 328–338.

16. Saunders, *Colonial Records*, 10:126–127.

17. Saunders, *Colonial Records*, 10:135.

18. Saunders, *Colonial Records*, 10:126–127.

19. "July 14, 1775 Georgia Assembly Petition to King George III," in Ronald G. Killion and Charles T. Waller, eds., *Georgia and the Revolution* (Atlanta, 1975), 152–153; John J. Zubly, *The Law Liberty: Sermon on American Affairs, preached at the opening of the Provincial Congress of Georgia. Addressed to the Right Honourable the Earl of Dartmouth. With an appendix, giving a concise account of the Struggles of Swisserland* [*sic*] *to Recover their liberty* (Philadelphia, 1775), vi; "Part of a Draft of an article or letter on the Quebec Act, 1774," Samuel Avery Papers, 1765–1782, manuscript collection 165, Manuscripts, New York Public Library. During the siege of Boston, a Maryland militiaman scoffed about "the King's Damnation day" when British ships fired their cannons to salute Coronation Day, September 22, the remembrance of George III's ascent to the Protestant throne. "McCurtin's Journal," in Thomas Balch, ed., *Papers Relating Chiefly to the Maryland Line during the Revolution* (Philadelphia, 1857), 17. For the situation in Virginia, see Holton, *Forced Founders*, 77–163, and see 33, 35–38, 209, for reaction to the Quebec Act in Virginia.

20. R. W. D. Connor, *History of North Carolina*, vol. 1: *The Colonial and Revolutionary Periods, 1584–1783* (New York, 1919), 350; Saunders, *Colonial Records*, 10:145.

21. For the committees in the land disputes, see Marjoleine Kars, *Breaking Loose Together: The Regulator Rebellion in Pre-Revolutionary North Carolina* (Chapel Hill, 2002), esp. 133–176, 179–191; and Brendan McConville, *These Daring Disturbers of the Public Peace: The Struggle for Property and Power in Early New Jersey* (Ithaca, 1999), 138–162. For committees in revolutionary Massachusetts, see Richard D. Brown, *Revolutionary Politics in Massachusetts: The Boston Committee of Correspondence and the Towns,*

1772–1774 (New York, 1976); Dirk Hoeder, *Crowd Action in Revolutionary Massachusetts, 1765–1780* (New York, 1977). For Philadelphia, see Richard Alan Ryerson, *The Revolution Is Now Begun: The Radical Committees of Philadelphia, 1765–1776* (Philadelphia, 1978); and for New York, see Edward Countryman, *A People in Revolution: The American Revolution and Political Society in New York, 1760 to 1790* (New York, 1989).

22. Thomas Jones to [?], June 28, 1775, folder 1.83, box 3, Johnston Family Series. For the first discussion of them, see Connor, *History of North Carolina*, 1:354–366.

23. Ashe, *History of North Carolina*, 1:421–422, 423, 473–474, 481–482. At 473n, Ashe makes an interesting distinction. He thinks that in North Carolina, the terms "convention" and "congress" did not mean the same thing. The conventions of August 1774 and April 1775 had only a moderator, not a delegated presiding officer, and sought redress, not rupture. Voting was by individual delegates. In the Congress of 1775, voting was by counties, and the congress acted as an ad hoc legislative body. Robert O. DeMond, *The Loyalists in North Carolina during the Revolution* (Durham, 1940), 64.

24. Saunders, *Colonial Records*, 10:26, 334.

25. Saunders, *Colonial Records*, 10:125–126, 229–230; for Pitt, see 37–38.

26. Saunders, *Colonial Records*, 10:213–214; for the creation of district committees, see 208. For the committees, also see Bessie Lewis Whitaker, *The Provincial Council and Committees of Safety in North Carolina*, James Sprunt Historical Monograph no. 8 (Chapel Hill, 1908), 1–49, esp. 2–3. The creation of six defensive districts, each with a committee, was foreshadowed by efforts late in the imperial period to divide the colony into six legal districts, each with its own superior court. That plan was created by a committee headed by the Edenton jurist Samuel Johnston, and he may have influenced the committee structure suggested at Hillsborough. Saunders, *Colonial Records*, 9:670, 881.

27. Saunders, *Colonial Records*, 10:212. The Surrey County committee declared that "any Member Behaving Disorderly either by Getting Drunk, Swearing, or any other Vice, shall be fined and subject to the same penalties as officers of the Court." Clearly, the Revolution had yet to create the new republican, enlightened man in Surrey County in late 1775, and indeed it never would. See Saunders, *Colonial Records*, 10:254–255. For the Pitt County committee, see Saunders, *Colonial Records*, 10:61. For political violence, see Charles Sellers, "Making a Revolution: The North Carolina Whigs, 1765–1775," in Joseph Carlyle Sitterson, ed., *Studies in Southern History*, vol. 39 of James Sprunt Studies in History and Political Science (Chapel Hill, 1957), 40.

28. Saunders, *Colonial Records*, 10:215.

29. Connor, *History of North Carolina*, 1:351 discusses the transfer of power to the extraordinary congresses / conventions; See Saunders, *Colonial Records*, 10:10, 11–12; for the new money supply, see 10:195. The Hillsborough delegates declared that anyone who refused the Congress's emergency public bills of credit "shall be treated as an enemy to his country."

30. See "In the Committee of New Bern, June 17, 1775," (New Bern, 1775) proclamation for use of the term "enemy of the Country."

31. Saunders, *Colonial Records*, 10:9–10, 34; DeMond, *Loyalists in North Carolina*, 65–66.

32. Robert Smith to Joseph Hewes, Edenton, May 23, 1775, folder 1.83, box 3, Johnston Family Series.

33. Robert Smith to Joseph Hewes, Edenton, May 23, 1775.

34. Samuel Johnston to Joseph Hewes, June 11, 1775, Johnston Family Series, Hayes Collection, Also cited in Sellers, "Making a Revolution," 42; DeMond, *Loyalists in North Carolina*, 64, 66–67. The committee of safety at Nansemond examined its own chairman, Colonel Riddick, who was considered timid. Committees throughout British America went through several waves of purges and resignations in 1774 and 1775. See Laura Page Frech, "The Wilmington Committee of Public Safety and the Loyalist Rising of February, 1776," *NCHR* 41 (January 1964): 21–33, esp. 22. See also Saunders, *Colonial Records*, 10:136. *The New York Journal; Or the General Advertiser*, January 4, 1776, 3.

35. Whitaker, *The Provincial Council*, 1–49, esp. 4–5.

36. Saunders, *Colonial Records*, 10:16–17, 141–151, 231–233; Ashe, *History of North Carolina*, 1:436, 468–469.

37. Ruth Blackwelder, "Attitude of North Carolina Moravians," 1:8–9. For the Committee of Safety's seizure of power at Edenton, see, for example, "The Committee of Safety for the District of Edenton 22nd Febry 1776," folder "Edenton District Committee of Safety," 1776, Edenton District, Records of the Superior Court, 1774–1776, DCR2, D 22, 28, State Archives of North Carolina (SANC); Whitaker, *The Provincial Council*, 46. Saunders, *Colonial Records*, 10:487.

38. Saunders, *Colonial Records*, 10:655–656.

39. "A Letter from the Revd. Mr. Earle, Miss., in North Carolina, dated Edenton, Augst. 30th, 1775, At a General Meeting of the Society for the Propagating the Gospel in Foreign Parts Held January 19th, 1776," microfilm, SPG Journals 1776, SANC.

40. Saunders, *Colonial Records*, 10:237–238. Kellie Slappery, "Rev. Daniel Earle," North Carolina History Project, https://northcarolinahistory.org/encyclopedia/rev-daniel-earle/. "A Letter from the Revd. Mr. Earle, Miss., in North Carolina, May 15, 1775, At a General Meeting of the Society for the Propagating the Gospel in Foreign Parts Held September 15th, 1775," microfilm, SPG Journals 1775, SANC. For an example of a North Carolina minister being removed from their pulpit, see "A Letter from Mr. Reed, Missy in N. Carolina, At a General Meeting of the Society for the Propagating the Gospel in Foreign Parts Held January 19th, 1776," microfilm, SPG Journals 1776, SANC. For the Reverend Earle's career as a fisherman, see the poem cited in Hugh Buckner Johnston, "The Journal of Ebenezer Hazard in North Carolina, 1777 and 1778," *NCHR* 36 (July 1959): 364–365.

41. In a 1772 proclamation, Josiah Martin issued careful orders to ministers on how to pray for the royal family. Saunders, *Colonial Records*, 6:520; Governor Josiah Martin, "Instructions from Martin as to Prayer," Colonial Governors Papers, vol. 8, Governor Josiah Martin, 1771–1775, SANC.

42. Rhys Isaac, *The Transformation of Virginia* (Chapel Hill, 1999), examines the harassment of unlicensed Baptist preachers in the Old Dominion. See also the antiquarian-style study by Lewis Peyton Little, *Imprisoned Preachers and Religious Liberty in Virginia: A Narrative Drawn Largely from the Official Records of Virginia*

Counties, Unpublished Manuscripts, Letters and Other Original Sources (Lynchburg, 1938), which gives a virtual catalogue of attacks on Baptists preachers.

43. Rev. L. C. Vass, *History of the Presbyterian Church of New Bern, N.C., with Resume of Early Ecclesiastical Affairs in Eastern North Carolina and Sketch of the Early Days of New Bern, N.C.* (Richmond, VA, 1886), 77–78, 87–88; for the congregation's reaction to his refusal to preach on the general fast day, see Saunders, *Colonial Records*, 10:115–116, 153.

44. Saunders, *Colonial Records*, 10:122; Bertie County, NC Genproject website, "Loyalists," https://sites.rootsweb.com/~ncbertie/loyalist.htm. In Orange County, the Reverend George Micklejohn was targeted after the loyalist disaster at Moore's Bridge. He was eventually exiled from Orange County. Saunders, *Colonial Records*, 10:646.

45. Saunders, *Colonial Records*, 10:134.

46. Saunders, *Colonial Records*, 10:553–554. John E. Tyler, "The Church of England in Colonial Bertie County" (typescript, SANC), 5.

47. Ashe, *History of North Carolina*, 1:564–565.

48. Records of the Proceedings of the Vestry of St. Paul's Church, Edenton, NC, 1701–1841, p. 262 (typescript from a handwritten copy made by the Reverend R. B. Drane, of Edenton), Church Records, Chowan County, SANC; For the formalization of the role of wardens in society, and managing church affairs, see Saunders, *Colonial Records*, 1:544–545, 558–562, 568–569.

49. Saunders, *Colonial Records*, 9:638–640, describes the chapels and the formal sanction given to the building of one in Currituck County in the northern Albemarle.

50. Crow, "Tory Plots," 2–3, discusses this. See also "A Letter from Rev. Mr. Earl Missy in N. Car. Dated Edenton April 20, 1777. At a General Meeting of the Society for Propagating the Gospel in Foreign Parts, Held March 20th, 1778," SPG Journal 1778, 288–289, microfilm, SANC; Bennett H. Wall, "Charles Pettigrew, First Bishop-Elect of the North Carolina Episcopal Church," *NCHR* 28 (January 1951): 18–20; for the ministers' efforts to avoid political issues, see "A Letter from the Rev. Mr. Pettigrew, Missy in N. Carolina, dated Edenton April 13th, 1776. At a General Meeting of the Society for Propagating the Gospel in Foreign Parts, Held Oct. 18th, 1776," SPG Journal 1776, 102–103, microfilm SANC; Vass, *History of the Presbyterian Church*, 77–78, 87–88; see Saunders, *Colonial Records*, 10:153, for the dismissal of the Reverend Reed of New Bern. For the quote from Willis, see 261, reel Z.5.234, SPG microfilms, SANC. Records of the Proceedings of the Vestry of St. Paul's Church, Edenton, N.C., 1701–1841, p. 262; the Edenton church apparently shut shortly after independence and did not reopen until at least 1778 (p. 265).

51. Brendan McConville, *The King's Three Faces: The Rise and Fall of Royal America* (Chapel Hill, 2006), 306–311, addresses the iconoclastic violence against royal symbols. See also David Waldstreicher, *In the Midst of Perpetual Fetes: The Making of American Nationalism, 1776–1820* (Chapel Hill, 1997), 30–31; Winthrop D. Jordan, "Familial Politics: Thomas Paine and the Killing of the King, 1776," *Journal of American History* 60 (1973): 294–308; Darrett B. Rutman, "George III: The Myth of a Tyrannical King," in Nicholas Cords and Patrick Gerster, eds., *Myth and the American Experience* (New

York, 1973); William D. Liddle, "'A Patriot King, or None': Lord Bolingbroke and the American Renunciation of George III," *Journal of American History* 55 (1979): 951–970; Peter Shaw, *American Patriots and the Rituals of Revolution* (Cambridge, MA, 1981); Benjamin Lewis Price, *Nursing Fathers: American Colonists' Conception of English Protestant Kingship, 1688–1776* (Lanham, 1999).

4. JULY FIFTH

1. W. C. Allen, *History of Halifax County* (Boston, 1918), 37. Fletcher Green, "Listen to the Eagle Scream: One Hundred Years of the Fourth of July in North Carolina (1776–1876)," *North Carolina Historical Review* [*NCHR*] 31, no. 3 (July 1954): 297.

2. For the problems with the salt supply, see R. L. Hilldrup, "The Salt Supply of North Carolina during the American Revolution," *NCHR* 22 (October 1945): 393–417. For problems with counterfeiting, see Walter Clark, ed., *The State Records of North Carolina* (Winston, 1895–1907), 11:317. Deposition of Daniel Legate, Edenton District Superior Court, Depositions from Persons in Bertie, Chowan, Hyde, Martin and Tyrrell Counties relative to charges against John Lewellen . . . and others for Treason, 1777, Misc. Records, 1699–1865, CRX box 4, Court Records, State Archives of North Carolina (SANC). J. R. B. Hathaway, ed., *North Carolina Historical and Genealogical Register* (Edenton, 1900–1903) (hereafter cited as *NCHGR*), 2:396–397.

3. Gordon S. Wood, *The Creation of the American Republic* (Chapel Hill, 1969), 363.

4. R. W. D. Connor, *History of North Carolina*, vol. 1: *The Colonial and Revolutionary Periods, 1584–1783* (New York, 1919), 86–87. William L. Saunders, ed., *The Colonial Records of North Carolina* (Raleigh, 1886–1890), 10:265; C. B. Alexander, "Richard Caswell: Versatile Leader of the Revolution," *NCHR* 23 (April 1946): 124.

5. Saunders, *Colonial Records*, 10:943–949; Gerald W. Thomas, *Rebels and King's Men: Bertie County in the Revolutionary War* (Raleigh, 2013), 98–99.

6. Clark, *State Records*, 11:421, 438.

7. Richard Caswell to Thomas Burke, New Bern, May 13, 1777, Governor Richard Caswell Correspondence, Governors Papers, vol. 1, January 10, 1777–September 20, 1777, 30–35, SANC (hereafter cited as Caswell Correspondence). See, generally, Caswell Correspondence, January 10, 1777–September 20, 1777: Richard Caswell to Thomas Burke, New Bern, May 13, 1777, Caswell Correspondence, 30–35. On July 17, 1777, Lt. Col. Robert Mebane wrote to Governor Caswell to report that the efforts of the officers of the state's Seventh Battalion to recruit more men had failed. The chief reason given by the recruiting officers, Mebane wrote, "is want of money." See also John Resch and Walter Sargent, eds., *War and Society in the American Revolution* (DeKalb, 2007), especially the excellent essays by Charles Neimeyer, Walter Sargent, John Resch, and Michael McDonnell. These essays make it clear that nowhere did mobilization occur without issue. An interesting essay by Wayne Lee in the same volume details the role of militia units in the internal fighting in North Carolina later in the war. See Wayne Lee, "Restraint and Retaliation: The North Carolina Militias and the Backcountry War of 1780–1782," in Resch and Sargent, *War and Society*, 163–190. For a general discussion of these changes, see John Shy, *A People Numerous and Armed:*

Reflections on the Military Struggle for American Independence (Oxford, 1976), 29–42, 117–132, 163–180, 213–244.

8. Deposition of Joseph Taylor, June 4, 1777, Oyer and Terminer, Edenton District, September 1777, Edenton District Records of the Superior Court, 1774–1779, SANC. For William Tyler, see *NCHGR,* 2:404, 567.

9. Deposition of William Hyman, July 4, 1777, Sworn before John Everitt, Edenton District Superior Court, Depositions from Persons in Bertie, Chowan, Hyde, Martin and Tyrrell Counties relative to charges against John Lewellen . . . and others for Treason, 1777, Misc. Records, 1699–1865, CRX box 4, SANC; *NCHGR,* 2:398; Deposition of Benjamin Harrison, Tyrrell County, July 16, 1777, Edenton District Superior Court, Depositions from Persons in Bertie, Chowan, Hyde, Martin and Tyrrell Counties relative to charges against John Lewellen . . . and others for Treason, 1777, Misc. Records, 1699–1865, CRX box 4, Court Records, SANC. Deposition of Stephen Garrett, Tyrrell County, July 16, 1777, Chowan County Papers, vol. 15, 1772–1777, 137, CR 024. 928.15, SANC.

10. Saunders, *Colonial Records,* 10:632. North Carolina had substantial Quaker and Moravian populations; the former were in place in substantial numbers in the Albemarle region, and they would generally not repudiate the pacifism that lay at their theological core. Baptists in the state also claimed pacifism as a tenet in some cases. See Saunders, *Colonial Records,* 10:699–700; for an incident with a Baptist minister, see 10:134. Such problems were hardly confined to North Carolina. See Michael McDonnell, "Fit for Common Service?," in Resch and Sargent, *War and Society,* 103–131.

11. For a clear account of the colony in the Seven Years War, see John R. Maass, *The French and Indian War in North Carolina: The Spreading Flames of War* (Charleston, SC, 2013).

12. Samuel Johnston Jr. to Joseph Hewes, Halifax, April 4, 1776, folder 1.88, box 4, Johnston Family Series, Hayes Collection, Wilson Library, University of North Carolina, Chapel Hill. Johnston worried to Hewes that "it seems a matter of uncertainty whether the French will join us or risqué [risk] a quarrel with Great Britain on our account." Samuel Johnston Jr. to Joseph Hewes, Halifax, April 11, 1776, folder 1.88, box 4, Johnston Family Series, Hayes Collection.

13. William Byrne, *History of the Catholic Church in the New England States* (Boston, 1899), 4; J. Thomas Scharf, *History of Maryland from the Earliest Period to the Present Day* (Hatboro, 1967), 221–222; Thomas Jones, *History of New York during the Revolutionary War, and of the Leading Events in the Other Colonies at That Period,* vol. 1 (New York, 1879), 92. Jones comments on the hypocrisy of Congress in denouncing the Quebec Act and then trying to enlist the Canadians in the rebellion. See also Amy Noel Ellison, "'Reverse of Fortune': The Invasion of Canada and the Coming of American Independence, 1774–1776" (PhD diss., Boston University, 2016). Clark, *State Records,* 11:421, 422, 423, and for a letter announcing the arrival of a large number of munitions from France, see 11:433; *The North Carolina Gazette,* July 11, 1777, 2. It is difficult to gauge the impact of newspaper stories among the semiliterate yeomen population. See also Elisha P. Douglass, "Thomas Burke, Disillusioned Democrat," *NCHR* 26 (April 1949): 150–186.

14. Don Higginbotham, ed., *The Papers of James Iredell*, vol. 1 (Raleigh, 1976), 448, 449n; for the French merchants throwing a ball, see 1:449–450.

15. Governor Richard Caswell to John Ashe, Esq., New Bern, July 3, 1777, Caswell Correspondence, July 5–6, pp. 48–52.

16. Governor Richard Caswell to Governor Patrick Henry, New Bern, June 10, 1777, Caswell Correspondence, 36–40; John Rutledge to Governor Richard Caswell, Charleston, June 25, 1777, Caswell Correspondence, 46–47; Higginbotham, *Papers of James Iredell*, 1:449n.

17. Deposition of Nathan Hallaway, July 4, 1777, Oyer and Terminer, Edenton District, September 1777, Edenton District Records of the Superior Court, 1774–1779, SANC.

18. Deposition of David Taylor, June 4, 1777, Oyer and Terminer, Edenton District, September 1777, Edenton District Records of the Superior Court, 1774–1779, SANC; Joseph Taylor swore "if the popish Religion was brought into the land that they were to take up arms to oppose them that brought it."

19. See Brendan McConville, "A Deal with the Devil: Revolutionary Anti-Popery, Francophobia, and the Dilemmas of Diplomacy," in Evan Haefeli, ed., *Against Popery: Britain, Empire, and Anti-Catholicism* (Charlottesville, 2020), 203–233.

20. John Brickell, *The Natural History of North Carolina* (Dublin, Ireland, 1737), 40; B. W. C. Roberts, "Cockfighting: An Early Entertainment in North Carolina," *NCHR* 42, no. 3 (July 1965): 306. Higginbotham, *Papers of James Iredell*, 1:176, 197–198, 204. Roberts, "Cockfighting," 309, describes the Wilmington, North Carolina, Jockey Club, founded in 1774, as dedicated to both horse racing and cockfighting. The club also apparently hosted gambling sessions that lasted until early in the morning, a practice bemoaned by some. For the presence of silk handkerchiefs in the region, see "The Estate of George Marshal, deceased," folder 1, John Nisbet Papers, Wilson Library, University of North Carolina, Chapel Hill (hereafter cited as Nisbet Papers). See also Ashe, *History of North Carolina*, 1:377–395.

21. James Iredell's papers reveal that the Albemarle gentry spent a considerable portion of their lives reading, often alone, the great works current among the refined in Europe. One will inventory from the region taken in 1775 revealed a reader who valued Locke, Pope, Swift, and Shakespeare as well as Enfield's *Sermons* and volumes on British history and military tactics. For an example of Iredell reading Blackstone, see Higginbotham, *Papers of James Iredell*, 1:193–194. Inventory, 1775, folder 1.81, Johnston Family Series, Hayes Collection. In North Carolina, literacy proved a determinate of status in Edenton and the Albemarle. Church ministers ran schools for young gentlemen, at least sporadically, in the Albemarle area beginning early in the eighteenth century. Many in Edenton, especially among the leaders, had some formal education. Ashe, *History of North Carolina*, 1:386–387, 389, 390. In 1765 Governor Tryon noted the extent of ignorance, as he called it, and blamed it on a lack of schools. See Saunders, *Colonial Records*, 7:104.

22. Higginbotham, *Papers of James Iredell*, 1:173.

23. For the rural enlightenment and the Protestant ministry's ambiguous relationship to it, see John Fea, *The Way of Improvement Leads Home: Philip Vickers Fithian and the Rural Enlightenment in America* (Philadelphia, 2009), 33–155.

24. See, for example, the depositions of Thomas Harrison (son of John) and Thomas Harrison Sr., July 14, 1777, Tyrrell County, Edenton District Superior Court, Depositions from persons in Bertie, Chowan, Hyde, Martin and Tyrrell Counties relative to charges against John Lewelling and others for treason, 1777, Beaufort, Bertie, Carteret, Chowan, Davidson, Davie, Edenton District, Forsyth, Guilford, Lenoir, Madison, and Pasquotank Counties, Misc. Records, 1699–1865, CRX box 4, SANC; Jeffrey J. Crow, "Tory Plots and Anglican Loyalty: The Llewelyn Conspiracy of 1777," *NCHR* 55 (January 1978): 6. For the broader tensions over these "worldly" heresies, see, for example, John Witherspoon, *Christian Magnanimity; a sermon, preached at Princeton, September 1775—the Sabbath Preceding the annual Commencement, and again with additions, September 23, 1787. To which is added, an address to the senior class, who were to receive the degree of Bachelor of Arts. By John Witherspoon, D.D. LLD, president of the College of New-Jersey* (Princeton, 1787), 1–2; Israel Evans, *A Discourse, Delivered at Easton, on the 17th of October, 1779, to the officers and soldiers of the Western Army, after their return from an expedition against the five nations of hostile Indians. By the Reverend Israel Evans, A. M. and Chaplain to General Poor's brigade. Now published at the particular request of the generals and field officers of that army, and to be distributed among the soldiers—Gratis* (Philadelphia, 1779), 5–6. For the American Enlightenment, see Henry May, *The Enlightenment in America* (New York, 1978); see also Robert Ferguson, *The American Enlightenment* (Cambridge, MA, 1997). Protestant yeomen generally eyed suspiciously any deviance from their understanding of Christianity.

5. CONVENTIONS OF THE PEOPLE

1. Several studies discuss state constitution making. For that which most directly addresses North Carolina, see Elisha Douglass, *Rebels and Democrats: The Struggle for Equal Political Rights and Majority Rule during the American Revolution* (New York, 1989), esp. 71–135. Douglass is correct in assuming that "democratic" impulses ran through the proto-state, though I find his efforts to link various issues strained. G. Alan Tarr, *Understanding State Constitutions* (Princeton, 1998), 60–93, examines the structural differences in state constitutions. Tarr follows the logic of constitutional development articulated by Donald Lutz in a range of works. See Donald S. Lutz, *Popular Consent and Popular Control: Whig Political Theory in the Early State Constitutions* (Baton Rouge, 1980); Lutz, *The Origins of American Constitutionalism* (Baton Rouge, 1988); Lutz, "The Purposes of American State Constitutions," *Publius* 12 (Winter 1982): 27–44; Willi Paul Adams, *The First American Constitutions: Republican Ideology and the Making of State Constitutions in the Revolutionary Era* (New York, 2001); Marc Kruman, *Between Authority and Liberty: State Constitution Making in Revolutionary America* (Chapel Hill, 1997); Gordon S. Wood, *The Creation of the American Republic, 1776–1787* (Chapel Hill, 1969), 65–161. Connecticut and Rhode Island effectively continued with their preexisting frames of government, stripping away imperial symbols and the loyalty oaths to the British monarchy. Of the governors in place in the thirteen colonies in 1773, only Connecticut's Jonathan Trumbull remained in place on January 1, 1777.

NOTES TO PAGES 84–87

2. William L. Saunders, ed., *The Colonial Records of North Carolina* (Raleigh, 1886–1890), 10:xix–xx. Saunders directly links this view about simplicity to Benjamin Franklin. Saunders's inclusion of Caswell in this is interesting. Once elected governor, Caswell became an advocate for a mixed government and for a strong executive. At the nation's dawn, many who would later be quite conservative revolutionaries embraced radical or unorthodox political ideas, only to abandon them as the Revolution unfolded and the war dragged on.

3. Saunders, *Colonial Records*, 10:xix. I follow here in some respects Samuel Ashe, *History of North Carolina*, vol. 1: *1584–1783* (repr., Raleigh, 1971), 557–559. I also draw on the text and annotation in *The Papers of James Iredell*. For a dated but still useful account of the origins of the constitution, see Earle H. Ketcham, "The Sources of the N.C. Constitution of 1776," *North Carolina Historical Review [NCHR]* 6, no. 3 (July 1929): 215–236. See also Fletcher Green, *Constitutional Development in the South Atlantic States, 1776–1860: A Study in the Evolution of Democracy* (New York, 1971), 48–49, for discussion of the constitutional controversies in the state.

4. Saunders, *Colonial Records*, 10:xix, 498–499; Ashe, *History of North Carolina*, 1:528–529; Don Higginbotham, ed., *The Papers of James Iredell*, vol. 1 (Raleigh, 1976), 350–351.

5. The assemblymen needed 100 acres and senators 300 acres to stand for office in this compromise. See Elisha Douglass, "Thomas Burke, Disillusioned Democrat," *NCHR* 26 (April 1949): 156–160.

6. See Winthrop D. Jordan, "Familial Politics: Thomas Paine and the Killing of the King, 1776," *Journal of American History* 60 (1973): 294–308. For broader discussions of the meanings and implications of the rebellion against patriarchy, see Peter Shaw, *American Patriots and the Rituals of Revolution* (Cambridge, MA, 1981), and especially Gordon S. Wood, *The Radicalism of the American Revolution* (New York, 1991), 145–168.

7. In *The King's Three Faces: The Rise and Fall of Royal America* (Chapel Hill, 2006), 306–312, I discuss this iconoclasm and its political implications.

8. For a view of the Interregnum's Commonwealth governments, see Austin Woolrych, *England without a King* (London, 1983), esp. 9–29, and Woolrych, *Commonwealth to Protectorate* (London, 1982), esp. 1–67. The influence of the constitutional experiments in Britain between 1649 and 1659 on the American revolutionaries is grossly underestimated. Clearly, the Council of State government instituted in 1649 in England after Charles I's execution foreshadowed the Pennsylvania Constitution of 1776 in many ways.

9. Ketcham, "The Sources," 225–226; Ashe, *History of North Carolina*, 1:530; Higginbotham, *Papers of James Iredell*, 1:356; Ketcham, "The Sources," 226. R. W. D. Connor, *History of North Carolina*, vol. 1: *The Colonial and Revolutionary Periods, 1584–1783* (New York, 1919), 375–376, suggests that the provisional assemblies in 1775 and 1776 had toyed with or experimented with plural executives.

10. Connor, *History of North Carolina*, 1:411; Francis Nash, *Hillsboro Colonial and Revolutionary* (Raleigh, 1903), 47; Ashe, *History of North Carolina*, 1:558, 564. Higginbotham, *Papers of James Iredell*, 1:420–421, reprints James Iredell's satirical "Creed of a Rioter," long believed to have been written in response to this disorder. Higginbotham questioned the piece's origins and whether the disorder was actually directed against Samuel Johnston, and whether the Iredell piece is about the electoral violence at all.

Higginbotham was engaging Robert L. Ganyard's, "Radicals and Conservatives in Revolutionary North Carolina: A Point at Issue, the October Election, 1776," *William and Mary Quarterly* 24 (October 1967): 568–587. It seems to me there was some disorder; there was a bitterly disputed election for convention delegates occurred in Guilford County. Although it was clear that some things happened, a committee of the convention insisted there was "no Riot or disorderly Behaviour in the Electors." See Saunders, *Colonial Records,* 10:921–922. R. W. D. Conner, *Revolutionary Leaders of North Carolina* (Chapel Hill, 1916), insists there was intense dispute, especially in Chowan County, and that Wylie Jones, who became a central figure in the unrest in 1777, led the radical, anti-Johnston faction in the struggle over the state constitution. See Kruman, *Between Authority and Liberty,* 20.

11. Saunders, *Colonial Records,* 10:819–820.

12. Ashe, *History of North Carolina,* 1, 564, 56in; Charles Francis Adams, ed., *The Works of John Adams,* vol. 4 (Boston, 1851), 203, 206, 208–209; see also Ketcham, "The Sources," 227, 228. Walter Clark, ed., *The State Records of North Carolina* (Winston, 1895–1907), 11:321–327; see 324–325 for Adams's attack on unicameralism.

13. Saunders, *Colonial Records,* 10:866–868.

14. Saunders, *Colonial Records,* 10:862, 868. Nash, *Hillsboro Colonial,* 47; Ashe, *History of North Carolina,* 1:563. William Hooper may well have been the source of these constitutional models. At the end of October 1776 he wrote from Philadelphia, where he served as a delegate to the Continental Congress, to the Halifax Congress, about "applying the experimental knowledge" he had gained by observation in Philadelphia, "to the benefit of our own state." Saunders, *Colonial Records,* 10:862.

15. Articles XII–XVI, North Carolina Constitution of 1776 (Avalon Project, Yale University); Ketcham, "The Sources," 218; 233–234. Articles V–VIII and XV, North Carolina Constitution of 1776 (Avalon Project, Yale University). For the defining of the governor's powers as being "for the Time being," see articles XVIII and XIX.

16. Depositions of Thomas Harrison (son of John), July 14, 1777, Tyrrell County, Edenton District Superior Court, Depositions from persons in Bertie, Chowan, Hyde, Martin and Tyrrell Counties relative to charges against John Lewelling and others for treason, 1777, Beaufort, Bertie, Carteret, Chowan, Davidson, Davie, Edenton District, Forsyth, Guilford, Lenoir, Madison, and Pasquotank Counties, Misc. Records, 1699–1865, CRX box 4, State Archives of North Carolina. Ernst Cassirer, *The Philosophy of the Enlightenment* (Boston, 1955); Peter Gay, *The Enlightenment: An Interpretation—The Rise of Modern Paganism* (New York, 1966); Henry May, *The Enlightenment in America* (New York, 1976); David Lundberg and Henry May, "The Enlightened Reader in America," *American Quarterly* 28 (1976); Charles Miller, *Jefferson and Nature: An Interpretation* (Baltimore, 1988); John Gray, *Enlightenment's Wake: Politics and Culture at the Close of the Modern Age* (London, 1995); Jonathan Israel, *Radical Enlightenment: Philosophy and the Making of Modernity, 1650–1750* (New York, 2002); James Schmidt, "Inventing the Enlightenment: Anti-Jacobins, British Hegelians, and the 'Oxford English Dictionary,'" *Journal of the History of Ideas* 64, no. 3 (July 2003): 441; Lorraine Daston and M. Stolleis, eds., *Natural Law and Laws of Nature in Early Modern Europe* (Surrey, 2008); Anthony J. La Vopa, "A New Intellectual History? Jonathan Israel's

Enlightenment," *Historical Journal* 52, no. 3 (2009): 717–738; Jonathan Israel, *A Revolution of the Mind: Radical Enlightenment and the Intellectual Origins of Modern Democracy* (Princeton, 2011); Anthony Pagden, *The Enlightenment: And Why It Still Matters* (New York, 2013); Nathalie Caron and Naomi Wolf, "American Enlightenments: Continuity and Renewal," *Journal of American History* (March 2013): 1072–1091; Jonathan M. Dixon, "Henry F. May and the Revival of the American Enlightenment: Problems and Possibilities for Intellectual and Social History," *William and Mary Quarterly*, 3rd. ser., 71, no. 2 (April 2014): 255–280.

17. For Robert Jones, Willie's father, see Ashe, *History of North Carolina*, 1:295, and James P. Beckwith Jr., "Robert (Robin) Jones, Jr.," NCPedia, https://www.ncpedia.org/biography/jones-robert-robin-jr.

18. Blackwell Pierce Robinson, "Willie Jones of Halifax," pt. 1, *NCHR* 18 (January 1941): 1, 144–145, 169–170; See also Samuel Elliott Morison, "The Willie Jones–John Paul Jones Tradition," *William and Mary Quarterly* 16, no. 2 (April 1959): 198–206.

19. Robinson, "Willie Jones of Halifax," 3. The meaning of this pledge is unclear. His various eccentricities were well known, though, in eastern North Carolina. In regard to his children, see Donna Kelly and Lang Baradell, eds., *The Papers of James Iredell*, vol. 3: *1784–1789* (Raleigh, 2003), 100n.

20. Saunders, *Colonial Records*, 8:583; Robinson, "Willie Jones of Halifax." For his ownership of large numbers of slaves, see Robinson, "Willie Jones of Halifax," 8. For his ownership of slaves in 1790, see Walter Clark, ed., *The State Records of North Carolina, 26th Census, 1790* (Goldsboro, 1905), 733.

21. W. C. Allen, *History of Halifax County* (Boston, 1918), 26–27; Ashe, *History of North Carolina*, 1:559; Saunders, *Colonial Records*, 10:283.

22. Although resident in Martin County, Hill owned lands in Bertie and Tyrrell Counties as well. His 1797 will makes no mention of Jesus Christ. It begins "in the name of God amen." "I Surrender my spiritual hart to my creator trusting in his mercies so to dispose of it as his infinite wisdom but knows." Last Will and Testament of Whitmel Hill, folder 1, Whitmel Hill Collection, 03099-z, Special Collections and Manuscripts, Wilson Library, University of North Carolina, Chapel Hill. For his self-referencing as an infidel, see David L. Swain, "Life and Letters of Whitmill Hill," *North Carolina University Magazine*, March 1861, 391. The letter was written in 1780.

23. Last Will and Testament of Whitmel Hill.

24. Last Will and Testament of Whitmel Hill; William S. Powell, ed., *Dictionary of North Carolina Biography* (Chapel Hill, 1979), 3:140–141; Saunders, *Colonial Records*, 10:283.

25. See ncrevwar.lostsoulsgenealogy.com/tories/johnwilliamllewellynar.htm; R. D. W. Connor, *Cornelius Harnett: An Essay in North Carolina History* (Raleigh, 1909), for Harnett's deathbed comments at 198–199; see also "A Son of the Enlightenment," North Carolina History Project website, Sam Hummel and Ed McCormick, curators. Conner, *Revolutionary Leaders*, 73.

26. For a discussion of Burke, see Douglass, "Thomas Burke, Disillusioned Democrat," 150–186, and see 153 for his religious views, and 153–154 for his views of himself as a global citizen.

27. Ashe, *History of North Carolina*, 1:562–563. For the declaration itself, see Saunders, *Colonial Records*, 10:870a; for additional information about Mecklenburg yeomen's views about what they understood as popery and heresy, see 10:239–241, "Instructions for the Delegates of Mecklenburg County proposed to the Consideration of the County." The instructions included orders to accept the "39 Articles of the Church of England excluding the 37th Article . . . and not to be imposed on the dissenters, by the act of toleration. . . . to be the Religion of the State to the utter exclusion forever of all and every other (falsely so called) Religion, whether Pagan or Papal. . . . You are moreover to oppose the establishing an ecclesiastical supremacy in the sovereign authority of the State. You are to oppose the toleration of popish idolatrous worship." Ashe, *History of North Carolina*, 1:566.

28. Ashe, *History of North Carolina*, 1:566, 567–568; Sarah McCulloh Lemmon, "The Genesis of the Protestant Episcopal Diocese of North Carolina, 1701–1823," *NCHR* 23 (October 1951): 450; Higginbotham, *Papers of James Iredell*, 1:425.

29. Ashe, *History of North Carolina*, 1:566, 568, 569.

6. THE HOUSE OF FEAR

1. Deposition of Daniel Legate, Edenton District Superior Court, Depositions from Persons in Bertie, Chowan, Hyde, Martin and Tyrrell Counties relative to charges against John Lewellen . . . and others for Treason, 1777, Misc. Records, 1699–1865, CRX box 4, Court Records, State Archives of North Carolina (SANC).

2. For the term "Brethren," see the Deposition of Michael Ward, Bertie County, July 9, 1777, Edenton District Superior Court, Depositions from persons in Bertie, Chowan, Hyde, Martin and Tyrrell Counties relative to charges against John Lewelling and others for treason, 1777, Beaufort, Bertie, Carteret, Chowan, Davidson, Davie, Edenton District, Forsyth, Guilford, Lenoir, Madison, and Pasquotank Counties, Misc. Records, 1699–1865, CRX box 4, SANC.

3. Deposition of Thomas Harrison, July 14, 1777, Edenton District Superior Court, Depositions from Persons in Bertie, Chowan, Hyde, Martin and Tyrrell Counties relative to charges against John Lewellen . . . and others for Treason, 1777, Misc. Records, 1699–1865, CRX box 4, Court Records, SANC. This was illiterate Thomas Harrison, who signed his deposition with an X. Thomas Harrison Sr. also believed that the fourteen assemblymen intended to introduce popery. See Deposition of Thomas Harrison Sr., July 14, 1777, Edenton District Superior Court, Depositions from Persons in Bertie, Chowan, Hyde, Martin and Tyrrell Counties relative to charges against John Lewellen . . . and others for Treason, 1777, Misc. Records, 1699–1865, CRX box 4, Court Records, SANC. "Deposition of William May Jr., June 19th, 1777 Sworn before me. . . . Robert Salley," Edenton District, Records of the Superior Court, 1774–1779, SANC; Deposition of Armel Holles, Oyer and Terminer, Edenton District, September 1777, Edenton District Records of the Superior Court, 1774–1779, SANC.

4. Examination of Peleg Belote, Bertie County, August 12, 1777, Edenton District Superior Court, Depositions from Persons in Bertie, Chowan, Hyde, Martin and

Tyrrell Counties relative to charges against John Lewellen ... and others for Treason, 1777, Misc. Records, 1699–1865, CRX box 4, SANC.

5. Deposition of Joseph Taylor, June 4, 1777, Oyer and Terminer, Edenton District, September 1777, Edenton District Records of the Superior Court, 1774–1779, SANC; Deposition of Nathan Hallaway, July 4, 1777, Oyer and Terminer, Edenton District, September 1777, Edenton District Records of the Superior Court, 1774–1779, SANC. Deposition of William Durrance, Depositions of Tyrrell County, July 14, 1777, Edenton District Superior Court, Depositions from Persons in Bertie, Chowan, Hyde, Martin and Tyrrell Counties relative to charges against John Lewellen ... and others for Treason, 1777, Misc. Records, 1699–1865, CRX box 4, Court Records, SANC; *NCHGR*, 2:209–210; Deposition of James Harrison, Tyrrell County, July 14, 1777, Edenton District Superior Court, Depositions from Persons in Bertie, Chowan, Hyde, Martin and Tyrrell Counties relative to charges against John Lewellen ... and others for Treason, 1777, Misc. Records, 1699–1865, CRX box 4, Court Records, SANC.

6. Deposition of John Stewart, July 19, 1777, Martin County, Edenton District Superior Court, Depositions from Persons in Bertie, Chowan, Hyde, Martin and Tyrrell Counties relative to charges against John Lewellen ... and others for Treason, 1777, Misc. Records, 1699–1865, CRX box 4, Court Records, SANC.

7. *NCHGR*, 2:211. Supplemental deposition of Daniel Legate (Legett), July 14, 1777, Edenton District Superior Court, Depositions from Persons in Bertie, Chowan, Hyde, Martin and Tyrrell Counties relative to charges against John Lewellen ... and others for Treason, 1777, Misc. Records, 1699–1865, CRX box 4, Court Records, SANC.

8. See Thomas L. Purvis, "High Born, Long-Recorded Families: Social Origins of the New Jersey Assemblymen, 1703–1776," *William and Mary Quarterly*, 3rd ser., 37, no. 4 (October 1980): 592–615; John Morrill, *The Revolt in the Provinces: Conservatives and Radicals in the English Civil War, 1630–1650* (London, 1977); Brendan McConville, *The King's Three Faces: The Rise and Fall of Royal America* (Chapel Hill, 2006), 156–157.

See Charles Lee Raper, *North Carolina: A Study in English Colonial Government* (New York, 1904), esp. 226. For the role of political fathers in dispensing patronage, see P. M. G. Harris, "Social Origins of American Leaders," in Donald Fleming and Bernard Bailyn, eds., *Perspectives in American History* (Cambridge, MA, 1969) 3:159–346; Bernard Bailyn, *The Origins of American Politics* (New York, 1968), 99; John M. Murrin and Gary Kornblith, "The Making and Unmaking of an American Ruling Class," in Alfred F. Young, ed., *Beyond the American Revolution: Explorations in the History of American Radicalism* (DeKalb, 1993), 27–79; Brendan McConville, *These Daring Disturbers of the Public Peace: The Struggle for Property and Power in Early New Jersey* (Ithaca, 1999), 111–115; Roger Champagne, "Family Politics versus Constitutional Principles: The New York Assembly Elections of 1768 and 1769," *William and Mary Quarterly* 20 (1963): 57–73; McConville, *The King's Three Faces*, 152–159.

Jessica Kross, "'Patronage Most Ardently Sought': The New York Council, 1665–1775," in Bruce C. Daniels, ed., *Power and Status: Officeholding in Colonial America* (Middletown, 1986), 218–219. Beyond the Kross essay, see those by Ronald K. Snell, Bruce Daniels, Lorena Walsh, Richard Ryerson, and Grace L. Chickering.

9. Deposition of Benjamin Harrison, son of Thomas, July 16, 1777, Tyrrell County, Edenton District Superior Court, Depositions from Persons in Bertie, Chowan, Hyde, Martin and Tyrrell Counties relative to charges against John Lewellen . . . and others for Treason, 1777, Misc. Records, 1699–1865, CRX box 4, Court Records, SANC. For Lewellen and Hays, see deposition of Thomas Harrison, son of John, Tyrrell County, July 14, 1777, Chowan County Papers, XV, 1772–1777, 133, CR 024. 928.15, SANC. For Daniel Legate, see the Deposition of Jerosiah Everett, Tyrrell County, July 15, 1777, Chowan County Papers, XV, 1772–1777, 135, CR 024. 928.15, SANC; *NCHGR,* 2:397.

10. Supplemental Deposition of Daniel Legate (Legett), July 14, 1777, Edenton District Superior Court, Depositions from Persons in Bertie, Chowan, Hyde, Martin and Tyrrell Counties relative to charges against John Lewellen . . . and others for Treason, 1777, Misc. Records, 1699–1865, CRX box 4, Court Records, SANC; *NCHGR,* 2:208, 209, 210–212, 214, 215, 390–391, 396–397, 397–398, 568–569, 571. Deposition of James Rawlings, Martin County, August 10, 1777, Oyer and Terminer, Edenton District, September 1777, Edenton District Records of the Superior Court, 1774–1779, SANC; Walter Clark, ed., *The State Records of North Carolina* (Winston, 1895–1907), 11:747; see also Raymond Parker Fouts, compiler, *Marriages of Bertie County, North Carolina, 1762–1868* (Baltimore, 1982), 61.

11. "To the Worshipful Justices of Newbern" from James Rawlings [no date], Oyer and Terminer, Edenton District, September 1777, Edenton District Records of the Superior Court, 1774–1779, SANC; *NCHGR,* 2:568, 396.

12. Martin County, Records of Deeds, Deed Book A, 1774–1787, SANC; Claiborne T. Smith Jr., "John Lewelling," NCpedia, https://www.ncpedia.org/biography /lewelling-john. District 5, Martin County Census, 1784, State Census Taken under Act of 1784, Martin-Wilkes, GO 131, SANC. District 1, Martin County Census, 1784, State Census Taken under Act of 1784, Martin-Wilkes, GO 131, SANC.

13. Additional Deposition of James Rawlins of Martin County, Oyer and Terminer, Edenton District, September 1777, Edenton District Records of the Superior Court, 1774–1779, SANC; Deposition of John Stewart, July 19, 1777, Martin County, Edenton District Superior Court, Depositions from Persons in Bertie, Chowan, Hyde, Martin and Tyrrell Counties relative to charges against John Lewellen . . . and others for Treason, 1777, Misc. Records, 1699–1865, CRX box 4, Court Records, SANC. For deference in an ethnically diverse society, see McConville, *These Daring Disturbers of the Public Peace,* 47–66, esp. 47–50; John Smolenski, "From Men of Property to Just Men: Deference, Masculinity, and the Evolution of Political Discourse in Early America," *Early American Studies* 3 (2005): 253–285; Richard Beeman, *The Varieties of Political Experience in Eighteenth-Century America* (Philadelphia, 2006), esp. 8–68.

14. Deposition of William Durrance, July 14, 1777, Tyrrell County, Edenton District Superior Court, Depositions from Persons in Bertie, Chowan, Hyde, Martin and Tyrrell Counties relative to charges against John Lewellen . . . and others for Treason, 1777, Misc. Records, 1699–1865, CRX box 4, Court Records, SANC; for Bird Land, see the Deposition of Bird Land, July 16, 1777, Tyrrell County, Edenton District

Superior Court, Depositions from Persons in Bertie, Chowan, Hyde, Martin and Tyrrell Counties relative to charges against John Lewellen . . . and others for Treason, 1777, Misc. Records, 1699–1865, CRX box 4, Court Records, SANC. Bird Land, like so many others involved with the Brethren, was illiterate.

15. Deposition of Armel Holles, Oyer and Terminer, Edenton District, September 1777, Edenton District Records of the Superior Court, 1774–1779, SANC. For James Harrison Jr., see Deposition of James Harrison, son of James Harrison, July 14, 1777, Tyrrell County, Edenton District Superior Court, Depositions from Persons in Bertie, Chowan, Hyde, Martin and Tyrrell Counties relative to charges against John Lewellen . . . and others for Treason, 1777, Misc. Records, 1699–1865, CRX box 4, Court Records, SANC. For Harrison Sr., see also the Deposition of Thomas Harrison Sr., Tyrrell County, July 14, 1777, Edenton District Superior Court, Depositions from Persons in Bertie, Chowan, Hyde, Martin and Tyrrell Counties relative to charges against John Lewellen . . . and others for Treason, 1777, Misc. Records, 1699–1865, CRX box 4, Court Records, SANC. *NCHGR*, 2:209–211, 212, 567, 214–215; Deposition of William Howard, July 15, 1777, Edenton District Superior Court, Depositions from Persons in Bertie, Chowan, Hyde, Martin and Tyrrell Counties relative to charges against John Lewellen . . . and others for Treason, 1777, Misc. Records, 1699–1865, CRX box 4, Court Records, SANC.

16. Deposition of James Rawlins of Martin County, Oyer and Terminer, Edenton District, September 1777, Edenton District Records of the Superior Court, 1774–1779, SANC. For example, John Stewart recalled discussing the Brethren with Samuel Black at Capt. Everett's muster. *NCHGR*, 2:217.

17. Deposition of John Stewart, July 19, 1777, Martin County, Edenton District Superior Court, Depositions from Persons in Bertie, Chowan, Hyde, Martin and Tyrrell Counties relative to charges against John Lewellen . . . and others for Treason, 1777, Misc. Records, 1699–1865, CRX box 4, Court Records, SANC. The further Deposition of Thomas Harrison, July 14, 1777, Edenton District Superior Court, Depositions from Persons in Bertie, Chowan, Hyde, Martin and Tyrrell Counties relative to charges against John Lewellen . . . and others for Treason, 1777, Misc. Records, 1699–1865, CRX box 4, Court Records, SANC.

18. Daniel Legate owned a hundred acres in Tyrrell County in 1784. Nothing in the record suggests that he was anything other than a yeoman. List of the Taxable Property in County Tyrrell 1784, G.A. 64.1., SANC. *NCHGR*, 2:394. When John Garrett (also referred to as McGarrett) recruited Lemuel Hyman, he referred him to Daniel Legate to be sworn in. Deposition of Benjamin Harrison, son of Thomas, July 16, 1777, Tyrrell County Edenton District Superior Court, Depositions from Persons in Bertie, Chowan, Hyde, Martin and Tyrrell Counties relative to charges against John Lewellen . . . and others for Treason, 1777, Misc. Records, 1699–1865, CRX box 4, Court Records, SANC. For Lewellen and Hays, see deposition of Thomas Harrison, son of John, Tyrrell County, July 14, 1777, Chowan County Papers, XV, 1772–1777, 133, CR 024. 928.15, SANC. For Daniel Legate, see Deposition of Jerosiah Everett, Tyrrell County, July 15, 1777, Chowan County Papers, XV, 1772–1777, 135, CR 024. 928.15, SANC; *NCHGR*, 2:397.

19. Deposition of Benjamin Harrison, son of Thomas, July 16, 1777, Tyrrell County, Edenton District Superior Court, Depositions from Persons in Bertie, Chowan, Hyde, Martin and Tyrrell Counties relative to charges against John Lewellen . . . and others for Treason, 1777, Misc. Records, 1699–1865, CRX box 4, Court Records, SANC. For Lewellen and Hays, see Deposition of Thomas Harrison, son of John, Tyrrell County, July 14, 1777, Chowan County Papers, XV, 1772–1777, 133, CR 024. 928.15, SANC. For Sherrard, see also *NCHGR*, 2:396–397. For Legate, see Deposition of Jerosiah Everett, Tyrrell County, July 15, 1777, Chowan County Papers, XV, 1772–1777, 135, SANC. For Tyler, see, for example, Deposition of William May, Sworn before Robert Salley, June 19, Oyer and Terminer, Edenton District, September 1777, Edenton District Records of the Superior Court, 1774–1779, SANC. For Garrett, see Deposition of Armel Holles, Oyer and Terminer, Edenton District, September 1777, Edenton District Records of the Superior Court, 1774–1779, SANC; and the deposition of William Howard reproduced in *NGHGR*, 2:567. The inclusion of John Stewart on this list is intriguing given that Stewart testified that he avoided actual membership, though he did seem to recruit people. Or it may be another Stewart, of whom we are unaware. For the senior wardens' identification, see Deposition of William May, Sworn before Robert Salley, June 19, Oyer and Terminer, Edenton District, September 1777, Edenton District Records of the Superior Court, 1774–1779, SANC. Deposition of Thomas Harrison Sr., Tyrrell County, July 14, 1777, Edenton District Superior Court, Depositions from Persons in Bertie, Chowan, Hyde, Martin and Tyrrell Counties relative to charges against John Lewellen . . . and others for Treason, 1777, Misc. Records, 1699–1865, CRX box 4, Court Records, SANC. In regard to Brimage, see also Deposition of Bird Land, July 16, 1777, Edenton District Superior Court, Depositions from Persons in Bertie, Chowan, Hyde, Martin and Tyrrell Counties relative to charges against John Lewellen . . . and others for Treason, 1777, Misc. Records, 1699–1865, CRX box 4, Court Records, SANC; for Brimage, see also *NCHGR*, 2:212. James Sherrard was called a "senior warden" by James Rawlings. See Deposition of Daniel Legate, August 13, 1777, Edenton District Superior Court, Depositions from Persons in Bertie, Chowan, Hyde, Martin and Tyrrell Counties relative to charges against John Lewellen . . . and others for Treason, 1777, Misc. Records, 1699–1865, CRX box 4, Court Records, SANC. Almost all the scholars who have touched on this episode have noted the connection of the Brethren's institutional structures to those of the Church of England. See, for example, Gerald W. Thomas, *Rebels and King's Men: Bertie County in the Revolutionary War* (Raleigh, 2013), 73–76.

20. Alan Watson, *Bertie County: A Brief History* (Raleigh, 1982), 67, addresses William Brimage's wealth. John Lewellen, Martin County, Records of Deeds, Deed Book A, p. 273, 1774–1787, SANC. Lewellen's deed was filed in 1780. District 5, Martin County Census, 1784, State Census Taken Under Act of 1784, Martin-Wilkes, GO 131, SANC. List of the Taxable Property in County Tyrrell 1784, G.A. 64.1, SANC. Deposition of Thomas Harrison Sr., Tyrrell County, July 14, 1777, Edenton District Superior Court, Depositions from Persons in Bertie, Chowan, Hyde, Martin and Tyrrell Counties relative to charges against John Lewellen . . . and others for Treason, 1777, Misc. Records, 1699–1865, CRX box 4, Court Records, SANC. For Brimage, see *NCHGR*, 2:212.

21. I determined this through an examination of the depositions in SANC, and those documents published in *NCHGR;* Clark, *State Records,* vol. 11.

22. Deposition of William Jordain, Oyer and Terminer, Edenton District, September 1777, Edenton District Records of the Superior Court, 1774–1779, SANC. For additional uses of the term "solicitor," see Deposition of Nathan Everett, Tyrrell County, July 15, 1777, Chowan County Papers, XV, 1772–1777, 135, CR 024. 928.15, SANC. See also Deposition of James Hollis, Tyrrell County, July 15, 1777, Chowan County Papers, XV, 1772–1777, 136, CR 024. 928.15, SANC.

23. Deposition of John Burkey, Oyer and Terminer, Edenton District, September 1777, Edenton District Records of the Superior Court, 1774–1779, SANC; Deposition of Salvanas Buttery, Oyer and Terminer, Edenton District, September 1777, Edenton District Records of the Superior Court, 1774–1779, SANC. Deposition of William Jordain, Oyer and Terminer, Edenton District, September 1777, Edenton District Records of the Superior Court, 1774–1779, SANC; Deposition of James Harrison, July 16, 1777, Misc. Records, 1699–1865, CRX box 4, Court Records, SANC.

24. Robert Smith to Governor Richard Caswell, July 31, 1777, Governor Richard Caswell Correspondence, Governors Papers, vol. 1, 94–96, SANC; Supplemental Deposition of Daniel Legate (Legett), July 14, 1777, Edenton District Superior Court, Depositions from Persons in Bertie, Chowan, Hyde, Martin and Tyrrell Counties relative to charges against John Lewellen . . . and others for Treason, 1777, Misc. Records, 1699–1865, CRX box 4, Court Records, SANC. Deposition of Thomas Harrison, son of John, July 14, 1777, Edenton District Superior Court, Depositions from Persons in Bertie, Chowan, Hyde, Martin and Tyrrell Counties relative to charges against John Lewellen . . . and others for Treason, 1777, Misc. Records, 1699–1865, CRX box 4, Court Records, SANC; Supplemental Deposition of Daniel Legate (Legett), July 14, 1777, Edenton District Superior Court, Depositions from Persons in Bertie, Chowan, Hyde, Martin and Tyrrell Counties relative to charges against John Lewellen . . . and others for Treason, 1777, Misc. Records, 1699–1865, CRX box 4, Court Records, SANC.

25. Robert Smith to Governor Richard Caswell, July 31, 1777, Governor Richard Caswell Correspondence, Governors Papers, vol. 1, 94–96, SANC; Deposition of Thomas Harrison, son of John, July 14, 1777, Edenton District Superior Court, Depositions from Persons in Bertie, Chowan, Hyde, Martin and Tyrrell Counties relative to charges against John Lewellen . . . and others for Treason, 1777, Misc. Records, 1699–1865, CRX box 4, Court Records, SANC.

26. Deposition of William Skyles, Oyer and Terminer, Edenton District, September 1777, Edenton District Records of the Superior Court, 1774–1779, SANC. Deposition of James Rawlins, Hyde County, August 6, Edenton District Superior Court, Depositions from Persons in Bertie, Chowan, Hyde, Martin and Tyrrell Counties relative to charges against John Lewellen . . . and others for Treason, 1777, Misc. Records, 1699–1865, CRX box 4, Court Records, SANC. Supplemental Deposition of Daniel Legate (Legett), July 14, 1777, Edenton District Superior Court, Depositions from Persons in Bertie, Chowan, Hyde, Martin and Tyrrell Counties relative to charges against John Lewellen . . . and others for Treason, 1777, Misc. Records, 1699–1865, CRX box 4, Court Records, SANC. *NCHGR,* 2:239, 393–395, 399, 401–402. Identifying associators

and their residence was difficult, as the line between associator and non-associator was often gray and the records too incomplete to make certain identifications in a number of cases. I drew on the depositions and other documents published in the *NCHGR;* Clark, *State Records,* vol. 11; Supplemental Deposition of Daniel Legate (Legett), July 14, 1777, Edenton District Superior Court, Depositions from Persons in Bertie, Chowan, Hyde, Martin and Tyrrell Counties relative to charges against John Lewellen . . . and others for Treason, 1777, Misc. Records, 1699–1865, CRX box 4, Court Records, SANC. For Henry Irwin's view of the situation in Tarborough, see Lt. Colonel Henry Irwin to Governor Caswell, Tarborough, July 16, 1777, Governor Richard Caswell Correspondence, July 14–16, 1777, Governors Papers, vol. 1, 58–59, SANC. Deposition of James Rawlins of Martin County, August 10, 1777, Oyer and Terminer, Edenton District, September 1777, Edenton District Records of the Superior Court, 1774–1779, SANC. The records of the Oyer and Terminer, Edenton District, September 1777, Edenton District Records of the Superior Court, 1774–1779, SANC; Deposition of John Brogdon, Windsor, July 1, 1777, Edenton District Superior Court, Depositions from Persons in Bertie, Chowan, Hyde, Martin and Tyrrell Counties relative to charges against John Lewellen . . . and others for Treason, 1777, Misc. Records, 1699–1865, CRX box 4, Court Records, SANC.

27. John Gray Blount to His Excellency Governor Richard Caswell, Contentney, July 5, 1777, Governor Richard Caswell Correspondence, July 5–6, Governor Papers I, 53–54, SANC; *NCHGR,* 2:393–395.

28. Affidavit of Benjamin Harrison, July 16, 1777, Tyrrell County, Edenton District Superior Court, Depositions from Persons in Bertie, Chowan, Hyde, Martin and Tyrrell Counties relative to charges against John Lewellen . . . and others for Treason, 1777, Misc. Records, 1699–1865, CRX box 4, Court Records, SANC. Hays owned 126 acres in the Parish of St. Andrews. Deed Book 4, pt. 1, 139-(189), The Deeds of Tyrrell County, North Carolina, 1760–1770 (transcript, 1991), SANC, 12. In February 1769 he purchased an additional 100 acres at the Flat Swamp. He was illiterate in 1769 when he left his mark on the transfer recorded August 1769. Deed 590-(312), Deed Book 4, pt. 2, The Deeds of Tyrrell County North Carolina 1760–1770 (transcript, 1991), SANC, 51.

29. Deposition of Thomas (X) Harrison, July 14, 1777, Tyrrell County, Chowan County Court Papers, XV, 1772–1777, 133, SANC. Deposition of Thomas Harrison (son of John), July 14, 1777, Tyrrell County; and further deposition of Thomas (X) Harrison (son of John), July 14, 1777, Tyrrell County Edenton District Superior Court, Depositions from Persons in Bertie, Chowan, Hyde, Martin and Tyrrell Counties relative to charges against John Lewellen . . . and others for Treason, 1777, Misc. Records, 1699–1865, CRX box 4, Court Records, SANC. For other claims for the movement's extension, see *NCHGR,* 2:393. Deposition of John Brogdon, Windsor, July 1, 1777, Edenton District Superior Court, Depositions from Persons in Bertie, Chowan, Hyde, Martin and Tyrrell Counties relative to charges against John Lewellen . . . and others for Treason, 1777, Misc. Records, 1699–1865, CRX box 4, Court Records, SANC; Deposition of Jonathan Adams, Tyrrell County, July 17, 1777, Chowan County Papers, XV, 1772–1777, 136, SANC; *NCHGR,* 2:395. The Deposition of James Rawlins, Edenton District Superior Court, Depositions from Persons in Bertie, Chowan, Hyde, Martin and

Tyrrell Counties relative to charges against John Lewellen ... and others for Treason, 1777, Misc. Records, 1699–1865, CRX box 4, Court Records, SANC. See also Deposition of John Brogdon, Windsor, July 1, 1777 Edenton District Superior Court, Depositions from Persons in Bertie, Chowan, Hyde, Martin and Tyrrell Counties relative to charges against John Lewellen ... and others for Treason, 1777, Misc. Records, 1699–1865, CRX box 4, Court Records, SANC. For other mentions of the Virginia connection, see *NCGHR*, 2:393. Governor Richard Caswell Correspondence, box 2, Correspondence, September 22, 1777–April 18, 1778, SANC.

30. Robert Smith to Governor Richard Caswell, July 31, 1777, Governor Richard Caswell Correspondence, Governors Papers, vol. 1, 94–96, SANC; Governor Richard Caswell Letterbook, 147–148, 1775–1779, GLB 1.1, SANC.

31. Deposition of James Rawlings, Oyer and Terminer, Edenton District, September 1777, Edenton District Records of the Superior Court, 1774–1779, SANC.

32. Deposition of James Rawlings, Oyer and Terminer, Edenton District, September 1777, Edenton District Records of the Superior Court, 1774–1779, SANC. Deposition of James Rawlings, Edenton District Superior Court, Depositions from persons in Bertie, Chowan, Hyde, Martin and Tyrrell Counties relative to charges against John Lewelling and others for treason, 1777, Beaufort, Bertie, Carteret, Chowan, Davidson, Davie, Edenton District, Forsyth, Guilford, Lenoir, Madison, and Pasquotank Counties, Misc. Records, 1699–1865, CRX box 4, SANC. *NCHGR*, 2:399; Deposition of Thomas Harrison, Senior, called to give further evidence, July 14, 1777, Tyrrell County, Edenton District Superior Court, Depositions from Persons in Bertie, Chowan, Hyde, Martin and Tyrrell Counties relative to charges against John Lewellen ... and others for Treason, 1777, Misc. Records, 1699–1865, CRX box 4, Court Records, SANC. In regard to the copying of the constitution, see Deposition of John Stewart, July 19, 1777, Martin County, Edenton District Superior Court, Depositions from Persons in Bertie, Chowan, Hyde, Martin and Tyrrell Counties relative to charges against John Lewellen ... and others for Treason, 1777, Misc. Records, 1699–1865, CRX box 4, Court Records, SANC.

33. William L. Saunders, ed., *The Colonial Records of North Carolina* (Raleigh, 1886–1890), 10:476. "State of North Carolina, June 17, 1777," Chowan County Papers, XV, 1772–1777, 126, CR 024. 928.15, SANC.

34. Deposition of James Harrison (son of James Harrison), July 15, 1777, Tyrrell County, Edenton District Superior Court, Depositions from persons in Bertie, Chowan, Hyde, Martin and Tyrrell Counties relative to charges against John Lewelling and others for treason, 1777, Beaufort, Bertie, Carteret, Chowan, Davidson, Davie, Edenton District, Forsyth, Guilford, Lenoir, Madison, and Pasquotank Counties, Misc. Records, 1699–1865, CRX box 4, SANC. Also in *NCHGR*, 2:214, 568.

35. *NCHGR*, 2:396; Examination of Peleg Belote, Bertie, August 12, 1777, Edenton District Superior Court, Depositions from Persons in Bertie, Chowan, Hyde, Martin and Tyrrell Counties relative to charges against John Lewellen ... and others for Treason, 1777, Misc. Records, 1699–1865, CRX box 4, Court Records, SANC. Further Deposition of Thomas Harrison (son of John), Tyrrell County, July 14, 1777, Edenton District Superior Court, Depositions from persons in Bertie, Chowan, Hyde, Martin

and Tyrrell Counties relative to charges against John Lewelling and others for treason, 1777, Beaufort, Bertie, Carteret, Chowan, Davidson, Davie, Edenton District, Forsyth, Guilford, Lenoir, Madison, and Pasquotank Counties, Misc. Records, 1699–1865, CRX box 4, SANC.

36. Supplemental Deposition of Daniel Legate (Legett), July 14, 1777, Edenton District Superior Court, Depositions from Persons in Bertie, Chowan, Hyde, Martin and Tyrrell Counties relative to charges against John Lewellen . . . and others for Treason, 1777, Misc. Records, 1699–1865, CRX box 4, Court Records, SANC. Eight swore one oath, 23 swore to the first two oaths, 6 swore three oaths, and 2 took four oaths, all of which he carefully noted. The remaining 13 had no notation next to their name, although it is clear that some of these people also became involved to varying degrees. Deposition of William Hyman, July 4, 1777, Edenton District Superior Court, Depositions from persons in Bertie, Chowan, Hyde, Martin and Tyrrell Counties relative to charges against John Lewelling and others for treason, 1777, Beaufort, Bertie, Carteret, Chowan, Davidson, Davie, Edenton District, Forsyth, Guilford, Lenoir, Madison, and Pasquotank Counties, Misc. Records, 1699–1865, CRX box 4, SANC. See also the efforts to recruit Nathan Hallaway [Hattaway], *NCHGR*, 2:569–570.

37. *NCHGR*, 2:209.

38. Deposition of James Rawlins of Martin County, August 10, 1777, Oyer and Terminer, Edenton District, September 1777, Edenton District Records of the Superior Court, 1774–1779, SANC.

39. *NCHGR*, 2:392. Deposition of Nathan Hallaway, July 4, 1777, Oyer and Terminer, Edenton District, September 1777, Edenton District Records of the Superior Court, 1774–1779, SANC. See also Deposition of John Brogdon, Windsor, July 1, 1777, Edenton District Superior Court, Depositions from Persons in Bertie, Chowan, Hyde, Martin and Tyrrell Counties relative to charges against John Lewellen . . . and others for Treason, 1777, Misc. Records, 1699–1865, CRX box 4, Court Records, SANC. For the efforts to recruit Hallaway, see Deposition of Nathan Hallaway, Oyer and Terminer, Edenton District, September 1777, Edenton District Records of the Superior Court, 1774–1779, SANC. Also in *NCHGR*, 2:569–570.

40. "Examination of John Clifton taken in the County Court of Bertie at the court held on the 12th day of August 1777," Oyer and Terminer, Edenton District, September 1777, Edenton District Records of the Superior Court, 1774–1779, SANC. For the spelling out of "Be True," see also "Examination of Nathan Hallaway, 4th July, 1777," taken before John Everett, Edenton District, September 1777, Edenton District Records of the Superior Court, 1774–1779, SANC. Deposition of John Brogdon, Windsor, July 1, 1777, Edenton District Superior Court, Depositions from Persons in Bertie, Chowan, Hyde, Martin and Tyrrell Counties relative to charges against John Lewellen . . . and others for Treason, 1777, Misc. Records, 1699–1865, CRX box 4, Court Records, SANC. *NCHGR*, 2:394, 393.

41. Deposition of Charles Rhodes, Tyrrell County, July 15, 1777, Chowan County Papers, XV, 1772–1777, 137. SANC; Deposition of Josiah Harrison, Tyrrell County, July 16, 1777, Chowan County Papers, XV, 1772–1777, 137, SANC. William Skyles also mentions INRJ "lettering" as it was known. Deposition of William Skyles, Windsor,

July 1, 1777, Edenton District Superior Court, Depositions from Persons in Bertie, Chowan, Hyde, Martin and Tyrrell Counties relative to charges against John Lewellen ... and others for Treason, 1777, Misc. Records, 1699–1865, CRX box 4, Court Records, SANC.

42. Deposition of John Brogdon, Windsor, July 1, 1777, Edenton District Superior Court, Depositions from Persons in Bertie, Chowan, Hyde, Martin and Tyrrell Counties relative to charges against John Lewellen ... and others for Treason, 1777, Misc. Records, 1699–1865, CRX box 4, Court Records, SANC. William Skyles also mentions hand signs and rubbing. Deposition of William Skyles, Windsor, July 1, 1777, Edenton District Superior Court, Depositions from Persons in Bertie, Chowan, Hyde, Martin and Tyrrell Counties relative to charges against John Lewellen ... and others for Treason, 1777, Misc. Records, 1699–1865, CRX box 4, Court Records, SANC. For Skyles (Skiles), see also *NCHGR*, 2:394, 393.

7. Becoming Known, Becoming Loyalists

1. "James Rawlins, of Martin County, fleeing from thence to Mattimuskeet, being there apprehended on a Report that he had a hand in a Conspiracy carried on against the State of North Carolina, Deposeth and Saith," Deposition of James Rawlins of Martin County, August 10, 1777, Oyer and Terminer, Edenton District, September 1777, Edenton District Records of the Superior Court, 1774–1779, State Archives of North Carolina (SANC).

2. J. R. B. Hathaway, ed., *North Carolina Historical and Genealogical Register* (Edenton, 1900–1903) (hereafter cited as *NCHGR*), 2:568; Deposition of John Stewart, July 19, 1777, Martin County, Edenton District Superior Court, Depositions from persons in Bertie, Chowan, Hyde, Martin and Tyrrell Counties relative to charges against John Lewelling and others for treason, 1777, Beaufort, Bertie, Carteret, Chowan, Davidson, Davie, Edenton District, Forsyth, Guilford, Lenoir, Madison, and Pasquotank Counties, Misc. Records, 1699–1865, CRX box 4, SANC.

3. Deposition of James Rawlins of Martin County, Oyer and Terminer, Edenton District, September 1777, Edenton District Records of the Superior Court, 1774–1779, SANC; Deposition of James Rawlings, Edenton District Superior Court, Depositions from persons in Bertie, Chowan, Hyde, Martin and Tyrrell Counties relative to charges against John Lewelling and others for treason, 1777, Beaufort, Bertie, Carteret, Chowan, Davidson, Davie, Edenton District, Forsyth, Guilford, Lenoir, Madison, and Pasquotank Counties, Misc. Records, 1699–1865, CRX box 4, SANC. Deposition of David Taylor, June 4, 1777, taken before John Everitt, Oyer and Terminer, Edenton District, September 1777, Edenton District Records of the Superior Court, 1774–1779, SANC. Deposition of Joseph Taylor, Sworn before John Everitt, June 4, 1777, Oyer and Terminer, Edenton District, September 1777, Edenton District Records of the Superior Court, 1774–1779, SANC.

4. Nathan Mayo would go on to be a Lt. Colonel in the Martin County militia and a state legislature representative for Martin County and then Edgecombe County. "James

Mayo," https://www.WikiTree.com; "Nathan Mayo," https://www.WikiTree.com; Walter Clark, ed., *The State Records of North Carolina* (Winston, 1895–1907), 20:272; "Nathan Mayo," https://www.rootsweb.com; The American Revolution in North Carolina, https://www.carolana.com/NC/Revolution/home.html. Rufus Nathan Grimes, *The Grimes-Llewellyn Families 1635–1972*, www.grimestree.net, 57–61. For Mayo's conversion, see ncrevwar.lostsoulsgenealogy.com/patriots/colonelnathanmayoar.htm.

5. Additional Deposition of James Rawlins of Martin County, Oyer and Terminer, Edenton District, September 1777, Edenton District Records of the Superior Court, 1774–1779, SANC; Deposition of Joseph Taylor, Sworn before John Everitt, June 4, 1777, Oyer and Terminer, Edenton District, September 1777, Edenton District Records of the Superior Court, 1774–1779, SANC; Affidavit of Thomas Harrison (son of John), July 14, 1777, Tyrrell County, Edenton District Superior Court, Depositions from Persons in Bertie, Chowan, Hyde, Martin and Tyrrell Counties relative to charges against John Lewellen . . . and others for Treason, 1777, Misc. Records, 1699–1865, CRX box 4, Court Records, SANC; *NCHGR*, 2:401; Blackwell Pierce Robinson, "Willie Jones of Halifax, Part II," *North Carolina Historical Review [NCHR]* 2 (April 1941): 133–134.

6. *NCHGR*, 2:401, 403. Carole Troxler, *The Loyalist Experience in North Carolina* (Raleigh, 1976), 12–14; Grimes, *The Grimes-Llewellyn Families*, 57–61. Claiborne T. Smith Jr., "John Lewelling," NCpedia, https://www.ncpedia.org/biography/lewelling-john. Lewellen owned lands directly abutting those of Nathan Mayo. J. R. B. Hathaway, the original editor of the depositions, claims that the first person to actually give the government information about the Brethren was William Mayo, brother of James and Nathan Mayo. But there is no deposition from William Mayo in SANC, and Hathaway does not reproduce it in his edition. However, James Rawlings did claim the same thing about William Mayo when he was deposed on August 10, 1777. See August 10 Deposition of James Rawlings of Martin County, September 1777, Llewelyn Treason Trial, Oyer and Terminer, Edenton District, September 1777, Edenton District Records of the Superior Court, 1774–1779, SANC. For the Mayo family's origins in Virginia, see "Nathan Mayo," https://wc.rootsweb.com › trees › nathan-mayo › individual.

7. For Lewellen's view of James Mayo, see Deposition of Thomas Best, September 9, 1777, Oyer and Terminer, Edenton District, September 1777, Edenton District Records of the Superior Court, 1774–1779, SANC. For Lewellen's anger toward the Mayo brothers and Whitmel Hill, see "To the Worshipful Justices of Newbern" from James Rawlings, [no date], Oyer and Terminer, Edenton District, September 1777, Edenton District Records of the Superior Court, 1774–1779, SANC.

8. Deposition of Thomas Best, September 9, 1777, Oyer and Terminer, Edenton District, September 1777, Edenton District Records of the Superior Court, 1774–1779, SANC; "To the Worshipful Justices of Newbern" from James Rawlings, [no date] Oyer and Terminer Edenton District, September 1777, Edenton District Records of the Superior Court, 1774–1779, SANC.

9. August 10 Deposition of James Rawlings of Martin County, September 1777, Llewelyn Treason Trial, Oyer and Terminer, Edenton District, September 1777, Edenton District Records of the Superior Court, 1774–1779, SANC; for Lewellen's continuing

anger, see Testimony of Henry Culpeper, Sworn before Blake Wiggins, September 3, 1777, Llewelyn Treason Trial, Oyer and Terminer, Edenton District, September 1777, Edenton District Records of the Superior Court, 1774–1779, SANC.

10. For the identities and roles of those he named as targets, see "Whitmell Hill," Biographical Dictionary of the United States Congress, https://bioguideretro .congress.gov/; William L. Saunders, ed., *The Colonial Records of North Carolina* (Raleigh, 1886–1890), 10:215; "Pitt County Regiment of Militia," The American Revolution in North Carolina, https://www.carolana.com/NC/Revolution/nc_pitt_county _regiment.html; Saunders, *Colonial Records*, 10:295, 531; *NCHGR*, 2:126. Whitmell Hill and Colonel Robert Salter were in contact with one another, so my suspicion is he is the "Salter" mentioned here. See John Gray Blount to His Excellency Governor Richard Caswell, Contentney, July 5, 1777, Governor Richard Caswell Correspondence, July 5–6, Governor Papers, vol. 1, 53–54, SANC.

11. Deposition of James Rawlins of Martin County, August 10, 1777, Oyer and Terminer, Edenton District, September 1777, Edenton District Records of the Superior Court, 1774–1779, SANC; "Examination of John Clifton taken in the County Court of Bertie at the Court held on the 12th day of August 1777," Oyer and Terminer, Edenton District, September 1777, Edenton District Records of the Superior Court, 1774–1779, SANC. Deposition of Henry Culpeper, September 3, 1777, Oyer and Terminer, Edenton District, September 1777, Edenton District Records of the Superior Court, 1774–1779, SANC.

12. Deposition of James Rawlins of Martin County, August 10, 1777, Oyer and Terminer, Edenton District, September 1777, Edenton District Records of the Superior Court, 1774–1779, SANC; "Examination of John Clifton taken in the County Court of Bertie at the Court held on the 12th day of August 1777," Oyer and Terminer, Edenton District, September 1777, Edenton District Records of the Superior Court, 1774–1779, SANC. The Deposition of William Skyles, Windsor July 1, 1777, at a Court held this Day for the Purpose of Enquiring into Sundry Suspicions Against persons below mentioned. . . . Edenton District Superior Court, Depositions from Persons in Bertie, Chowan, Hyde, Martin and Tyrrell Counties relative to charges against John Lewellen . . . and others for Treason, 1777, Misc. Records, 1699–1865, CRX box 4, Court Records, SANC; Deposition of Thomas Best, September 9, 1777, Oyer and Terminer, Edenton District, September 1777, Edenton District, Records of the Superior Court, 1774–1779, SANC.

13. Deposition of David Taylor, June 4, 1777, taken before John Everitt, Oyer and Terminer, Edenton District, September 1777, Edenton District Records of the Superior Court, 1774–1779, SANC.

14. "Examination of John Clifton taken in the County Court of Bertie at the Court held on the 12th day of August 1777," Oyer and Terminer, Edenton District, September 1777, Edenton District Records of the Superior Court, 1774–1779, SANC.

15. "Examination of John Clifton taken in the County Court of Bertie at the Court held on the 12th day of August 1777," Oyer and Terminer, Edenton District, September 1777, Edenton District Records of the Superior Court, 1774–1779, SANC. The effort to recruit William May also reveals the sudden turn toward Loyalist militancy.

NOTES TO PAGES 135-139

Approached by William Tylor [Tyler], May swore to help "keep out popish Religion, if we could." He also pledged himself to help those drafted unwillingly into the state forces. But as May's conversation with Tyler continued, it took a more hostile turn against the state government. Tyler declared the Brethren "sofishantly strong" to oppose "any power that should offer the state oath." *NCHGR*, 2:404. Gerald Thomas suggests that the militant turn was driven by the new Assembly's April meeting, which created a new loyalty oath and passed a new militia law. There is reasonable logic to this, but Lewellen and others had been organizing on the basis of resistance to heresy, popery, and forced drafts, and the depositions repeatedly reference the confrontation between Mayo and Lewellen. They nowhere discuss the militia law, though the oath was an issue. See Gerald W. Thomas, *Rebels and King's Men: Bertie County in the Revolutionary War* (Raleigh, 2013), 71-73.

16. *NCHGR*, 2:396. Hodge was illiterate, and mentions at the end of his deposition an effort to teach him to "letter," which, unsurprisingly, apparently failed.

17. *NCHGR*, 2:211, 215. Further Testimony of James Harrison, Tyrrell County, July 16, 1777, Edenton District Superior Court, Depositions from persons in Bertie, Chowan, Hyde, Martin and Tyrrell Counties relative to charges against John Lewelling and others for treason, 1777, Beaufort, Bertie, Carteret, Chowan, Davidson, Davie, Edenton District, Forsyth, Guilford, Lenoir, Madison, and Pasquotank Counties, Misc. Records, 1699-1865, CRX box 4, SANC.

18. Deposition of Salvinas Buttrey, Oyer and Terminer, Edenton District, September 1777, Edenton District Records of the Superior Court, 1774-1779, SANC. I use the quote from Lewellen here with certain trepidation. It originates from a Mayo family genealogy done at some point in the past. For a variety of reasons I believe it to be a fragment from a document no longer in the collections of SANC. See ncrevwar .lostsoulsgenealogy.com/tories/johnwilliamllewellynar.htm.

19. Deposition of Thomas Best, September 9, 1777, Oyer and Terminer, Edenton District, September 1777, Edenton District Records of the Superior Court, 1774-1779, SANC. Deposition of James Rawlins of Martin County, Oyer and Terminer, Edenton District, September 1777, Edenton District Records of the Superior Court, 1774-1779, SANC.

20. *NCHGM*, 2:400.

21. Brendan McConville, *The King's Three Faces: The Rise and Fall of Royal America* (Chapel Hill, 2006), 175-182, discusses provincial slave royalism and, paradoxically, the fear that slaves would run off to the Catholic enemy. See also Jill Lepore, *New York Burning: Liberty, Slavery and Conspiracy in Eighteenth-Century Manhattan* (New York, 2005); for some interesting ideas about the political meaning of slave unrest, see Marcus Rediker and Peter Linebaugh, *The Many-Headed Hydra: Sailors, Slaves, Commoners, and the Hidden History of the Revolutionary Atlantic* (New York, 2013), 135-139, 190-203, 241-242. Peter Wood, *Black Majority: Negroes in Colonial South Carolina from 1670 through the Stono Rebellion* (New York, 1974), remains a classic study of slave resistance in the Carolinas. See also Philip Morgan, *Slave Counterpoint: Black Culture in the Eighteenth-Century Chesapeake and Low Country* (Chapel Hill, 1998); and Anthony Parent, *Foul Means: The Formation of a Slave Society in Virginia, 1660-1740* (Chapel Hill,

2003). Barry Gaspar, *Bondsmen and Rebels: A Study in Master-Slave Relations in Antigua* (Durham, 1993); Winthrop Jordon, *Tumult and Silence at Second Creek: An Inquiry into a Civil War Slave Conspiracy* (Baton Rouge, 1993). I have also benefited from conversations with Peter Silver of Rutgers University concerning purported slave unrest in the 1730s and early 1740s.

22. *The Newport Mercury,* May 29, 1775, 3. On fear of slaves in the Hudson River Valley, see Michael E. Groth, "Black Loyalists and African American Allegiance in the Mid-Hudson Valley," in Joseph S. Tiedemann, Eugene R. Fingerhut, and Robert W. Venables, eds., *The Other Loyalists: Ordinary People, Royalism and the Revolution in the Middle Colonies, 1763–1787* (Albany, 2009), 85–86. On fear of slaves in other northern states, see, for example, *Pennsylvania Archives,* 1st ser., vol. 6 (Philadelphia, 1853), 792.

23. I parallel here Woody Holton's treatment of the issue in Holton, *Forced Founders: Indians, Debtors, Slaves and the Making of the American Revolution in Virginia* (Williamsburg, 1999), esp. 133–163, and am influenced by Michael McDonnell's extended treatment of the impact of war on Virginia society and race relations; see Michael McDonnell *The Politics of War: Race, Class and Conflict in Revolutionary Virginia* (Chapel Hill, 2007). As early as August 1775, newspapers were carrying accounts of slaves fleeing to the British navy in the Norfolk area. See *Pennsylvania Evening Post,* August 15, 1775, 2. Patriot leaders long invoked Dunmore's actions to legitimate independence and their own actions during a long and bloody war. See, for example, Clark, *State Records,* 13:432–433; and *The North Carolina Gazette,* June 6, 1778, "The Grand Jury for the district of Edenton to the Honorable James Iredell, Esq., one of the Judges of the superior Court held at Edenton." See also James C. David, *Dunmore's New World: The Extraordinary Life of a Royal Governor in Revolutionary America* (Charlottesville, 2013), 94–108; Philip D. Morgan and Andrew Jackson O'Shaughnessy, "Arming Slaves in the American Revolution," in Christopher Brown and Philip D. Morgan, eds., *Arming Slaves from Classical Times to the Modern Age* (New Haven, 2006), 180–108; Alan Taylor, *American Revolutions: A Continental History, 1750–1804* (New York, 2016), 146–151; Sylvia Frey, "Between Slavery and Freedom: Virginia Blacks in the American Revolution," *Journal of Southern History* 49 (August 1983): 375–398; Robert A. Olwell, "'Domestick Enemies': Slavery and Political Independence in South Carolina, May 1775–March 1776," *Journal of Southern History* 55 (February 1989): 33–34; McConville, *The King's Three Faces,* 175–182.

24. Marvin L. Michael Kay and Lorin Lee Cary, *Slavery in North Carolina, 1748–1775* (Chapel Hill, 1995), 19, 22, 221, 226–227. Saunders, *Colonial Records,* 5:320, provides a breakdown of the slave population in the colony by county in 1754 as part of the General List of Taxables. See also W. Neil Franklin, "Agriculture in Colonial North Carolina," *NCHR* 3 (October 1926): 549. Perhaps the best examination of slave unrest in North Carolina is Jeffrey Crow, "Slave Rebelliousness and Social Conflict in North Carolina, 1775 to 1802," *William and Mary Quarterly,* 3rd ser., 37 (January 1980): 79–102. See also R. H. Taylor, "Slave Conspiracies in North Carolina," *NCHR* 5 (January 1928): 20–34, esp. 30–31. Also useful is Alan Watson, "Impulse towards Independence: Resistance and Rebellion among North Carolina Slaves, 1750–1775," *Journal of Negro History* 63 (Fall 1978): 317–328; Alan D. Watson, "North Carolina Slave Courts,

1715–1785," *NCHR* 60 (January 1983): 24–36; Donna J. Spindal, *Crime and Society in North Carolina, 1663–1776* (Baton Rouge, 1989). *In the Committee at New Bern,* May 31, 1775, folder 1.83, box 3, Johnston Family Series, Hayes Collection, Wilson Library, University of North Carolina, Chapel Hill.

25. Saunders, *Colonial Records,* 10:11–12, 21, 22, 24–25.

26. Leora H. McEachern and Isabel M. Williams, eds., *Wilmington–New Hanover Safety Committee Minutes, 1774–1776* (Wilmington, 1974), 45, 47; Don Higginbotham, ed., *The Papers of James Iredell,* vol. 1 (Raleigh, 1976), 313; Saunders, *Colonial Records,* 10:118.

27. McEachern and Williams, *Safety Committee Minutes,* 45, 47. Saunders, *Colonial Records,* 10:43, 138; Robert O. DeMond, *The Loyalists in North Carolina during the Revolution* (Durham, 1940), 73–74. Martin's reply to Lewis Henry DeRosset about the issue only served to further tensions. On June 24, 1775, Martin declared in regard to arming slaves, "I never conceived a thought of that nature," but then went on to declare that only "the actual and declared rebellion of the King's subjects" could lead him to encourage the slaves to violence, a passage the New Bern committee of safety described as "very alarming." Saunders, *Colonial Records,* 10:137–138, 138a; *Pennsylvania Evening Post,* September 12, 1775, 1.

28. Michael J. Crawford, *The Having of Negroes Is Become a Burden: The Quaker Struggle to Free Slaves in Revolutionary North Carolina* (Gainesville, 2010), 49, 51. Saunders, *Colonial Records,* 10:87; for other measure taken against slaves, see 10:11–12, 22, 24–25, 87, 569. See also, DeMond, *Loyalists in North Carolina,* 71.

29. Evangeline Walker Andrews, ed., *Journal of a Lady of Quality* (New Haven, 1934), 199, 199n; Richard Cogdell to? Chatham, July 15, 1775, Richard Cogdell Papers, SANC; see also Henry T. King, *Sketches of Pitt County: A Brief History of the County* (Raleigh, 1911), 65–67. For another example, see "New Bern, Aug. 6, 1775," *The New York Gazette, and the Weekly Mercury,* August 21, 1775, 2; Richard Cogdell to [?] Chatham, July 15, 1775, Richard Cogdell Papers, SANC; Saunders, *Colonial Records,* 10:95. Hugh T. Lefler and William S. Powell, *Colonial North Carolina: A History* (New York, 1973), 180; Andrews, *Journal,* 199. In McConville, *The King's Three Faces,* 175–183, I suggest that a slave royalism in some British American populations encouraged unrest at times.

30. Deposition of James Rawlings, Edenton District Superior Court, Depositions from persons in Bertie, Chowan, Hyde, Martin and Tyrrell counties relative to charges against John Lewelling and others for treason, 1777, Beaufort, Bertie, Carteret, Chowan, Davidson, Davie, Edenton District, Forsyth, Guilford, Lenoir, Madison, and Pasquotank Counties, Misc. Records, 1699–1865, CRX box 4, SANC.

31. Deposition of James Rawlings, Edenton District Superior Court, Depositions from persons in Bertie, Chowan, Hyde, Martin and Tyrrell Counties relative to charges against John Lewelling and others for treason, 1777, Beaufort, Bertie, Carteret, Chowan, Davidson, Davie, Edenton District, Forsyth, Guilford, Lenoir, Madison, and Pasquotank Counties, Misc. Records, 1699–1865, CRX box 4, SANC. Deposition of James Rawlins of Martin County, Folder Oyer and Terminer, Edenton District, September 1777, Edenton District Records of the Superior Court, 1774–1779, SANC. See Wayne Lee, *Crowds and Soldiers in Revolutionary North Carolina: The Culture of Violence in Riot and War* (Gainesville, 2001) 171.

32. Jeffrey J. Crow, "Tory Plots and Anglican Loyalty: The Llewelyn Conspiracy of 1777," *NCHR* 55 (January 1978): 11. Crow makes an excellent point here by dating the Taylor brothers' depositions as among the first to be given. This is also noted in Troxler, *The Loyalist Experience,* 12−14. However, by June others started to come forward; the idea of assassinating the state's governor seemed no more palatable to many. For the continued fear of slave uprising in the Albemarle, see "To the Sheriff of Chowan County, Greeting, Court Summoned to sit to hold trial for Negroe Grainge and His Sentence, 1783," Beaufort, Bertie, Carteret, Chowan, Davidson, Davie, Edenton District, Forsyth, Guilford, Lenoir, Madison, and Pasquotank Counties, Misc. Records, 1699−1865, CRX box 4, SANC. Grainge, the slave in question, was believed to be "endeavouring to stir up the Slaves for the Diabolical purpose of murdering their masters."

33. Henry Irwin to Richard Caswell, Tarborough, July 16, 1777, Governor Richard Caswell Correspondence, Governors Papers, vol. 1, January 10, 1777−September 20, 1777, SANC, 58−59.

34. William Wallace, Tyrrell County, September 8, Edenton District Superior Court, Depositions from Persons in Bertie, Chowan, Hyde, Martin and Tyrrell counties relative to charges against John Lewellen . . . and others for Treason, 1777, Misc. Records, 1699−1865, CRX box 4, Court Records, SANC.

35. William Wallace, Tyrrell County, September 8, 1777, Edenton District Superior Court, Depositions from Persons in Bertie, Chowan, Hyde, Martin and Tyrrell counties relative to charges against John Lewellen . . . and others for Treason, 1777, Misc. Records, 1699−1865, CRX box 4, Court Records, SANC. Deposition of Thomas Best, September 9, 1777, Oyer and Terminer, Edenton District, September 1777, Edenton District Records of the Superior Court, 1774−1779, SANC. *NCHGR,* 2:402, 405. For Salter as a member of the Committee of Safety in Pitt, see Saunders, *Colonial Records,* 10:99. Robertson may have joined the committee after July 1775, or he may have been in the state government in another role, but in 1775 he served as a lieutenant in Pitt County's 15th Militia company.

36. Henry Irwin to Richard Caswell, Tarborough, July 16, 1777, Governor Richard Caswell Correspondence, Governors Papers, vol. 1, January 10, 1777−September 20, 1777, SANC, 58−59. In regard to Irwin's military service, see John Burke O'Donnell Jr., "Irwin, Henry," NCpedia, https://www.ncpedia.org/biography/irwin-henry.

37. Deposition of Thomas Stubbs Sr., July 14, 1777, Tyrrell County Depositions from persons in Bertie, Chowan, Hyde, Martin and Tyrrell Counties relative to charges against John Lewelling and others for treason, 1777, Beaufort, Bertie, Carteret, Chowan, Davidson, Davie, Edenton District, Forsyth, Guilford, Lenoir, Madison, and Pasquotank Counties, Misc. Records, 1699−1865, CRX box 4, SANC. Deposition of Nathan Everett, Tyrrell County, July 15, 1777, Chowan County Papers, XV, 1772−1777, 135, SANC. See also Deposition of James Hollis, Tyrrell County, July 15, 1777, Chowan County Papers, XV, 1772−1777, 136, SANC.

38. Deposition of Benjamin Harrison, July 16, Tyrrell County, Edenton District Superior Court, Depositions from persons in Bertie, Chowan, Hyde, Martin and Tyrrell Counties relative to charges against John Lewelling and others for treason, 1777, Beaufort,

Bertie, Carteret, Chowan, Davidson, Davie, Edenton District, Forsyth, Guilford, Lenoir, Madison, and Pasquotank Counties, Misc. Records, 1699–1865, CRX box 4, SANC.

39. Deposition of Nathan Everett, Tyrrell County, July 15, 1777, Chowan County Papers, XV, 1772–1777, 135, CR 024. 928.15, SANC. See also Deposition of James Hollis, Tyrrell County, July 15, 1777, Chowan County Papers, XV, 1772–1777, 136, CR 024. 928.15, SANC.

40. *NCHGM*, 2:213, 217.

41. Deposition of William Harrison, Tyrrell County, July 15, 1777, Chowan County Papers, XV, 1772–1777, CR 024, 928.15, 134. SANC.

42. Deposition of William Harrison, Tyrrell County, July 15, 1777.

43. "Examination of John Clifton taken in the County Court of Bertie at the court held on the 12th day of August 1777," Oyer and Terminer, Edenton District, September 1777, Edenton District Records of the Superior Court, 1774–1779, SANC.

44. "Deposition of John Wheatly.... Sworn before me this 4th day of July 1777," Oyer and Terminer, Edenton District, September 1777, Edenton District Records of the Superior Court, 1774–1779, SANC; Deposition of Salvinus Buttery, Oyer and Terminer, Edenton District, September 1777, Edenton District Records of the Superior Court, 1774–1779, SANC.

45. Deposition of Thomas (X) Harrison, July 14, 1777, Tyrrell County, Chowan County Court Papers, XV, 1772–1777, 133, SANC. For Hyman, see *NCHGM*, 2:397–398. James Harrison claimed that Legate knew of, and approved of, the efforts to contact Lord Howe. Further Testimony of James Harrison, Tyrrell County, July 16, 1777, Edenton District Superior Court, Depositions from persons in Bertie, Chowan, Hyde, Martin and Tyrrell Counties relative to charges against John Lewelling and others for treason, 1777, Beaufort, Bertie, Carteret, Chowan, Davidson, Davie, Edenton District, Forsyth, Guilford, Lenoir, Madison, and Pasquotank Counties, Misc. Records, 1699–1865, CRX box 4, SANC. *NCHGM*, 2:211, 391. Thomas Harrison, son of John, later testified that as the Brethren became a conspiracy, exactly what was known and where the movement was going became increasingly confused. Deposition of Thomas Harrison, son of John, Tyrrell County, July 14, 1777, Edenton District Superior Court, Depositions from Persons in Bertie, Chowan, Hyde, Martin and Tyrrell Counties relative to charges against John Lewellen ... and others for Treason, 1777, Misc. Records, 1699–1865, CRX box 4, Court Records, SANC. Second Deposition of Thomas Harrison, Senior, July 14, 1777, Edenton District Superior Court, Depositions from Persons in Bertie, Chowan, Hyde, Martin and Tyrrell Counties relative to charges against John Lewellen ... and others for Treason, 1777, Misc. Records, 1699–1865, CRX box 4, Court Records, SANC. Even Legate claimed he had never been "acquainted with the general plan at all," though there is ample reason to doubt his statement.

46. Deposition of John Collins, July 1777, Edenton District Superior Court, Depositions from persons in Bertie, Chowan, Hyde, Martin and Tyrrell Counties relative to charges against John Lewelling and others for treason, 1777, Beaufort, Bertie, Carteret, Chowan, Davidson, Davie, Edenton District, Forsyth, Guilford, Lenoir, Madison, and Pasquotank Counties, Misc. Records, 1699–1865, CRX box 4, SANC; another copy exists

in Oyer and Terminer, Edenton District, September 1777, Edenton District Records of the Superior Court, 1774–1779, SANC. *NCHGM,* 2:575.

47. Deposition of James Rawlins, August 6, 1777, Edenton District Superior Court, Depositions from persons in Bertie, Chowan, Hyde, Martin and Tyrrell Counties relative to charges against John Lewelling and others for treason, 1777, Beaufort, Bertie, Carteret, Chowan, Davidson, Davie, Edenton District, Forsyth, Guilford, Lenoir, Madison, and Pasquotank Counties, Misc. Records, 1699–1865, CRX box 4, SANC; Deposition of James Rawlins of Martin County, August 10, 1777, Oyer and Terminer, Edenton District, September 1777, Edenton District Records of the Superior Court, 1774–1779, SANC. "To The Worshipful Justices of New Bern . . . from James Rawlins," Oyer and Terminer, Edenton District, September 1777, Edenton District Records of the Superior Court, 1774–1779, SANC; *NCHGM,* 2:399–400.

48. Deposition of Mary Walker, July 15, 1777, Oyer and Terminer, Edenton District, September 1777, Edenton District Records of the Superior Court, 1774–1779, DCR2, D 22, 28, SANC; Deposition of Elizabeth Ward, Tyrrell County, July 15, 1777, Oyer and Terminer, Edenton District, September 1777, Edenton District Records of the Superior Court, 1774–1779, DCR2, D 22, 28, SANC; *NCHGR,* 2:571.

49. Robert Smith to Governor Richard Caswell, Edenton, July 31, 1777, Governor Richard Caswell Correspondence, January 10, 1777–September 20, 1777, Governors Papers, vol. 1, 94–96, SANC; *NCHGM,* 2:249.

50. *Boston Gazette and Country Journal,* September 2, 1776, 2.

8. THE SWORD AND THE SCALE

1. Deposition of Daniel Austin, Oaths of Daniel Austin, Cornelius Austin and John Smith against William Brimage, Beaufort, Bertie, Carteret, Chowan, Davidson, Davie, Edenton District, Forsyth, Guilford, Lenoir, Madison, and Pasquotank Counties, Misc. Records, 1699–1865, CRX, box 4, State Archives of North Carolina (SANC). J. R. B. Hathaway, ed., *North Carolina Historical and Genealogical Register* (Edenton, 1900–1903) (hereafter cited as *NCHGR*), 2:571–572. See also Gerald W. Thomas, *Rebels and King's Men: Bertie County in the Revolutionary War* (Raleigh, 2013), 83–84; Alan Watson, *Bertie County: A Brief History* (Raleigh, 1982), 67–68. Crow also mentions it. These accounts, like my own, draw on the depositions given by the Austin brothers.

2. For Brimage at the Hillsborough Congress, see William L. Saunders, ed., *The Colonial Records of North Carolina* (Raleigh, 1886–1890), 10:164.

3. Jacob Blount to Governor Caswell, Canterbury, July 6, 1777, Governor Richard Caswell Correspondence, Governors Papers, vol. 1, 53–54, January 10, 1777–September 20, 1777, SANC; [Jacob?] Blount to Governor Richard Caswell, Governor Richard Caswell Correspondence, Governors Papers, vol. 1, 53, July 10, 1777–September 20, 1777, SANC.

4. *NCHGR,* 2: 437,438; Deposition of John Smith, Oaths of Daniel Austin, Cornelius Austin and John Smith against William Brimage, Beaufort, Bertie, Carteret, Chowan, Davidson, Davie, Edenton District, Forsyth, Guilford, Lenoir, Madison, and Pasquotank Counties, Misc. Records, 1699–1865, CRX, box 4, SANC. Walter Clark, ed.,

The State Records of North Carolina (Winston, 1895–1907), 11:555; Affidavit of John Stewart, July 19, Martin County, Edenton District Superior Court, Depositions from persons in Bertie, Chowan, Hyde, Martin and Tyrrell Counties relative to charges against John Lewelling and others for treason, 1777, Beaufort, Bertie, Carteret, Chowan, Davidson, Davie, Edenton District, Forsyth, Guilford, Lenoir, Madison, and Pasquotank Counties, Misc. Records, 1699–1865, CRX box 4, SANC. For Brimage being on parole when he fled, see Major D. Barrow to Gov. Caswell, New Bern, August 4, Governor Richard Caswell Correspondence, Governors Papers, vol. 1, 100–103, January 10, 1777–September 20, 1777, SANC. For an example of the paroles extended to gentlemen among the Highlanders, see Saunders, *Colonial Records*, 10:503, and for Brimage's appointment as deputy attorney general at New Bern in February 1771, see 8:508–511.

5. David Barrow to Governor Richard Caswell, New Bern, July 28, 1777, Governor Richard Caswell Correspondence, Governors Papers, vol. 1, 85–89, January 10, 1777–September 20, 1777, SANC; Clark, *State Records*, 11:539, 543. *NCHGR*, 2:437.

6. *NCHGR*, 2:436–437, 438–439.

7. Deposition of Daniel Austin, Oaths of Daniel Austin, Cornelius Austin and John Smith against William Brimage, Beaufort, Bertie, Carteret, Chowan, Davidson, Davie, Edenton District, Forsyth, Guilford, Lenoir, Madison, and Pasquotank Counties, Misc. Records, 1699–1865, CRX, box 4, SANC. *NCHGR*, 2:571–573, 574. Clark, *State Records*, 11:537–538, 539.

8. Deposition of Daniel Austin, Oaths of Daniel Austin, Cornelius Austin and John Smith against William Brimage, Beaufort, Bertie, Carteret, Chowan, Davidson, Davie, Edenton District, Forsyth, Guilford, Lenoir, Madison, and Pasquotank Counties, Misc. Records, 1699–1865, CRX, box 4, SANC. *NCHGR*, 2:571–573, 574; I assume this is the reference in regard to a "New" inlet that appeared in the 1730s, and not to the New Currituck inlet, which had formed around 1713. It is, though, not entirely clear. Alan D. Watson, *Tyrrell County: A Brief History* (Raleigh, 2010), 20, mentions the New Currituck inlet as a passage through the barrier islands, though one not suitable for large ships. The New Inlet disappeared in 1922, only to reemerge in 1933, again disappeared and reemerged again in the second decade of this century.

9. Clarke, *State Records*, 11:330; E. Milton Wheeler, "Development and Organization of the North Carolina Militia," *North Carolina Historical Review* [*NCHR*] 41, no. 3 (July 1964): 307–323. For example, the Congress of April 4, 1776, ordered 1,500 more minutemen enrolled from Edenton District, New Bern District, Halifax District, and Wilmington District. W. C. Allen, *History of Halifax County* (Boston 1918), 34–35.

10. *North Carolina Gazette*, October 6, 1775, 3; Saunders, *Colonial Records*, 10:704.

11. Governor Richard Caswell Letterbook, 121, 1775–1779 GLB 1.1, SANC. For the Wilmington militia, see *NCHGR*, 2:234.

12. Clarke, *State Records*, 11:521–523.

13. *NCHGR*, 2:244; Governor Richard Caswell Letterbook, 95, 1775–1779 GLB 1.1, SANC. Caswell acknowledged that "want of money" made recruiting almost impossible. See Richard Caswell to?, New Bern, June 17, 1777, Governor Richard Caswell Correspondence, Governors Papers, vol. 1, January 10, 1777–September 20, 1777, SANC,

43–45. In July 1777 a Major J. B. Ashe reported that he believed the governor would be "astonished" at the "Vast arrears" owed the state line's Ninth Regiment. *NCHGR*, 2:239.

14. Colonel David Smith to Governor Richard Caswell, Cross Creek, July 26, 1777, Governor Richard Caswell Correspondence, Governors Papers, vol. 1, July 10, 1777–September 20, 1777, SANC, 72–77; Archibald Henderson, *North Carolina: The Old North State and the New* (Chicago, 1941), 1:327–346, gives an overview of the issues during the war years. In regard to interpretation, I draw here in a general sense on John Shy, *A People Numerous and Armed: Reflections on the Military Struggle for American Independence* (Ann Arbor, 1990), and Wayne Lee's *Crowds and Soldiers*.

15. Richard Caswell to?, New Bern, April 20, 1777, folder 1, Richard Caswell Papers, Wilson Library, University of North Carolina, Chapel Hill.

16. Deposition of Daniel Austin, July 30, Oaths of Daniel Austin, Cornelius Austin and John Smith against William Brimage, Beaufort, Bertie, Carteret, Chowan, Davidson, Davie, Edenton District, Forsyth, Guilford, Lenoir, Madison, and Pasquotank Counties, Misc. Records, 1699–1865, CRX, box 4, SANC; Clark, *State Records*, 11:551–552; *NCHGR*, 2:571–573, 574.

17. *NCHGR*, 2:571–574, 245; Samuel Ashe, *History of North Carolina*, vol. 1: *1584–1783* (repr., Raleigh, 1971), 577. Deposition of Cornelius Austin, July 30, Oaths of Daniel Austin, Cornelius Austin and John Smith against William Brimage, Beaufort, Bertie, Carteret, Chowan, Davidson, Davie, Edenton District, Forsyth, Guilford, Lenoir, Madison, and Pasquotank Counties, Misc. Records, 1699–1865, CRX, box 4, SANC. *NCHGR*, 2:571–573, 574.

18. Deposition of Daniel Austin, July 30, 1777, Oaths of Daniel Austin, Cornelius Austin and John Smith against William Brimage, Beaufort, Bertie, Carteret, Chowan, Davidson, Davie, Edenton District, Forsyth, Guilford, Lenoir, Madison, and Pasquotank Counties, Misc. Records, 1699–1865, CRX, box 4, SANC. *NCHGR*, 2:571–573, 574.

19. Deposition of Daniel Austin, July 30, 1777; Deposition of Cornelius Austin, Oaths of Daniel Austin, Cornelius Austin and John Smith against William Brimage, Beaufort, Bertie, Carteret, Chowan, Davidson, Davie, Edenton District, Forsyth, Guilford, Lenoir, Madison, and Pasquotank Counties, Misc. Records, 1699–1865, CRX, box 4, SANC. *NCHGR*, 2:571–573, 574.

20. Ashe, *History of North Carolina*, 1:328. See also C. B. Alexander, "The Training of Richard Caswell," *NCHR* 23, no. 1 (January 1946): 28–29, for Caswell's role in reforming the legal system in 1762. For the context that encouraged these legal changes, see John M. Murrin, "Anglicizing an American Colony: The Transformation of Provincial Politics" (PhD diss., Yale, 1966); Leonard Woods Larabee, *Royal Government in America: A Study of the British Colonial System before 1783* (New Haven, 1930); Jack P. Greene, "Metropolis and Colonies: Changing Patterns of Constitutional Conflict in the Early Modern British Empire, 1607–1763," in *Negotiated Authorities: Essays in Colonial Political and Constitutional History* (Charlottesville, 1994), 43–77.

21. Ashe, *History of North Carolina*, 1:328. Disputes between governors and lower houses were of course common in provincial America. For North Carolina, see A. Roger Ekirch, *"Poor Carolina": Politics and Society in Colonial North Carolina, 1729–1776* (Chapel Hill, 1981), esp. 120, 125, 205–208. For the Regulation and the legal / administrative order,

see Marjoleine Kars, *Breaking Loose Together: The Regulator Rebellion in Pre-Revolutionary North Carolina* (Chapel Hill, 2002), 30–34, 69–71, 73–75, 136, 141, 148–152, 159–160, 167–168, 170–174, 194–195.

22. Ashe, *History of North Carolina*, 1:411–414, gives a direct account of the problems with courts late in the imperial period. See also Alexander, "Training of Richard Caswell," 29–30.

23. For these tensions in 1774, see Josiah Martin to Samuel Martin, January 27, 1774, reel Z.5. 168P, 274–276, 77b. Additional Manuscripts, The Martin Papers: Papers of Col. Samuel Martin Sr., Samuel Martin Jr., Sir Henry Martin, Bart and Adm. Sir Thomas Byam Martin, Correspondence of Samuel Martin Jr. and Josiah Martin the Younger, December 21, 1752–November 19, 1785, microfilm, SANC, filmed from Additional Manuscripts, ADD. Ms. 41,361, British Library, London. Saunders, *Colonial Records*, 9:641. See also "A Letter from the Revd Mr. Reed, Missy in Craven County, N. Carolina Jany 7, 1774 At a General Meeting of the Society for the Propagating the Gospel in Foreign Parts Held May 20th, 1774," microfilm, SPG Journals, SANC; Reed's letter in its entirety can be found in Society for the Propagation of the Gospel Letters, ser. B, 5–6, 1761–1782, see "To The Revd. Doctor Burton, at Abington Street Westminster." Ashe, *History of North Carolina*, 1:408. For conflict between the Council and the Assembly over the establishment of superior courts, see Saunders, *Colonial Records*, 9:768–770. For demands from the towns early in 1774 for courts to be established, see Saunders, *Colonial Records*, 9:827. For royal instructions in regard to the Superior Courts, see Saunders, *Colonial Records*, 9:856. For Harvey's communication to Governor Martin in regard to the courts and the imperial crisis, see "To His Excellency Josiah Martin....," March 24, 1775, Colonial Governors Papers, vol. 8, Governor Josiah Martin, 1771–1775, SANC. For the continuation of debate even as the empire collapsed, see Saunders, *Colonial Records*, 9:853, 857, 879–880.

24. Saunders, *Colonial Records*, 10:215–216. Alan D. Watson, "The Committees of Safety and the Coming of the American Revolution in North Carolina, 1774–1776," *NCHR* 73, no. 1 (April 1996): 151. The third Provisional Congress placed the legal system under the control of the local committees of safety. With this, courts stopped meeting in many places. According to antiquarian historian Francis Nash, all courts except the local JP courts stopped meeting by mid-1775. This may not have been entirely true, but there was a widespread collapse of the legal order. Francis Nash, *Hillsboro, Colonial and Revolutionary* (Raleigh, 1903), 40; Saunders, *Colonial Records*, 10:127–129. This collapse can be traced through the records of the Edenton District, Records of the Superior Court, 1774–1779. The Oyer and Terminer meetings continued into 1775, but each session did less business, and in 1776 the Committee of Safety seized the court function entirely. See Oyer and Terminer, Edenton District, 1776, Edenton District Records of the Superior Court, 1774–1779, SANC. The Oyer and Terminer sessions resumed with the trials associated with the Gourd Patch conspiracy. See Oyer and Terminer, Edenton District, September 1777, Edenton District Records of the Superior Court, 1774–1779, SANC.

25. Trial, Appearance, and Reference Docket, Court of Pleas and Quarter Sessions, 1771–1775, 1778–1781, Chowan County, CR 24.308.3, SANC. For the March sessions at

Edenton, see Don Higginbotham, ed., *The Papers of James Iredell*, vol. 1 (Raleigh, 1976), 345–346, 365–367. The last king's attorney at Edenton was the wily Iredell, future associate Supreme Court justice and architect of the Eleventh Amendment. His ability to stay within the order while also rebelling against it was remarkable indeed. Alexander, "Training of Richard Caswell," 31. For the committees of safety acting as both civil and political court or arbitrator, see the records of the Edenton District Committee of Safety, 1776, Edenton District Records of the Superior Court, 1774–1779, SANC. In that year the committee assumed judicial power like that of a superior court.

26. See, for example, of the breakdown of the courts in Tyrrell County, State Docket, County Court, 1762–1785, CR 096 307.1, SANC; and Tyrrell County Court Minutes, 1735–1778, vol. 3, 51, microfilm. Tyrrell apparently had no regularly erected county courts, between February 1775 and the autumn of 1777, although sporadic meetings did occur. Clark, *State Records*, 11:434, and see 424 for an example of those petitioning from jail; Nash, *Hillsboro, Colonial and Revolutionary*, 40. Michael J. Crawford, *The Having of Negroes Is Become a Burden: The Quaker Struggle to Free Slaves in Revolutionary North Carolina* (Gainesville, 2010), 63, 64, 64n, reveals the courts at work in Perquimans County Courts of Pleas and Quarter Sessions in mid-July 1777. On the significance of the courts in shaping the provincial social order, I draw here on Rhys Isaac, *The Transformation of Virginia, 1740–1790* (Williamsburg, 1999), 88–94, 131–135, 230–242, 278–292; and A. G. Roeber, *Faithful Magistrates and Republican Lawyers: Creators of Virginia Legal Culture, 1680–1810* (Chapel Hill, 1981).

27. For Nash's comments, see Clark, *State Records*, 11:453. Richard Caswell to Thomas Burke, New Bern, May 13, 1777, Governor Richard Caswell Correspondence, Governors Papers, vol. 1, January 10, 1777–September 20, 1777, 30–35, SANC. Higginbotham, *Papers of James Iredell*, 1:445n. James Iredell and Samuel Johnston repeatedly lamented the lack of a working legal structure; see Higginbotham, *Papers of James Iredell*, 1:444, for an example. For the April 1777 failure of the court bill, see Clark, *State Records*, 11:470–471.

28. Watson, *Tyrrell County*, 11–12: North Carolina had forty-five or so attorneys in the late 1760s. A. Maclaine to Governor Richard Caswell, Wilmington, January 14, 1778, 38–40, box 2, Governor Richard Caswell Correspondence, Governors Papers, vol. 2, September 22, 1777–April 18, 1778, SANC. In 1779 the magistrates in Tyrrell decided to simply ignore any case in which one or no participants could be found. See Watson, *Tyrrell County*, 54.

29. *NCHGR*, 2:235. For the efforts to staff the courts, see James Iredell to Samuel Johnston, Edenton, December 4, 1777, folder 1.92, box 4, Johnston Family Series, Hayes Collection, Wilson Library, University of North Carolina, Chapel Hill.

30. Governor Richard Caswell Letterbook, 51–52, 1775–1779 GLB 1.1, SANC.

31. Chas. Bonafield to Governor Richard Caswell, Edenton, July 31, 1777, Governor Richard Caswell Letterbook, 147, 1775–1779 GLB 1.1, SANC.

32. Clark, *State Records*, 11:434, and see 424 for an example of those petitioning from jail; Nash, *Hillsboro, Colonial and Revolutionary*, 40; Clark, *State Records*, 11:551–552; see also *NCHGR*, 2:245. These personnel problems help explain why officials had eagerly

offered Brethren like John Lewellen and William Brimage positions in the new order. They had served in the empire's legal order and had some sense of how a court worked.

33. John Ancrum to His Excellency Rich. Caswell, Gov. of North Carolina, Wilmington, April 4, 1777, Governor Richard Caswell Letterbook, 56, 1775–1779 GLB 1.1, SANC. Later that summer Sampson Moseley, appointed a judge in the Court of Admiralty at the port of Brunswick, complained to Governor Caswell that he had received neither his commission nor the "directions laid down" by the Continental Congress on how to constitute the court. Sampson Moseley to Richard Caswell, Moseley Hall, August 25, 1777, Governor Richard Caswell Correspondence, Governors Papers, vol. 1, January 10, 1777–September 20, 1777, 125–127, SANC.

34. Hillsborough District Oyer and Terminer, December 1777, Hillsborough District Court Superior Courts, SANC; Clark, *State Records,* 11:92.

35. Clark, *State Records,* 11:551–552, 555, 603–604; *NCHGR,* 2:438.

36. Governor Richard Caswell Letterbook, 191–192, 1775–1779 GLB 1.1, SANC; W. Brimage to His Excellency Rich. Caswell, October 11, 1777, Governor Richard Caswell Correspondence, October 11–28, 1777, Governors Papers, vol. 2, 8–11, SANC; *NCHGR,* 2:439.

37. Clark, *State Records,* 11:562.

38. *NCHGR,* 2:400.

39. *NCHGR,* 2:566–567. Thomas, *Rebels and King's Men,* 85–86, which also gives an account of Rawlings's flight; *North Carolina Gazette,* September 12, 1777.

40. For his August 13 deposition, see Deposition of Daniel Legate, Edenton District Superior Court, Depositions from Persons in Bertie, Chowan, Hyde, Martin and Tyrrell Counties relative to charges against John Lewellen ... and others for Treason, 1777, Misc. Records, 1699–1865, CRX box 4, Court Records, SANC; Letter from Danl. Legett, December 4, 1777, 22–26, box 2, Governor Richard Caswell Correspondence, Governors Papers, vol. 2, September 22, 1777–April 18, 1778, SANC; for his indictment, see "Indictment for Misprision of Treason against Daniel Legate, Evidences for the State Thomas Harrison son of John, Benjamin Harrison son of Thomas, Charles Rhodes, William Harrison, Daniel Garret," September 16, Court of Oyer and Terminer, Edenton District, Court Papers, District of Edenton, 1751–1787, CCR 141, SANC. For Thomas Harrison's deposition, see Deposition of Thomas Harrison, July 14, 1777, Tyrrell County, Chowan County Court Papers, XV, 1772–1777, 133, SANC. *NCHGR,* 2:390–391, 396–397; Higginbotham, *Papers of James Iredell,* 1:463–464. "Indictment for Misprision of Treason against Absalom Leggett, Evidences for the State William Chiles, William Burkitt, Robert Knox," September 16, Court of Oyer and Terminer, Edenton District, Court Papers, District of Edenton, 1751–1787, CCR 141, SANC.

41. "Indictment for Misprision of Treason against William Tyler, Evidences for the State Thomas Best and John Carter," September 16, Court of Oyer and Terminer, Edenton District, Court Papers, District of Edenton, 1751–1787, CCR 141, SANC.

42. For Skiles and the others, see *NCHGR,* 2:393–396; Bond of Recognizance, Oyer and Terminer, Edenton District, September 1777, Edenton District Records of the Superior Court, 1774–1779, SANC.

43. Wm Houston, James Kenan Joseph Dickson to Richard Caswell, Duplin Court House, July 17, 1777. They had captured Richard Brocas and were searching for Felix Kennan, both of whom they obviously believed to be Protestant associators. Governor Richard Caswell Correspondence, Governors Papers, vol. 1, January 10, 1777–September 20, 1777, 60–63, SANC. They believed this because of the testimony of William Wheatey. See Wm Houston, James Kenan Joseph Dickson to Richard Caswell, Duplin Court House, July 17, 1777, Governor Richard Caswell Correspondence, Governors Papers, vol. 1, January 10, 1777–September 20, 1777, 60–63, SANC.

44. Higginbotham, *Papers of James Iredell*, 1:462–463, 463n, 464n; Meeting of the Superior Court, State of North Carolina, Edenton District, September 16, 1777, Court Papers, 40, District of Edenton, 1751–1787, SANC; *NCHGR*, 2:249.

45. Prisoner and witness list, Meeting of the Superior Court, State of North Carolina, Edenton District, September 16, 1777, Court Papers, 44, District of Edenton, 1751–1787, SANC. Clark, *State Records*, 11:776–777, 816. For the death sentence, see Walter Clark, *Minutes of the North Carolina Council of State: Colonial and State Records of North Carolina*, vol. 22 (Chapel Hill, 1907), 929. The Lewellen and Culpepper families were intermarried to some degree. See ncrevwar.lostsoulsgenealogy.com/tories /johnwilliamllewellynar.htm for Lewellen's claim about Caswell's spiritual views.

46. For Legate's August 13 deposition, see Deposition of Daniel Legate, Edenton District Superior Court, Depositions from Persons in Bertie, Chowan, Hyde, Martin and Tyrrell Counties relative to charges against John Lewellen . . . and others for Treason, 1777, Misc. Records, 1699–1865, CRX box 4, Court Records, SANC; For his arrest in August, see *NCHGM*, 2:247. "Letter from Danl. Legett, 4 Decr 1777," 22–26, box 2 Governor Richard Caswell Correspondence, Governors Papers, vol. 2, September 22, 1777–April 18, 1778, SANC; *NCHGR*, 2:390–391, 396–397; Higginbotham, *Papers of James Iredell*, 1:463–464. For those called to testify, see prisoner and witness list, Meeting of the Superior Court, State of North Carolina, Edenton District, September 16, 1777, Court Papers, 44, District of Edenton, 1751–1787, SANC. For the debate over the difference between treason and misprision of treason, see Clark, *State Records*, 12:52.

47. Prisoner and witness list, Meeting of the Superior Court, State of North Carolina, Edenton District, September 16, 1777, Court Papers, 44, District of Edenton, 1751–1787, SANC. For William Lewellen's indictment, see The State versus William Lewellen, October 10, 1777, Court of Oyer and Terminer, Edenton District, Court Papers, District of Edenton, 1751–1787, CCR 141, SANC. For the Bertie men who were forced to give bond on September 20, see State of North Carolina, Edenton, Oyer and Terminer, Edenton District, September 1777, Lewelyn Treason Trial, Edenton District, Records of the Superior Court, 1774–1779, SANC.

48. Clark, *State Records*, 11:816, 551–552, 562, 12:119.

49. Clark, *State Records*, 11:205, 562.

50. I follow the logic of Don Higginbotham here in his examination of Iredell's correspondence. See Higginbotham, *Papers of James Iredell*, 1:464–465, 465n2, for the resumption of circuit riding in the autumn of 1777.

51. Higginbotham, *Papers of James Iredell,* 1:466–467, 467n, lxxviii–lxxix. James Iredell rode the superior court circuit once; its rigors and demands drove him from office. Blackwell Pierce Robinson, "Willie Jones of Halifax, Part II," *NCHR* 2 (April 1941): 132. "Abner Nash to Newbern," April 25, 1778, folder 1, Abner Nash Papers, Wilson Library, University of North Carolina, Chapel Hill.

9. The Return of the Father

1. "Letter from Danl. Legett to Governor Richard Caswell, 4 Decr., 1777," 22–26, box 2, Governor Richard Caswell Correspondence, Governors Papers, vol. 2, September 22, 1777–April 18, 1778, State Archives of North Carolina (SANC). See also J. R. B. Hathaway, ed., *North Carolina Historical and Genealogical Register* (Edenton, 1900–1903) (hereafter cited as *NCHGR*), 2:390–391. This letter was the second of two pleas Legate made for mercy. For his August 13 deposition, see Deposition of Daniel Legate, Edenton District Superior Court, Depositions from Persons in Bertie, Chowan, Hyde, Martin and Tyrrell Counties relative to charges against John Lewellen . . . and others for Treason, 1777, Misc. Records, 1699–1865, CRX box 4, Court Records, SANC; for his arrest in August, see *NCHGR,* 2:247. "Letter from Danl. Legett to Governor Richard Caswell, 4 Decr., 1777," 22–26, box 2, Governor Richard Caswell Correspondence, Governors Papers, vol. 2, September 22, 1777–April 18, 1778, SANC. See *NCHGR,* 2:393, for Absalom's version of the oath as administered to William Skyles (Skiles); see 2:394 for his statement against the state government as given to John Allen; for his advocating for attacks on those who accepted the draft, see 2:395.

2. Donald Lutz has argued that a kind of retrenchment of authority began in New York in the autumn of 1777. His view that running governments during a brutal war delivered a cold dose of reality to the revolutionaries is indeed correct. See Lutz, *Popular Consent and Popular Control: Whig Political Theory in the Early State Constitutions* (Baton Rouge, 1980); Lutz, *The Origins of American Constitutionalism* (Baton Rouge, 1988); and Lutz, "The Purposes of American State Constitutions," *Publius* 12 (Winter 1982): 27–44. For a discussion that highlights the weakening of the executives, see Gordon S. Wood, *The Creation of the American Republic, 1776–1787* (Chapel Hill, 1969), 127–151.

3. C. B. Alexander, "Richard Caswell: Versatile Leader of the Revolution," *North Carolina Historical Review [NCHR]* 23, no. 2 (April 1946): 128–129. Caswell apparently blamed Cornelius Harnett for advocating for limiting the governor's powers. The North Carolina State Constitution, 1776, sections 8 and 9, addresses the issue of the appointing power.

4. C. B. Alexander, "The Training of Richard Caswell," *NCHR* 23, no. 1 (January 1946): 13, 15–16, 21, 22. Caswell's father served in the Maryland assembly and as a militia captain. See also Charles R. Holloman, "Richard Caswell," NCpedia, https://www.ncpedia.org/biography/caswell-richard-0.

5. For Governor Josiah Martin's views on Caswell's motivations in joining the rebellion, see William L. Saunders, ed., *The Colonial Records of North Carolina* (Raleigh, 1886–1890), 10:1061, 232; Alexander, "Richard Caswell," 119–120; R. D. W. Connor,

Revolutionary Leaders of North Carolina (Raleigh, 1916) 82–92. See also Saunders, *Colonial Records*, 10:444, 452–453.

6. Alexander, "Richard Caswell," 128–129. For John Adams's views in this moment, see Adams, *Thoughts on Government Applicable to the Present State of the American Colonies* (Philadelphia, 1776). Adams was writing in response to *Common Sense*.

7. The strategic use of mercy was an ancient practice. Julius Caesar was, ironically, perhaps its most powerful advocate until some of those he had pardoned murdered him on the Ides of March. For the retention of this power, see Ketcham, "The Sources of the N.C. Constitution of 1776," *NCHR* 6 (July 1929): 215–236, esp. 218.

8. R. W. D. Connor, *History of North Carolina*, vol. 1: *The Colonial and Revolutionary Periods, 1584–1783* (New York, 1919), 317–318, discusses Tryon's use of both punishment and mercy. Marjoleine Kars, *Breaking Loose Together: The Regulator Rebellion in Pre-Revolutionary North Carolina* (Chapel Hill, 2002), also discusses the Regulation's aftermath. For the pleas for pardons for the Regulators, see Samuel Ashe, *History of North Carolina*, vol. 1: *1584–1783* (repr., Raleigh, 1971), 397.

9. Saunders, *Colonial Records*, 10:684–685.

10. Saunders, *Colonial Records*, 10:549; for the Declaration, see 10:547–549; for women and children associated with loyalism being expelled from a community, see 10:631; for another example of loyalist women appealing to political fathers for mercy, see 10:841.

11. Saunders, *Colonial Records*, 10:971.

12. *NCHGR*, 2:245.

13. For the efforts to strip the governor of war-making powers in 1780–1781, see John S. Watterson III, "The Ordeal of Governor Burke," *NCHR* 48, no. 2 (1971): 96. The assembly established a Board of War at the governor's expense, only to dissolve it at the beginning of 1781 and extend almost dictatorial powers to the governor during the British invasion. See also Abner Nash to Thomas Burke, July 5, 1781, reel 5, Thomas Burke Papers, Wilson Library, University of North Carolina, Chapel Hill. See Watterson, "The Ordeal," 105–106; and Elisha P. Douglass, "Thomas Burke, Disillusioned Democrat," *NCHR* 26 (April 1949): 150–186, esp. 175.

14. Letter from John B. Beasly to Governor Richard Caswell, December 2, 1777, 22–26, box 2, Governor Richard Caswell Correspondence, Governors Papers, vol. 2, September 22, 1777–April 18, 1778, SANC.

15. Joseph Blount, Robt. Smith and Chas Bondfield to Gov. Caswell, Edenton, September 30, 1777, box 2, Governor Richard Caswell Correspondence, Governors Papers, vol. 2, September 22, 1777–April 18, 1778, SANC.

16. Letter from John B. Beasly to Governor Richard Caswell, December 2, 1777, 22–26, box 2, Governor Richard Caswell Correspondence, Governors Papers, vol. 2, September 22, 1777–April 18, 1778, SANC. See also Legate's plea. Walter Clark, ed., *The State Records of North Carolina* (Winston, 1895–1907), 11:816. Brendan McConville, *These Daring Disturbers of the Public Peace: The Struggle for Property and Power in Early New Jersey* (Ithaca, 1999), 196–200, describes the manipulation of gentry benevolence and gender norms by the yeomanry in riot-wracked New Jersey in the 1740s and 1750s.

17. Thomas Hall to Richard Caswell, September 23, 1777, 1–4, box 2, Governor Richard Caswell Correspondence, Governors Papers, vol. 2, September 22, 1777–April 18, 1778, SANC; also in Clark, *State Records*, 11:776–777.

18. Thomas Hall to Richard Caswell, September 23, 1777.

19. Thomas Hall to Richard Caswell, September 23, 1777; Clark, *State Records*, 22:929.

20. Thomas Hall to Richard Caswell, September 23, 1777.

21. "Letter from Danl. Legett, 4 Decr 1777," 22–26, box 2, Governor Richard Caswell Correspondence, Governors Papers, vol. 2, September 22, 1777–April 18, 1778, SANC; *NCHGR*, 2:390–391, 396–397; William Skyles deposition, July 1, 1777, Bertie County. Skyles implicates Legate in the turn toward a bloody coup. See also the affidavit of James (X) Harrison, who swore he heard Legate invoke General Howe. *NCHGR*, 2:393–394, 210–211.

22. "To the Worshipful Justices of Newbern" from James Rawlings, [no date], Oyer and Terminer, Edenton District, September 1777, Edenton District Records of the Superior Court, 1774–1779, SANC. *NCHGR*, 2:401.

23. *North Carolina Gazette*, September 12, 1777.

24. Jeffrey J. Crow, "Tory Plots and Anglican Loyalty: The Llewelyn Conspiracy of 1777," *NCHR* 55 (January 1978): 14n.

25. Don Higginbotham, ed., *The Papers of James Iredell*, vol. 1 (Raleigh, 1976), 459n; Clark, *State Records*, 12:274, 277–278, 22:929.

26. Clark, *State Records*, 12:278.

27. US Census, North Carolina, 1790, https://archive.org/details/1790_census. Claiborne T. Smith Jr., "John Lewelling," NCpedia, https://www.ncpedia.org/biography/lewelling-john.

28. Clark, *State Records*, 12:329.

29. Governor Richard Caswell Correspondence, Governors Papers, vol. 2, Correspondence, September 22, 1777–April 18, 1778, SANC. For Bogg's involvement with the Brethren, see William Skiles deposition, July 1, 1777, Bertie County. There is a claim filed with the loyalist commission in 1798 by "John Bogg of Edenton" for nearly 400 pounds in losses, plus interest. Although the first names differ, the location and circumstances the man describes suggest that John Bogg and Thomas Bogg are the same person, or closely related. See "To the Commisioners for carrying into Effect the Sixth Article of the Treaty of Amity . . . Between his Brittannic Majesty and the United States of America, The Memorial of John Boggs of the parish of Arigs and County of Air in that part of Great Britain Called Scotlant," reel Z.5.180P, bundle 5, microfilm, SANC, derived from Treasury Papers, American Loyalist Claims, Claimant Papers, Public Record Office, London.

30. Crow, "Tory Plots," 14n. See also Tax List, Bertie County, 1774, General Assembly Papers, G.A. 11.1, SANC. Ebenezer Hazard, the traveler who found 1777 Edenton so underwhelming, believed that many of those convicted in September 1777 would be exiled. But there is no evidence that that occurred. Hugh Buckner Johnston, "The Journal of Ebenezer Hazard in North Carolina, 1777 and 1778," *NCHR* 36, no. 3 (July 1959): 364.

31. Clark, *State Records*, 11:603–604; Alan Watson, *Bertie County: A Brief History* (Raleigh, 1982), 67–68; Gerald W. Thomas, *Rebels and King's Men: Bertie County in the Revolutionary War* (Raleigh, 2013), 89–90. In 1780 Brimage sent his fellow exiled associator Captain Thomas Bogg under a flag of truce from Bermuda to North Carolina to transport his wife to Bermuda. Bogg apparently accomplished this task. See Clark, *State Records*, 15:129; Bertie County, NC Genproject website, "Loyalists," https://sites.rootsweb.com/~ncbertie/loyalist.htm.

10. AFTERMATHS

1. New Bern, January 14, 1778, 38–40, box 2, Governor Richard Caswell Correspondence, Governors Papers, vol. 2, September 22, 1777–April 18, 1778, State Archives of North Carolina (SANC). For the order to guard the magazine and prison at Halifax, see Richard Caswell to General Jones, Dobbs County, August 23, 1777, Governor Richard Caswell Correspondence, Governors Papers, vol. 1, January 10, 1777, to September 20, 1777, SANC, 125–127. For Robert Smith's efforts to guard the magazine, see J. R. B. Hathaway, ed., *North Carolina Historical and Genealogical Register* (Edenton, 1900–1903) (hereafter cited as *NCHGR*), 2:244–245, 249.

2. John Shy, *A People Numerous and Armed: Reflections on the Military Struggle for American Independence* (Oxford, 1976), 1–42, 245–294, speaks to the issues of allegiance and militia in the revolutionary period. See also Michael McDonnell, "Fit for Common Service?," in John Resch and Walter Sargent, eds., *War and Society in the American Revolution* (DeKalb, 2007), 103–131. For a good scholarly account of the North Carolina militia later in the war, see Wayne E. Lee, "Restraint and Retaliation: The North Carolina Militias and the Backcountry War of 1780–1782," in Resch and Sargent, *War and Society*, 163–190. In that same volume, see also vii–viii and Resch and Sargent, "Changing Meanings of the American Revolution," 291–300.

3. Dobbs County, 1778, Criminal Action Papers, Superior Court, New Bern District, SANC.

4. Walter Clark, ed., *The State Records of North Carolina* (Winston, 1895–1907), 12:48.

5. "At a Superior Court of Law, begun and held in the town of New Bern in and for the district of New Bern, in the year of our Lord one thousand seven hundred and seventy eight and in the second year of our independence, before the Honorable Samuel Ashe and Samuel Spencer, Esquires, judges of said courts," Craven County, 1778, Criminal Action Papers, Superior Court, New Bern District, SANC.

6. Clark, *State Records*, 13:429–430.

7. Clark, *State Records*, 14:267.

8. Clark, *State Records*, 14:267. *NCHGR*, 2:195. For Caswell's exasperation with the situation, see Clark, *State Records*, 14:151.

9. Clark, *State Records*, 14:319.

10. Clark, *State Records*, 14:169–170.

11. "Petition of the Sundry Inhabitants of Bertie Co. in favor of William Berkitt," January 30, 1779, Misc. Petitions, box 1, General Assembly Records, January–February 1779, Joint Papers, SANC; Deposition of William Burket, Bertie County,

Edenton District Superior Court, Depositions from Persons in Bertie, Chowan, Hyde, Martin and Tyrrell Counties relative to charges against John Lewellen ... and others for Treason, 1777, Misc. Records, 1699–1865, CRX, box 4, Court Records, SANC. Berkitt's petition is one of a few hints that tension over the Brethren, its turn toward loyalism, and its suppression caused lasting division in the community.

12. Samuel Ashe, *History of North Carolina*, vol. 1: *1584–1783* (repr., Raleigh, 1971), 661–662, 661n.

13. Ashe, *History of North Carolina*, 1:662.

14. The neoclassical scholarship fixated on the centrality of classical notions of civic virtue to the revolutionary generation. Bizarrely, though, they then, except for John Shy and a handful of others, ignored military issues.

15. *NCHGR*, 2:576–577.

16. Drafts and Enlistments, Martin County, 1779, 5–15, Military Collections, SANC.

17. William K. Boyd, *The History of North Carolina*, vol. 2: *The Federal Period, 1783–1860* (Chicago, 1919), 9; John Wheeler, ed., *The Narrative of Colonel David Fanning (A Tory in the Revolutionary War with Great Britain) Giving an Account of His Adventures in North Carolina from 1775 to 1783, as Written by Himself, with an Introduction and Explanatory Notes* (Richmond, 1861), 41–42.

18. Correspondence of J. Simpson, Sec to Commissioner for Peace, 1780–1781, box 13, English Records, British Public Record Office (SANC microfilm).

19. *Boston Gazette and Country Journal*, July 28, 1777, 2; Clark, *State Records*, 11:512.

20. *Boston Gazette and Country Journal*, July 28, 1777, 2.

21. *Boston Gazette and Country Journal*, January 27, 1777, 1.

22. "The Examination & Confession of Nathan Mayo, Craven County, State of North Carolina," Oyer and Terminer, New Bern, September 1777, Criminal Action Papers, Superior Court, New Bern District, SANC. See also "State of North Carolina, Pitt County, I here with send you the body of Nathan Mayo Planter for murdering Thomas Clark," Minutes of the Superior Court, New Bern District, SANC. Criminal Action Papers, 1761–1782, folder 1780, Superior Court, New Bern District, SANC.

23. "The Examination & Confession of Nathan Mayo," Craven County, State of North Carolina, Oyer and Terminer, New Bern, September 1777, Criminal Action Papers, Superior Court, New Bern District, SANC. See also "State of North Carolina, Pitt County, I here with send you the body of Nathan Mayo Planter for murdering Thomas Clark," Minutes of the Superior Court, New Bern District, SANC. Criminal Action Papers, 1761–1782, folder 1780, Superior Court, New Bern District, SANC.

24. "Examination & Confession of Nathan Mayo." Having shot someone in his front yard proved not to inhibit Mayo's political career. He continued on as a JP, became a representative to the state assembly, and remained an officer in the militia. See wc.rootsweb.ancestry.com/cgi-bin/igm.cgi?op=GET&db=jmljr&id=I119035.

25. Saunders, *Colonial Records*, 10:471.

26. "Taken before me Michael [Messfet?]," Salisbury District Superior Court, Criminal Actions, Treason, 1777, DSCR 207.326.1, SANC.

27. Deposition of P. Robertson, 1778, Criminal Action Papers, Superior Court, New Bern District, SANC.

28. Minutes of the Superior Court, New Bern District, SANC. Criminal Action Papers, 1761–1782, folder 1779, Superior Court, New Bern District, SANC.

29. Clark, *State Records*, 11:835–836.

30. Clark, *State Records*, 11:835–836.

31. Walter Clark, ed., *The State Records of North Carolina, 26th Census, 1790* (Goldsboro, 1905), 729.

32. Clark, *State Records . . . 26th Census,* 729.

33. "John William Llewellyn II," WikiTree, https://www.wikitree.com/wiki/Llewellyn-100. Joseph Biggs, Lemuel Burkitt, Jesse Reed compilers, *History of the Kehukee Baptist Association,* published and printed by George Howard (Tarborough Free Press, 1834); Will of Col. Nathan Mayo. This will was signed by him on December 2, 1808, and probated in the May term of court in 1811. Ref. Edgecombe Co. Wills, 7:29.

Conclusion

1. *Royal Gazette* (New York), June 13, 1778, 3.

2. Benedict Arnold, "To the Inhabitants of America," (New York, 1780). For the most recent studies of Arnold, see Nathaniel Philbrick, *Valiant Ambition: George Washington, Benedict Arnold, and the Fate of the American Revolution* (New York, 2017); Stephen Brumwell, *Turncoat: Benedict Arnold and the Crisis of American Liberty* (New Haven, 2018); and Joyce Lee Malcolm, *The Tragedy of Benedict Arnold* (New York, 2018).

M a n u s c r i p t s

The collections of two manuscript repositories, the State Archives of North Carolina and the Wilson Library at the University of North Carolina at Chapel Hill, were vital to my study of what happened in eastern North Carolina at the opening of the American Revolution. At the State Archives, the Edenton District Superior Court, Depositions from Persons in Bertie, Chowan, Hyde, Martin and Tyrrell counties relative to charges against John Lewellen . . . and others for Treason, 1777, Misc. Records, 1699–1865, CRX box 4, contains the depositions that are central to my examination of the beliefs and actions of the Brethren. Also valuable were the Bertie County Criminal Papers; Bertie County Court Minutes, 1763–1780; Governor Richard Caswell Letterbook, 191–192, 1775–1779 GLB I.I; Governor Richard Caswell, Correspondence, Governors Papers, vol. I, January 10, 1777–September 20, 1777; Governor Richard Caswell Correspondence, box 2; Chowan County Court (Superior) Papers; Chowan County Papers, XV, 1772–1777; Oyer and Terminer, Edenton District, September 1777, Edenton District Records of the Superior Court, 1774–1779; Oyer and Terminer, Edenton District, September 1777, Edenton District Records of the Superior Court, 1774–1779; and the Tyrrell County Records, County Court Minutes, 1770–1782, pt. 1, 1770–1782. There are another forty-five manuscript groups there that speak to issues raised in the book, and I consulted them as appropriate.

The collection of the Wilson Library also contains manuscript collections that speak to the situation in North Carolina at the time of independence. The Johnston Family Series in the Hayes Collection; the Richard Caswell Papers; the Whitmel Hill Collection; the James Iredell Papers; St. Paul's Episcopal Church Records; and the Jones Letters in Eccles Family Papers were valuable to this study. Each contains materials that concern the views of the Albemarle gentry as the Revolution unfolded; some of those gentry would go on to play central parts in the Revolution in the state.

Published Sources

The most important published primary sources for the study of North Carolina in the colonial and revolutionary period is William L. Saunders, *The Colonial Records of North Carolina*, vols. 1–10, published in Raleigh, North Carolina, at the end of the nineteenth century. These volumes contain official correspondence, correspondence between officials, some court-related documents, materials from the committees of safety and popular conventions that emerged in 1774 and continued on after independence, and papers from the newly independent state government; these all provide a powerful base for examining the beginnings of the Revolution in North Carolina. The continuation of this series, *The State Records of North Carolina Published Under the Supervision of the Trustees of the Public Libraries by Order of the General Assembly*, published in volumes 11 to 28 (including two index volumes), under the editorial direction of Walter Clark between 1895 and 1906, are equally valuable as a source for following the course of the Revolution in North Carolina.

Robert Cain, ed., *The Colonial Records of North Carolina*, 2nd ser., vol. 10: *Records of the Executive Council, 1755–1775* (Raleigh, 1994), and Robert J. Cain and Jan-Michael Poff, eds., *The Colonial Records of North Carolina*, 2nd ser., vol. 11: *The Church of England in North Carolina: Documents, 1742–1763* (Raleigh, 2007), were also essential to examining the issues raised in this study. The Church of England in North Carolina documents, although not extending up to the Revolution, proved invaluable for establishing the changes in religious structures in the colony after 1740 that played into the unrest in 1777. And R. B. Hathaway, ed., *North Carolina Historical and Genealogical Register*, vol. 2, published at Edenton, North Carolina, in 1901, printed many, though not all, of the depositions taken from the Brethren and their supporters in 1777.

A variety of websites address the period and the figures in the unrest. The most valuable of these is NCpedia Online, NCmuseumofhistory.org, and the North Carolina History Project Online.

Secondary Sources

This movement lasted perhaps six months at the most as a formal structure, and for this reason most scholars have ignored it. Those who have examined it have seen it as one in a series of would-be, failed tory uprisings in North Carolina. Jeffrey J. Crow's short, thoughtful 1978 piece "Tory Plots and Anglican Loyalty: The Llewelyn Conspiracy of 1777," *North Carolina Historical Review* 55 (January 1978): 1–17, is the only article devoted solely to this movement. Crow's piece is well drawn, and, like all good historical scholarship, based on a careful, measured reading of the primary sources. But we diverge regarding his two essential points—that the movement was primarily a loyalist plot, and that it was driven by the desire to save the Church of England—as well as regarding what sparked the movement, and in regard to its broader meaning.

Another well-thought-through local study is Gerald W. Thomas, *Rebels and King's Men: Bertie County in the Revolutionary War* (Raleigh, 2013), 67–88. Thomas parallels Crow's central points about the conspiracy—that what happened in eastern North Carolina was a loyalist plot, and that many were motivated by a desire to defend the Church of England's status. Thomas's focus is on Bertie County, but he recognizes that the movement spread into two other counties south of the sound. Although I disagree with them about important points, both of these studies are serious and scholarly, based on primary sources, and aim to show how the Revolution played out on the local level. They are the sorts of quality local studies that have become, unfortunately, increasingly uncommon as publishing has contracted and state and local historical journals have faced financial retrenchment or even extinction.

There are a number of useful studies of provincial and revolutionary North Carolina. Noeleen McIlvenna, *A Very Mutinous People: The Struggle for North Carolina, 1660–1713* (Chapel Hill, 2009), is the most recent study of the unsettled proprietary period of North Carolina's history. Harry Roy Merrens, *Colonial North Carolina in the Eighteenth Century: A Study in Historical Geography* (Chapel Hill, 1964), gives a detailed account of North Carolina's various regions in the provincial period. A. Roger Ekrich, *Poor Carolina: Politics and Society in Colonial North Carolina, 1729–1776* (Chapel Hill, 2011), examines the rise and fall of royal government in the colony, and its relation to social change. Marjoleine Kars, *Breaking Loose Together: The Regulator Rebellion in Pre-Revolutionary North Carolina* (Chapel Hill, 2002), is the most detailed study of the agrarian rebellion in the interior that dominated political life in North Carolina between 1765 and 1771.

The issue of slavery is addressed extensively in Marvin L. Michael Kay and Lorin Lee Cary, *Slavery in North Carolina, 1748–1775* (Chapel Hill, 1995), and Michael J. Crawford, *The Having of Negroes Is Become a Burden: The Quaker Struggle to Free Slaves in Revolutionary North Carolina* (Gainesville, 2010). Perhaps the best examination of slave unrest in North Carolina is Jeffrey Crow, "Slave Rebelliousness and Social Conflict in North Carolina, 1775 to 1802,"

William and Mary Quarterly, 3rd ser., 37 (January 1980): 79–102. See also R. H. Taylor, "Slave Conspiracies in North Carolina," *North Carolina Historical Review* 5 (January 1928): 20–34, esp. 30–31. Also useful is Alan Watson, "Impulse towards Independence: Resistance and Rebellion among North Carolina Slaves, 1750–1775," *Journal of Negro History* 63 (Fall 1978): 317–328, and Watson, "North Carolina Slave Courts, 1715–1785," *North Carolina Historical Review* 60 (January 1983): 24–23.

Finally, students of early North Carolina will soon find themselves dependent on the articles and research notes published in *The North Carolina Historical Review.* Decade after decade, the journal has produced quality pieces based on original sources that illuminate different parts of North Carolina's long and complex history. I have found myself repeatedly indebted to the many students of that history who have published in that and other journals, and these debts are evident in my endnotes.

Acknowledgments

A friend once said to me that writing a book is a cry for help. There is probably a lot of truth in that, and certainly no book gets written without help. I would like to thank the staffs of the State Archives of North Carolina in Raleigh and the Wilson Library of the University of North Carolina in Chapel Hill for their steady assistance in finding and retrieving sources for this project. Their collective knowledge of North Carolina's early history allowed me to make continual progress on my research.

I would also like to thank Kathleen McDermott of Harvard University Press for her assistance, and I would especially like to thank the press's two readers, Woody Holton and Frank Cogliano. Their close reading and friendly support improved the manuscript and let me reconsider some aspects of it.

As scholars we live in scholarly communities, and I was greatly aided by mine. I inflicted earlier versions of this manuscript on my former graduate students Heather Schwartz, Robert Shimp, Amy Ellison, Katie Moore, Alex Buckley, and Christina Carrick, and each offered useful criticism of a messy draft. I am especially grateful to my friends in early American history, Michael McDonnell and Kate Grandjean, who both pointed out numerous issues with the manuscript and made strong suggestions on how to fix it. Their remarks on both substance and style have been critical and to the point, and thus extremely helpful. Criticism improves manuscripts, for certain.

My friend and radio co-host Loren Samons once again suffered through two readings of an early draft of a McConville manuscript, now the third time he has done so. After thirty-five years of close friendship, he should know better than to ask about my work, but happily he has not yet come to that realization. His perceptive reading helped me shape a protean mass of pages into a working book manuscript. And even though Brad Thompson, Robert Johnston, and Brian Keegan escaped reading the manuscript, their friendship surely sustained me as I wrote it.

When a scholar researches and writes a book, no one lives it more than their family. Each tangled endnote or frustrating paragraph somehow makes itself known to them. To Kristen Murphy and Griffin McConville, I give my love and thanks for long tolerating an often distracted and occasionally absent husband and father. I may write the books, but they make it worthwhile.

INDEX

Albemarle region, 1–3, 5, 7, 51, 54–55, 57, 66–67, 69–72, 74–75, 77–78, 80, 83, 99–100, 101–104, 106, 107, 108, 110–117, 120, 123, 126, 127–128, 130–132, 134, 136–138, 148, 170, 172, 180, 186–187, 190, 195, 199, 203, 209, 214, 258n32; politics and government of, 12–13, 84; economy and demography of, 13–23, 41–42, 66, 70–72; churches and religion in, 26–27, 29–42, 59–64, 78, 83, 228n22, 229nn29,34, 235n49, 237n10; literacy in, 38, 40–41, 238n21. *See also individual counties and towns*

Albemarle Sound, 13, 19, 34, 36, 37, 152, 184

Anglican Church. *See* Church of England

Anti-popery. *See* Popery, and anti-popery

Archdale, John (proprietor governor of North Carolina, 1695–1696), 31

Arnold, Benedict, 212

Article 32 (North Carolina State Constitution, 1776), 98, 105, 213

Association, the, 3, 41, 69, 102, 107, 113, 117, 120, 122, 145, 171, 195, 200, 229n34, 232n11

Balance (British Constitution), 65

Baptists, 35, 229n34, 234n42, 237n10

Bayley, Thomas (Church of England minister), 32

Belote, Peleg (Brethren), 104, 122, 124; as senior warden for Brethren, 112

Berkeley, William, 12

Bertie County, North Carolina, 3, 14–15, 19, 36–37, 39, 55, 62–63, 69, 93, 95, 101–102, 107, 111–115, 120, 122, 150, 152, 159, 167, 169, 171–172, 188–189, 199. *See also* Windsor

Best, Thomas, 133, 170

B-E-T-R-U-E (as Brethren code), 123–124, 126

Bible, 3, 78, 83, 90, 92, 96–97, 99, 103, 122, 213

Bicameral government. *See* Unicameral government

Bishop of London, 32–34, 61

Black, Samuel (Brethren), 110–111

Blount, Nathaniel (Church of England minister), 62

Board of Trade (London), 21

Bogg, Thomas (Bog, Boggs), 188, 269n29, 270n31

Book of Common Prayer, 39, 123, 229n28

Boston Tea Party, 45–48

Brethren, 3, 4, 9, 14, 19, 23–24, 27, 42, 49, 60, 62, 64, 71, 73, 83, 93, 102–103, 105, 107–108, 111–116, 120–122, 124, 126–127, 129, 131, 133–134, 136–138, 144–147, 149–150, 153, 156, 158, 160, 168–170,

Brethren (*continued*)
172–175, 178, 183–184, 188–191, 193–194,
199–200, 214, 247n19, 253n6, 254n15,
259n45, 264n32, 270n11; codes and
signs, 123–126, 189; defections from,
144–148

Brimage, William, 9, 15, 109, 111–113,
150–152, 157–159, 166–167, 189, 264n32,
270n31; flight of, 150–152, 157–159,
166–167

British Empire, 2, 4–5, 17, 27, 40, 47, 70, 176

Burke, Thomas, 70, 74, 163, 201; as a
Catholic, 96–97

Bute County, residents supporting the
Brethren, 115

Buttery, John, and militia service, 200

Buttrey, Salvanas (Buttany or Buttery,
Salvinas), 9, 114, 135, 147

Byrd, William, 17, 18, 33

Cape Fear District, 21, 141

Carolina proprietors, 12

Carter, John (Brethren), 26, 108

Cary's Rebellion, 31

Caswell, Richard (governor of North
Carolina), 1, 4, 75, 114, 138, 143, 148–152,
155–156, 167, 172, 174–178, 180–187, 188,
191, 195–196, 201, 208, 217; plot to
assassinate, 49, 133, 143, 148, 149;
recruitment of troops, 70, 236n7,
261n13; on form of government, 84,
88, 240n2; religious beliefs of, 96,
135, 171; on legal system, 160–165;
early career of, 176–178; considers
mercy for Brethren, 179–187

Catholics, 2, 4, 28–30, 39–40, 42, 44–51,
57, 67, 72–76, 80, 86, 92, 96–97, 103–105,
139, 210, 212–213, 225n5, 229n34

Charles I (king of England, Scotland,
and Ireland), 11, 46

Charles II (king of England, Scotland,
and Ireland), 11, 13, 39

Chesapeake Region, 20, 21, 139, 220n7,
223n20

Chowan County, 18; Superior Court in,
162, 169; militia of, 195. *See also*
Edenton

Christian Trinity, 78, 92, 97, 101, 103,
124–125; denounced by state leaders,
3, 78, 97, 135

Church of England (Anglican Church,
Anglicans), 24–39, 42, 59–60, 62–64,
78, 98, 101, 106, 111, 130, 209, 229n34,
243n27, 247n19; ministers of, 17, 31, 35,
41, 61, 63, 113, 161; preaching circuits
of, 26, 35–38, 41–42, 59, 62–64, 113,
227n21, 232n11, 267n51; chapels of,
26–27, 35–39, 41–42, 62, 64, 113, 227n21,
232n11, 235n49; lay readers in, 27, 35,
38–39, 41, 44, 60, 63–64, 110, 185;
Society for the Propagation of the
Gospel (SPG) as arm of, 30, 32–33,
36, 37, 39, 64, 227n21; and Vestry Act
of 1701, 31; and Vestry Act of 1764,
34; ministers of persecuted by
committees of safety, 59–65

Church of Rome, 28, 50, 210, 212

Committees of safety, 43–44; and seizure
of power, 52–67, 101, 121, 123, 126,
130–133, 135, 141–142, 153–154, 160, 162,
172–173, 187, 197, 203–204, 234n34,
263nn24,25; as persecutors of clergy,
59–64

Continental Congress, Second. *See*
Second Continental Congress

Convention Parliament (1689), 28

Cooper, Anthony Ashley (Earl of
Shaftsbury, Carolina Proprietor), 12

Corn, 19, 21, 23, 42, 106, 109

County Conventions, 53

Courts: Provincial, 47, 105–106, 150;
Royal Admiralty Courts, 160–163;
under Republican government,
163–165, 169, 171–173, 181, 193, 263n24;
Republican Admiralty Courts, 165;
oyer and terminer courts, 162, 165,
170, 177, 186

Craven County, 168, 184, 193–194

Dobbs, Arthur (governor), 19–20, 33–34, 40, 91, 151, 227n19

Drafts, 68–72; and resistance to drafts, 69–72

Drafts, forced, and resistance to, 2, 7, 70–72, 75, 100, 102–103, 107, 128, 133, 135, 136, 145, 147, 153, 177, 189, 191, 193, 195–196, 198, 254n15

Drummond, William (proprietary governor of North Carolina, 1664–1667), 12

Eden, Charles (governor), 31

Edenton, North Carolina, 17–18, 22, 33–34, 36, 48, 64, 74, 78, 95, 116–117, 119, 160, 162, 164, 167, 169, 171–172, 180, 185, 188, 238n21, 263n25; militia in, 148, 190. *See also* St. Paul's Church

Edgecombe County, 37, 115, 144, 252. *See also* Tarborough

Enlightenment and Enlightened views, 3, 5, 6, 77–79, 81, 90, 92, 97–99, 103–104, 127–128, 137, 198, 210, 212, 218n7, 233n27

Eton College, 91–92

France, 4, 28–29, 31, 43, 47, 67, 72–74, 76, 104, 108, 134, 139, 194, 212

French people, attitudes toward, 28, 29, 40, 42, 47–49, 73–76, 80, 103–104, 107, 113, 128–129, 133, 166, 189, 194, 195, 210, 212, 237n12

Fourteen Delegates, the: as spiritual and political threat, 3, 79, 83, 90–91, 103–104, 106, 117, 126, 149, 212, 243n27; membership, 91–97; political actions, 97

Fundamental Constitution of 1698 (North Carolina), 31

Garrett, John (McGarrett) (Brethren), 9, 104, 112, 171, 246n18

George I (king of Great Britain), 28

George II (king of Great Britain), 45

George III (king of Great Britain), 46, 50, 134, 232n19

Georgian architecture, 18

Glorious Revolution, 27, 28, 46, 51, 53, 73, 225n3

Gourd Patch Conspiracy, 1, 2, 4, 6, 144, 209, 229n34, 263n24

Halifax (county and town), North Carolina, 19, 36, 62, 66, 93, 95, 115, 120, 133, 135, 143, 151, 180, 204, 223n22, 229n34 270n1; Halifax County, 19, 36, 93; Provincial Congress at, 62, 180; Declaration of Independence read in Halifax Town, 66; Committee of Safety in, 93; Brethren recruit in, 115, 120; powder magazine in, 133, 135; plan to assassinate Governor Caswell at Halifax Town, 142–143; Halifax jail, 151, 204

Harrison, Thomas (X), 147, 243n3

Harrison, Thomas (son of John), 115, 145

Harrison, Thomas, Jr., 106, 135

Harrison, Thomas, Sr., 23, 104, 106, 109–112, 145, 243n3

Harrison, William, and the Brethren, 145–146

Haw River, North Carolina, Brethren recruit members at, 116

Hayes, James (Brethren), 148; as senior warden, 106, 112; traveling to build the Brethren, 116

Hazard, Ebenezer, 18

Heretical beliefs, 3, 40, 67, 78, 81, 90–91, 98, 101, 103–105, 117, 126, 129–130, 135, 146, 149, 173, 189, 212, 229n34

Heretics, 9, 98, 103, 107, 113, 123, 126, 128–129; Arians as, 91; Socinians as, 91

Herring, 22, 60, 224n26

Hessians, 201

Hill, Whitmel, 10, 91, 93, 96, 98–99, 104, 130–132, 187, 242n22, 274

Hillsborough, North Carolina, 162, 164, 165; conventions in, 55, 58, 96, 150, 154, 233nn26,29

Hooper, William, 85, 87, 88, 241n14

Howe, William Viscount (commander of British forces in North America), 135, 136, 143, 145, 147, 168–169, 202, 205

Hyde, Ann, 28

Hyde County, 19, 36, 168

Hyman, Louis, 71

Hyman, William (Brethren), 71, 147

Indigenous peoples, 29; Croatan, 13; Tuscarosa, 13; Siouan, 13

INRJ—Jesus Nazarenus, Rex Judorum (as Brethren symbol), 125–126

Iredell, James, 48–49, 78, 87–88, 141, 169, 170, 172

James II (King of England, Scotland, and Ireland), 28, 57

Jones, Thomas, 237n13

Jones, Wylie, 84, 91–93, 96, 98, 104, 130–131, 168, 172–173, 240n10; and celibacy, 92, 98, 104

Jordan-Armistead House, 15–16

Keith, George, 32

Land, Bird, 109, 245n14

Legate, Absalom (Leggett, Leget, Legett, Leggatt, Legit), 115–116, 133, 168–169, 171

Legate, Daniel (Leggett, Leget, Legett, Leggatt, Legit), 9, 101–102, 104, 106–107, 109–114, 116, 122, 125, 135, 145–146, 168, 171, 175, 184, 246n18, 259n45, 267n1, 269n21; as senior warden for the Brethren, 112

Lewellen, Frances, 108

Lewellen, John, 1–2, 24–25, 26, 102, 107–109, 111–112, 114, 116, 120, 124, 128–138, 142–144, 147–148, 151, 157, 167–168, 208–209, 254n15, 255n18;

name of, 9, 24; church at which a communicant, 41, 225n28; as leader of the Brethren, 107–109, 111–112; trial of, 170–172, 224n27, 229n34; sentence and pleading for, 181–186, 202; legal knowledge of, 264n32

Lewellen, Mary, pleading for mercy for John Lewellen, 182–183

Lewellen, Sussanah (Mayo), weddings of, 209

Lewellen, William, 115, 120, 171

Lewellen Conspiracy. See Gourd Patch Conspiracy

Locke, John, 12

Loyalists, 1, 2, 4, 6, 44, 49, 58, 129, 133, 135–137, 139, 143–149, 151, 157–158, 180, 183, 187–189, 191, 193–194, 197–198, 200–202, 205, 209, 211–212, 217n2, 219n8, 235n44, 254n15, 268n10, 269n29, 275–276

Martin, Josiah (royal governor of North Carolina), 21, 43–44, 141, 161, 177, 180, 234n26

Martin County, North Carolina, 2, 24, 27, 41, 93, 96, 101–103, 105, 107–110, 112, 115, 130, 132, 134, 168, 183–184, 200, 208, 225n28, 242n22Maryland, 13, 22, 176, 220nn6,7, 232n19, 267n4

Mary of Modena, 28

May, William (Brethren), 104; arrested, 143–144

Mayo, James (committeeman), 129–133, 148–149, 151, 181, 185, 253n6

Mayo, Nathan (committeeman), 130, 132–133, 183, 202–203, 208–209, 230, 252n6, 272; as executor of Lewellen will, 207–208

Mayo, William, 131, 253n6

Mercy, as political tool, 175–187

Methodists, 35, 64

Militia: and the suppression of the conspiracy, 1, 151, 167; instability of, 7, 153–157, 162, 198–202; Brethren organizing at musters of, 26, 101, 109; and committees of safety, 54–55; failure to muster, 68, 154, 156, 191; resistance to forced service, 68–72, 121, 191–198; officers of targeted by the Brethren leadership, 132–133; musters of and rumors about the Brethren's arrests, 146; Edenton militia guarding jailed Brethren, 148, 190

Native Americans, 29. *See also* Indigenous peoples
Naval stores, 22–23
New Bern, North Carolina, 51, 61, 151, 205; Provincial Congress at, 54–55; committee of safety at, 140–141; breakdown of legal system at, 163
Norfolk County, Virginia, 24
North Carolina Provincial Congresses (1774–1776): First Provincial Congress (New Bern, August 1774), 54–55; Second Provincial Congress (New Bern, April 1775), 233n23; Third Provincial Congress (Hillsborough, August–September 1775), 55, 68, 162; Fourth Provincial Congress (Halifax, April–May 1776), 62, 83–85, 180; Fifth Provincial Congress (Halifax, November–December 1776), 69, 87, 89, 93, 98–99, 102–103, 109–110, 133, 177

Oaths, 3, 47, 90, 91, 97–98, 105, 110–111, 117, 120–125, 143, 145–146, 189, 239n1, 251n36; state oath as anti-Christian, 135; state oath as not anti-Christian, 147

Pasquotank County, North Carolina, 22, 32
Pennsylvania, 11, 30, 86–89, 93, 176
Perquimans County, North Carolina, 22, 48, 95, 159, 264n26

Pitt County, North Carolina, 51, 55, 62, 104, 115, 130, 132, 141, 144, 161, 202, 223, 258, 271
Popery, 8, 26–27, 29, 39–40, 48, 50, 73, 75–76, 81, 97, 100, 104, 106–108, 126, 129–130, 133, 134, 136, 178, 210, 212, 225n5, 254n15; and anti-popery, 30, 44, 46, 50, 51, 72–73, 80, 105, 135–136, 232n11
Population growth, 22
Portsmouth, Virginia, 24, 116
Presbyterians, 35, 229n34
Provincial Congresses. *See* North Carolina Provincial Congresses

Quakers (Society of Friends), 13, 30–32, 40
Quebec Act, 46–50, 52–53, 76, 212, 237n13
Queen Anne's War (1702–1713), 31

Rawlings, James (Brethren, Church of England Lay Reader), 26–27, 75, 101–102, 107–109, 116, 121, 123, 129, 132–134, 142, 147–148, 168, 184–185, 225n1, 247n19, 253n6; name of, 9; as lay reader, 26–27, 35, 38, 41
Republicanism, 7, 81, 178, 180, 212, 223n20

St. Paul's Church, Edenton (Church of England), 18, 34, 36, 59, 63, 222n16, 228n22
Second Continental Congress, 1, 56, 58, 61, 69–70, 74–75, 85, 87, 93, 131, 141, 165, 177, 191, 201, 211–212, 241n14, 265n33
Seven Years War (1754–1763), 40, 47, 73, 226n6
Sherrard, James (Brethren), 10, 102, 107–108, 112, 122, 124, 136, 147, 247n19
Silk handkerchiefs, 77–78, 238n20
Slaves, African and African American, 13–17, 19, 21, 23, 71, 92–93, 109, 112, 138–143, 167, 170, 176, 181, 185–186, 200, 222n13, 255n21
Solicitors (as recruiters for the Brethren), 113, 114, 117, 120, 123, 147

South Carolina, 12, 16, 18, 32, 41, 56, 75, 80, 89, 116, 195, 199–200

Sticks (as political signal), 124–125, 189

Stuart, Mary (queen of England), 28, 40

Tarborough, Edgecombe County, 115, 144

Taylor, David (Brethren), 9, 75, 133, 142, 143, 238n18

Tobacco, 13–14, 17–24, 74, 77, 220n7; and British tobacco concerns, 20

Tory (political identity), 7, 9, 44, 58, 129–132, 134, 137–139, 142, 150–152, 157, 167–168, 172, 177, 184, 191, 193, 203, 275

Tryon, William (Royal governor of North Carolina and New York), 33–34, 177, 227n19, 229n28

Tyler, William (Brethren), 143–144, 146; arrested, 143–144; and charged with misprision of treason, 168, 169

Tyrrell County, 3, 14, 19, 22, 24, 48, 55, 71, 102, 106–107, 109, 111–112, 114–115, 120, 122, 145, 148, 171, 222n13, 227n21

Unicameral (single house) government, 84, 86–88, 241n12

University of Pennsylvania, 93

Virginia, 11–13, 15–19, 21–22, 24, 32–33, 61, 80, 89, 91, 102, 116–118, 130, 139, 158, 205, 220n7, 222n13, 223nn20,21, 227n20, 229n34, 232n19, 249n29, 256n23

Wardens (Brethren leaders), 112–117, 120–124, 135, 146–147, 235, 247, senior wardens, 102, 112–117, 120–122, 135, 150, 168

Wheat and wheat cultivation, 8–9, 19, 21–24, 109, 145, 151, 223n21

Whig (political identity), 7, 49, 54, 57, 141, 191, 198, 202

Whitefield, George, 33

William and Mary, 28, 31

Windsor, Bertie County, North Carolina, 14, 95, 119, 147, 160